GAYS AND LESBIANS IN THE MILITARY

SOCIAL PROBLEMS AND SOCIAL ISSUES

An Aldine de Gruyter Series of Texts and Monographs

SERIES EDITOR

Joel Best

Southern Illinois University at Carbondale

GAYS AND LESBIANS IN THE MILITARY

Issues, Concerns, and Contrasts

Wilbur J. Scott and Sandra Carson Stanley
EDITORS

ALDINE DE GRUYTER
New York

About the Editors

Wilbur J. Scott is Professor of Sociology, University of Oklahoma. The author of *The Politics of Readjustment: Vietnam Veterans since the War* (Aldine), Dr. Scott's reach on the sociology of politics, social movements, and military sociology has been widely published in professional journals.

From 1968 to 1969, Dr. Scott served in Vietnam as a platoon leader with the Fourth Infantry Division. He received his Ph.D. from Louisiana State University.

Sandra Carson Stanley is Associate Professor of Sociology, Towson State University. The author of *Women in the Military*, she has written extensively on such diverse subjects as military sociology and gerontology. Dr. Stanley received her Ph.D. from the University of Maryland.

Copyright © 1994 Walter de Gruyter, Inc., New York.
All rights reserved. No part of this publication may be reproduced or transmitted in any form, or by any means, electronic or mechanical, including photocopy, recording, or any information storage or retrieval system, without permission in writing from the publisher.

ALDINE DE GRUYTER
A division of Walter de Gruyter, Inc.
200 Saw Mill River Road
Hawthorne, New York 10532

This publication is printed on acid-free paper ∞

Library of Congress Cataloging-in-Publication Data

Gays and lesbians in the military / Wilbur J. Scott and Sandra Carson
    Stanley.
        p.   cm. — (Social problems and social issues)
    Includes bibliographical references and index.
    ISBN 0-202-30540-6 (acid-free paper).
    1. United States—Armed Forces—Gays. 2. Lesbians—United States.
I. Scott, Wilbur J., 1946–   . II. Stanley, Sandra Carson.
III.   Series.
UB418.G38G36   1994
355'.008'664—dc20   94-29004
                                                                 CIP

Manufactured in the United States of America

10 9 8 7 6 5 4 3 2 1

TO THOSE WHO SERVE

Contents

Introduction

Sexual Orientation and Military Service

WILBUR J. SCOTT and SANDRA CARSON STANLEY

Homosexuals have served in the U.S. military throughout its history. They have not, however, served openly. Traditionally the military has removed service members, homosexual or not, who committed "sodomy" (i.e., oral or anal sex between same-sex partners). Homosexuals as a category, "sodomists" or not, were excluded for the first time during the Second World War on the advice of military psychiatrists. Nonetheless, unit commanders had discretion and, given the enormous manpower needs of the wartime military, many homosexuals served in World War II, often with distinction and without difficulty.

The official ban on their service did not appear until 1950, when Congress enacted the Uniform Code of Military Justice (UCMJ). (Service members who engage in oral or anal sex with opposite-sex partners are also in violation of UCMJ's sodomy statute.)[1] Policy changes since then have become more restrictive. In its waning days, the Carter administration advanced the phrase, "homosexuality is incompatible with military service," and in 1981 the Reagan administration incorporated this language into a presidential directive. Though unit commanders often still had the final say in cases of discreet homosexuals who also were good troops, the military occasionally rooted out and discharged homosexual service members who had been serving effectively and unobtrusively. Between 1980 and 1990, the U.S. military expelled an average of about 1,500 service members per year under the separation category "homosexuality."

A number of recent events have focused attention on the issue and generated widespread debate. Several service members have by now come "out of the closet" to challenge the policy. However, the controversy flared to intense levels in 1992 when President-elect Bill Clinton announced, without consulting the Joint Chiefs of Staff, that he would honor his campaign pledge to lift the ban. The Joint Chiefs of Staff, led by General Colin Powell, publicly opposed the policy, as did Senator Sam Nunn (D-Ga.), and many Republicans in

Congress led by Senator Bob Dole (R-Kans.). Other opinion leaders and organizations, including gay and lesbian groups, lauded the president. Radio and television talk shows, the editorial pages of newspapers, and phone calls to politicians carried opinions for and against the change, and reflected wide interest and intense feelings. Adding to the controversy, a federal court ruling in January, 1993, rendered the military's ban unconstitutional and, that same month, the U.S. Navy revealed that an American sailor who was beaten to death by shipmates while on shore leave in October 1992 previously had requested a discharge on grounds of homosexuality.

Though much has been said and written, there is a paucity of literature to inform decision-makers and other interested persons. Some recent works do contribute to substantive understanding by providing accounts and histories of gays and lesbians in the U.S. military.[2] For example, historian Allan Berube details the experience of gays during the Second World War in *Coming Out Under Fire: The History of Gay Men and Women in World War Two*, and Randy Shilts covers the story from Vietnam through the Persian Gulf war in *Conduct Unbecoming: Lesbians and Gays in the U.S. Military*. Berube writes in a scholarly style familiar to academics; Shilts, in the manner of the journalist he was. These offerings are valuable because they move the stories of homosexuals in the military from the fringes of minority history to mainstream social history. Further, they offer an array of conjecture and evidence that invites more systematic and rigorous assessment.

Two other volumes, published in 1993, address the topic from different perspectives.[3] In *Exclusion: Homosexuals and the Right to Serve*, Major Melissa Wells-Petry (U.S. Army) presents a thorough examination of legal and constitutional considerations related to the military service of homosexuals. *Gays: In or Out?* is a sourcebook that includes two previously published works. One is the U.S. Government Accounting Office report on Department of Defense policy on homosexuality. The other is a reprint of "Military Necessity and Homosexuality," a self-published manuscript by Colonel Ronald Ray (U.S. Marine Corps Reserves).

While these works (along with others) represent a beginning, much more is needed. We seek to fill a portion of the void with this edited volume. Its purpose is to provide a balanced and scholarly presentation of the debate for use by university professors in their coursework, and by policymakers and administrators in other settings. We have used our understanding of status politics as a guide in planning the book. Social scientists refer to conflicts over wealth and money as *class politics*, and conflicts over values and styles of life as *status politics*.[4] Here, as with class politics, it is often useful to think of "haves" and "have-nots": some values and styles of life are strongly preferred by dominant groups and incur favor or prestige, while others are not and do not. The term *status politics* applies to instances in which protagonists seek to change the way target groups think about a particular issue, or to change associated practices and behaviors. Those who wish to preserve previously favored beliefs or arrangements usually counter these efforts. The resulting tug-of-war is carried out within various institutional or organizational arenas and at the interpersonal level as well.

The status politics perspective suggests some general observations and potential lines of inquiry. Beliefs and practices often change at different rates. For instance, attitudes toward gays and lesbians may become more accommodating, or less so, without altering the treatment afforded them or behaviors permitted by them. Sometimes practices change first and alterations in belief follow (as in the desegregation of the military). Also, beliefs and practices may change more quickly and be less contested in some arenas than others. For example, Dick Cheney, the secretary of defense under President George Bush, stated recently that he would oppose a ban prohibiting the of hiring homosexuals as civilian employees in the Department of Defense, but he supported the exclusion of gays from the military. Often, advances or setbacks in one arena may be used to induce or to preclude changes in another. In fact, one fear among opponents of President Clinton's initiative, and a hope among many who support it, is that the acceptance of gays and lesbians in the military will lead to expanded civil rights in other arenas.

More than anything, however, the status politics perspective suggests that the process is inherently political. Changing the prestige hierarchy of beliefs and styles of life means that disfavored ideas and arrangements must gain equal prominence with, or displace entirely, those heretofore favored. Hence challenges require concerted action. Protagonists must agitate for the change because adherents of previously favored attributes seldom give up or share positions of privilege without a struggle. At stake in this particular controversy is the assumed and exclusive dominance of heterosexuality and a related complex of values and practices, both within the military and in the larger society. This pits champions of "traditional" sex, gender, and/or family patterns against those who favor contemporary modifications that have already occurred or are about to take place.

It is in this context that we address the issue of gays and lesbians in the military. These observations suggest two interrelated tasks for the book: First, the book should address the status of gays and lesbians within the broader society and establish the historical and cultural context. Second, it should explore the dimensions and concerns surrounding the status of gays in the U.S. military and the militaries of other countries. We have identified and contacted the foremost scholars and opinion leaders who have expertise in these areas and solicited from them original contributions for this volume.[5] The papers presented in this book reflect their considered opinions and analyses about the many issues and dimensions of the debate.

Establishing the Context of the Debate

Part I provides the background and context of the controversy. The contributions give overviews of the gay and lesbian liberation movements, the evolution of the policy on homosexuals in the U.S. military, social science research on homosexuals and military service, and a commentary on the U.S. military as an agent of social change.

Margaret Cruikshank sets the stage with her discussion of gay and lesbian social movements. She details the diversity of initiatives among American homosexuals in three areas: sexual freedom and political and ideological movements. She argues that gay liberation as a sexual freedom movement is a consequence, rather than a cause, of recent changes in gender roles and the family. The open politicization of the gay community, on the other hand, she traces to the 1969 Greenwich Village riot at the Stonewall Inn; the battle of ideas, she says, has successfully introduced words such as *homophobia* and *heterosexism* into the lexicon of American life. Finally, she describes several conflicts that divide contemporary gay communities and undermine a unified response. She concludes that the integration of gays into the military should weaken the exclusion of homosexuals in other institutional spheres.

David Burrelli shifts the focus to the narrower issue of changes in the military's policy on service by homosexuals. He considers both legal restrictions and administrative practices. Administrative rules reside in Department of Defense regulations, legal restrictions in the sodomy statute of UCMJ. Burrelli reviews the history of these policies, examines administrative and congressional attempts to find a resolution, and comments on the scope of the controversy. In closing, he provides a classification of the proposed resolutions (based on whether military or civil rights concerns are paramount) and notes the awkward, perhaps untenable features of the 1994 compromise resolution.

David Segal, Paul Gade, and Edgar Johnson summarize information on homosexuals in the military from two areas of research: the study of foreign militaries and attitudinal data from military personnel and civilians. There is, they report, a growing and impressive array of evidence. Almost all other Western industrial democracies have dealt with the issue. Segal and his associates report that the militaries of these nations reflect (but lag behind) changes in the status of homosexuals in their respective societies. There are, however, many variations in the policies and practices. Likewise, there are by now several surveys of service members and civilians, both here and abroad. Segal, Gade, and Johnson argue that these survey findings, and the experiences of other nations that have addressed the issue, provide significant references for making sense and policy in the current debate in America.

Charles Moskos, Jr., concludes this section with a discussion of the all-volunteer force, changes in the post-cold war era, and the military as an agent of social change. Prior to 1974, he notes, universal conscription brought together as soldiers and sailors racial, ethnic, and class groupings that otherwise would have been socially isolated from each other. The current composition of a military based on voluntarism is more tightly tied to recruitment policy. Moskos reviews the history of racial integration of the military after World War II, and gender integration after 1974 with the shift to an all-volunteer force. These changes were necessary for military reasons, he contends, though they were not without their problems. Moskos argues that lifting the exclusionary ban of homosexuals will evoke similar problems while lacking military necessity.

Homosexuals in the U.S. Military: A Clash of Worldviews

Part II contains contrasting perspectives on the service of open homosexuals in the U.S. military. These views reflect reason and emotion and advance arguments drawn from two fundamentally different worldviews: One is "traditional" and steeped in moral and religious tenets; the other is "progressive," secular, and relativistic. Both have a long history in American political life.[6]

Laura Miller presents interview material on the views of soldiers from eight military bases in the United States and from Operation Restore Hope in Somalia. She finds both worldviews among active-duty soldiers' opinions on the exclusionary ban; however, the traditional position is much more prevalent among them than the progressive one. Male soldiers, she reports, feel much more intensely than servicewomen about the issue and are much more adamantly opposed to lifting the ban. She offers possible reasons for these findings and identifies them as elements of cultural warfare resulting from a clash of worldviews.

The contributions of Colonel Ray and Barry Adam reflect these contrasting worldviews. Ray bases his strong opposition to lifting the ban on his professional experience in the military and on religious convictions. He believes that the issue involves principles of virtue and morality: Lifting the ban, he says, would subvert a moral principle. He observes a critical crisis in America: "a cultural war over the meaning of freedom." The clash is between the proponents of absolute freedom and subjective choice and proponents of freedom grounded in conformity and moral conviction. The issue of gays in the military, he concludes, is part of a long-term trend toward the homosexualization of America.

Adam, on the other hand, maintains that the debate over gays in the

military has little to do with the lives of lesbians and gay men (but agrees that
the controversy is not only about homosexuality and the military). Homosexuality is an issue, he argues, because it poses a threat to the peculiar image of
masculinity that imbues the U.S. military from its warrior archetype and its
overall defense policy. Adam compares variations in the cultural patterns of
men in the military and finds no inherent connection between homosexuality and the military. The patterns range from viewing homosexuality as necessary for a strong military to seeing it as an obstacle against such. Adam
concludes that the issue requires a rethinking of both the exclusionary policy
and American defense policy.

Homosexuals in the U.S. Military: Critical Analyses

Frequent comparisons have been made of the integration process for
groups previously excluded from the military. Part III offers analyses of the
challenge and resistance these initiatives have posed for the displacement of
traditional roles in the U.S. military and the construction of suitable new
ones.

Garry Rolison and Thomas Nakayama focus on the substance of the controversy's discourse. They review similarities in how the issues were defined
prior to the integration of African Americans into the U.S. military and the
current construction of these issues in the case of homosexuals. Unlike General Powell (and others) who dismiss the analogy, Rolison and Nakayama
argue that the similarities are substantial and significant. They identify three
ways in which the discourse over the exclusion of homosexuals is "defensive:"
it protects the military, hypermasculinity, and heterosexuality. All three elements are symbols of the many recent changes that have displaced traditional power arrangements. Hence, they conclude, the stout defense of them
against further erosion of power.

M. C. Devilbiss in turn claims that the "persistent presence" of women
and of gay men and lesbians, as well as the military's dependence on them,
are two of the best-kept military secrets. She compares the military experiences of these two relatively invisible (and overlapping) groups. She urges
the reader to view her five comparisons as "historical stages" or themes in
the military's attempt to deal with the "women" issue and the "gay" issue.
Devilbiss offers two hypotheses about how organizational power and values
in the military have limited the access of these groups. She concludes that an
institutional "change of heart" is necessary for the military to use fully the
talents of servicewomen and of gay and lesbian service members.

Judith Stiehm examines the military's ban on homosexuals as a reflection
of the "cyclops effect"—the unintended consequences for servicewomen of

military policy based only on observations of servicemen. She believes that policy should have a broader grounding than knowledge about one group (straight men). Stiehm discusses the military's role as a socializing agent in shaping the views of the young (mainly men) on homosexuality, and the institution's role in nurturing the homosexual subculture. She describes the relationship between the military and gay men, and the differences between gay and lesbian subcultures and the responses to them. Stiehm concludes that the key issue is the *response* to gay men, not gay men themselves, and that rules made by men, for men, have been disproportionately punitive to servicewomen.

Evidence from the Militaries of Other Nations

Part IV introduces evidence from the militaries of four Western industrial nations: Canada, Israel, the United Kingdom, and the Netherlands. The military experiences of homosexuals in these countries reflect characteristics of the nation's military, the broader society it serves, and the relationship between the two.

Rosemary Park presents the case of Canada, whose military has a long history of opposing homosexuals serving within its ranks. In 1992, however, the Canadian Forces changed this policy and now allow gays and lesbians to enlist in the military and to serve openly. The Defence Ministry instituted the new policy after amendments to the Canadian Charter of Rights and Freedoms, the supreme law of Canada, established the rights of homosexuals. The policy applies the same rules of conduct to both heterosexual and homosexual personnel, and makes clear that military officers are to take the lead in implementing the policy. The focus of implementation is upon changing the behavior of service members rather than changing their attitudes toward homosexuality. To date, very few homosexual soldiers or sailors have made public their sexual orientation.

Reuven Gal discusses the policy and practices in the Israeli Defense Forces (IDF). The IDF removed all restrictions on military service by homosexuals in June 1993. Though Israeli society is characterized by cultural and ethnic diversity, Gal notes that Israelis share a common religion and have strong ties to the state and its armed forces. The universal conscription system applies to all groups and to men and women, and all service members are expected to place the demands of military life above personal inconveniences. Official policy has never exempted homosexuals from the military, but there were restrictions on their assignments before 1993. However, enforcement of these restrictions rested with unit commanders and often were not enforced if military performance was excellent. With other, more pressing problems facing Israeli society, Gal contends, rights of homosexuals in general and the issue of their service in the military have never been a major issue.

Gwyn Harries-Jenkins and Christopher Dandeker provide a review of the situation in the United Kingdom, the one most like that found in the United States. Historically the British have excluded homosexuals from military service and they still do. Prior to 1967, the military justified exclusion on the basis of the Sexual Offences Act, which criminalized same-sex sex between men (but not women). Though neither the act nor military law currently prohibits sodomy, the ban continues for reasons of "military necessity." British military culture also is highly traditional, i.e., staunchly antihomosexual. Service personnel may be promptly dismissed either for homosexual feelings (orientation) or homosexual behavior. However, attitudes in British society have become more accepting of homosexuality, and since 1991 homosexuality has not been a bar to obtaining a security clearance for civil service employees.

The Netherlands has the military with the most open policy on service by homosexuals and has conducted the most research on the issue. Marion Andersen-Boers and Jan van der Meulen describe the Dutch case. The Dutch Ministry of Defence dropped sexual orientation as a bar to service in 1974 and since then has adopted a far-reaching policy. It includes the recruitment of gay men and lesbians to military service and the development of training programs designed to alter the attitudes—not simply to change the behavior—of the heterosexual majority. Despite these initiatives, Andersen-Boers and van der Meulen characterize the posture among Dutch military personnel as "tolerance at a distance." What this means is that service members have accepting attitudes toward homosexuals but still practice discrimination informally at an interpersonal level. As in Canada, very few service members are openly gay.

Implications for Policy

The final section contains three papers that develop specific policy recommendations. Lawrence Korb served as the assistant secretary of defense from May 1981 through September 1985. During that period, he was responsible for the Department of Defense (DoD) directive that advanced the statement (prepared earlier under the Carter administration), "homosexuality is incompatible with military service." Korb explains in his paper the circumstances and considerations that led him since then to change his position. He now feels that the military would be better served by dropping the exclusionary ban entirely. In particular, he was persuaded by a 1988 DoD report, the so-called PERSEREC report, that concluded gay men and lesbians are as suitable for military service as heterosexuals. Korb ends by detailing six lessons that may be derived from the controversy and that should serve as guidelines for resolving it.

Lifting the ban, however, incurs many problems over which the military itself has no control. Allan Futernick explores these pitfalls. Constitutional and legal issues connected with the status of homosexuals, unlike the cases of Canada or the Netherlands, have not been resolved in American society. For instance, the Supreme Court upheld the constitutionality of Georgia's sodomy law in Bowers v. Hartwick. Currently, twenty-seven states prohibit homosexual relations between consenting adults, and fourteen states (and the UCMJ) hold that oral and/or anal sex constitute sodomy for all individuals. States and cities also vary in prohibiting discrimination in hiring and housing, recognizing partner rights, and the like. Futernick provides a checklist of the legal issues that must be resolved before the military and military personnel face a stable enough climate to implement the lifting of the exclusionary ban.

Finally, Donald Horner, Jr., and Michael Anderson ask the question: Should the military receive a mandate to lift the exclusionary ban, what guidance might officials draw from the previous experiences of integrating blacks and women into the armed services? They review the similarities and differences of these integration experiences with an eye toward policy implications. For example, as in the current debate, the military integrated blacks into the armed forces prior to a resolution of the issue, legally or otherwise, in the larger society—military installations in the deep South especially were surrounded by totally segregated communities. Horner and Anderson develop six policy recommendations that might serve as a guide should military leaders be asked to lift the ban.

Acknowledgments

First and foremost, we, as editors, are deeply grateful to our contributors for their informative and thought-provoking analyses. They are the experts, and the usefulness of this volume lies in the deliberations and insights they have provided. We appreciate too the guidance and efforts of executive editor Richard Koffler and his staff at Aldine de Gruyter. We also thank our colleagues at the University of Oklahoma, Towson State University, and the Inter-University Seminar on the Armed Forces and Society for their intellectual stimulation and encouragement, and our friends and families for their support during what has been a hectic year.

Finally, we express appreciation to the Department of Sociology, University of Oklahoma, for logistical support, and to Annette Chappel, Dean of the College of Liberal Arts, and Dean Esslinger and the Faculty Development Committee at Towson State University for the valuable gift of time.

Notes

1.   In two instances, personnel have been dismissed from military for heterosexual sodomy. These two cases also were instances of "fraternization," i.e., sex between service members directly related in the chain of command.

2.   Allan Berube, *Coming Out Under Fire: The History of Gay Men and Women in World War Two* (New York: Free Press, 1990); Randy Shilts, *Conduct Unbecoming: Lesbians and Gays in the U.S. Military—Vietnam to the Persian Gulf* (New York: St. Martin's, 1993). For a review of these books, see Wilbur J. Scott and Sandra Carson Stanley, "Gays and Lesbians in the U.S. Military: A Review of Recent Books," *Armed Forces and Society,* 20 (Summer, 1994): 633–37.

3.   Melissa Wells-Petry, *Exclusion: Homosexuals and the Right to Serve* (Washington, DC: Regenery Gateway, 1993); and Ronald D. Ray and the United States General Accounting Office, *Gays: In or Out? The U.S. Military & Homosexuals—A Sourcebook* (Washington, DC: Brassey, 1993). For a review, see Scott and Stanley, "Gays and Lesbians."

4.   See, for example, Joseph Gusfield, *Symbolic Crusade: Status Politics and the American Temperance Movement* (Urbana: University of Illinois Press, 1970); Seymour Martin Lipset and Earl Rabb, *The Politics of Unreason: Right-Wing Extremism in America, 1790-1970* (Chicago: University of Chicago Press, 1970); Kristen Luker, *Abortion and the Politics of Motherhood* (Berkeley University of California Press, 1984); and James Davison Hunter, *Culture Wars: The Struggle to Defend America* (New York: Basic Books, 1991).

5.   Only one of the seventeen papers in this volume has appeared elsewhere. The paper, "From Citizen's Army to Social Laboratory," by Charles Moskos, Jr., was published in the *Wilson Quarterly* 17 (Winter, 1993): 83–94. Moskos, the country's foremost military sociologist, originally prepared it in 1993 as a position paper for advising the Joint Chiefs of Staff and Congress's armed services committees.

6.   For a detailed discussion of these worldviews in historical perspective, see Hunter, *Culture Wars*, 107–32.

PART I

Establishing the Context of the Debate

Chapter 1

Gay and Lesbian Liberation: An Overview

MARGARET CRUIKSHANK

In the demonology of right-wing extremists, gay liberation is a simple threat, a monolithic evil. In fact, the movement is far more complicated than its enemies suppose. Sometimes it is so fluid, complex, and diverse that it is barely classifiable as "the gay movement," a phrase that suggests more cohesiveness and focus than often characterize the work of lesbian and gay male activists and their allies. Like the Right, the mainstream mass media presents a grossly oversimplified version of gay and lesbian liberation as a white, male-centered, special-interest group. One way to arrive at a more accurate view of the movement is to examine it from three perspectives: as a sexual freedom movement, as a political movement, and as a movement of ideas.[1]

In practice, of course, these strands are interwoven. A good example is the furor over ending the ban on gay men and lesbians in the military. When Senator Sam Nunn (D-Ga.) was photographed bending over bunks crowded close together on a navy submarine, he was signaling fear of uncontrolled homosexual behavior. (The Tailhook scandal showed the military's high tolerance for uncontrolled heterosexual behavior.) To conservative viewers the photograph equated gay sex with excess. Thus the fight about the ban is about stigmatized sexual behavior. But the effort to end the ban is not only about sex, it is also about discrimination and second-class status, and thus is inherently political.

Finally, the debate between the military and the gay community also involves ideas: The reason the military fights so hard on this issue is that the formal and public acceptance of gay people into its ranks (as opposed to the hypocritical tacit acceptance) also advances the idea that gay people are equal to heterosexuals. In the abstract this idea might not be so objectionable to mainstream America, but in this concrete instance it signifies that gay men can be just as good at soldiering as heterosexuals. It is this inference that has proven loathsome to the military establishment. If what they do can be done by the despised "Other," what is the unique value of their work?

Military leaders may fear that homosexuals in the armed forces may not be as malleable as their heterosexual counterparts. However, Randy Shilts's book, *Conduct Unbecoming*, demonstrates that many gay men and women in the military, in order to prove themselves, are the hardest-working, highest-achieving, and most patriotic soldiers and sailors.[2] In any case, a fight over sexual behavior and political power would be intense, but it would not be as highly charged as the current debate with its underlying clash of ideas. Is homosexuality acceptable or is it not? By its ludicrous attempt to enforce celibacy upon gay men and lesbians in the armed services, the military establishment mistakenly thinks it can separate identity from behavior. The idea behind this interdiction is that gay people, being inferior, have no fundamental right to sexual expression. Thus, paradoxically, the military stand upholds second- class status for gay people at the very time that challenges to that status have forced a softening of the ban.

Gay Liberation as a Sexual Freedom Movement

Gay liberation, like women's control of reproduction, is one aspect of the broad shift from family/church control over sexuality to individual control. It inevitably grows out of the idea that the ends of sexual expression are pleasure and personal happiness rather than procreation. Several trends in the past one hundred years are significant for indirectly encouraging homosexuality: (1) the change from a rural to an urban society, (2) the decline of the traditional family, (3) changing views of sex, (4) the emancipation of women, and (5) the growth of capitalism.

When most people lived on farms, they came into contact with a relatively small number of people, who were much like themselves. Thus it was difficult to imagine alternatives to their parents' and grandparents' lives. Throughout the twentieth century, the young who moved from the country to the city met people different from themselves, including homosexuals, and experienced a new sense of freedom. City life offered anonymity and privacy, conditions conducive to finding sexual partners. As large cities grew, their hidden homosexual populations grew as well, and this growth was a necessary precondition to the development of homosexual life in the second half of the twentieth century.

The city not only offered a wide range of potential sexual partners and a wider social life, it also created possibilities for living permanently outside the traditional family structure. While the extended or nuclear family pattern was nearly universal, few people could break away. In rural families, young people played an important economic role because their labor was needed to sustain the family farm or small business. As cities grew and more people had job opportunities away from their birthplaces, family control over them declined. The invention of the car increased the mobility of young people and gave them a place away from home for sexual experimentation. Cities became more accessible. Young people new to them saw that not everyone lived in a male-female couple, and many remained single. Friendship groups took on some of the functions of the family for homosexuals who settled in cities.

The importance of the family had to diminish considerably before homosexuality could become widespread. Homosexuality is therefore one of the results of a weakened family structure, not a cause. Where young people are influenced by their peers and the media as much as by their families, they have the freedom to make life choices different from those of their parents. No longer the employer of young people, the family cannot be the sole arbiter of behavior. Under these conditions, homosexuality is a possible life choice for those aware of same-sex attractions. When families were more dominant, homosexuality could only be aberrant behavior except for a few unusually strong, autonomous, or rich individuals who could make it a way of life.

Since the 1960s, cohabitation, divorce, birth control, and abortion have greatly altered families. However, decades before then, the forces weakening the family were already beginning to create conditions favorable to the formation of homosexual identity. In the 1860s, Walt Whitman's "Calamus" poems shocked readers by their explicit references to male homosexuality, but the poems were equally radical for their vision of male comrades forming their own societies. Whitman saw that large numbers of men could thrive outside the family system, singly, in pairs, and in groups. He understood that the traditional family could not encompass all of the forms of modern emotional and sexual life.

The first stirrings of feminism in nineteenth-century England and America also helped create a climate in which a few women felt free to choose other women for partners. As women challenged oppressive notions about their inferiority or the inevitability of male domination, they naturally reexamined the institution of marriage. Some found female lovers and life partners while attending college; others learned to accept erotic love between women as natural, whatever their own sexual preference. The idea that women could be fulfilled only by heterosexual marriage remained virtually unassailable until the late 1960s, however, because of Freud's influence and because economic pressure forced most women to marry. Nevertheless, the belief that woman are inherently equal to men had as a corollary the belief that some women appropriately choose other women as emotional and sexual partners. Not everyone who believed in women's emancipation went that far, of course, but the groundwork was laid for future extensions of the notion of women's equality.

The most important influence on lesbian sex in the past two decades has been the "second wave" of the women's movement. Women rebelled against sexual repression and the stereotyped views of themselves as either virgins or whores. They no longer subordinated their sexual needs to those of men. In this context, sex between women could be celebrated rather than shrouded in secrecy. Even heterosexual women nervous at the association between feminism and lesbianism could see that sexual freedom for women had to be for all women. Moreover, if women were entitled to sexual pleasure on their own terms, then people in general were entitled to define "normal" sexual behavior for themselves.

Finally, the growth of capitalism has helped to create both the economic and the psychological conditions that encourage homosexuality.[3] The decline of the family as a producer of goods and the concentration of goods and services in large urban centers brought about a population shift favorable to the formation of homosexual communities. With its emphasis on an ever-growing need for new products, capitalism tends to make sex itself a commodity, now that it is no longer an activity controlled by the family or by religious precepts. Sex sells products. As traditional sources of meaning such as family, religion, and community life become less important in defining who we are, sex becomes more important. Thus the quest for sexual satisfaction is likely to be far more significant for us than for our grandparents, and for some the quest will lead inevitably to homosexuality, not as a transitory experience, as it may have been in the nineteenth century, but as a life choice. Encouraged by capitalism to see ourselves as consumers with an infinite variety of choices, we tend not to stay in unhappy relationships but readily move on to new ones. Consequently, today we have more opportunity to discover whether or not we are homosexual. And we know that, if marriage does not suit us, we have an option besides remaining single.

Gay sex is just sex. Until this proposition is widely accepted, the sexual aspect of gay liberation will have to be highlighted. The newspaper photo alluded to earlier illustrates a puritanical fear of the hidden or mysterious dimensions of sex; it is an emblem of heterosexual America's anxieties. Until these lessen, homosexual conduct will continue to be distorted, trivialized, and condemned. But as time passes and more heterosexuals have the opportunity to meet open lesbians and gay men at work, at school, or in their neighborhoods, the perception that gay sex is evil or unnatural may gradually disappear. On the other hand, fear of difference is deeply ingrained and, when fear of sex is added to it, the result is a powerful impulse to repress or deny one's own difference and to attack it in others.

By now the view that lesbian and gay sex is just sex might have become widely accepted if the AIDS epidemic had not appeared in the second decade of gay liberation. AIDS and HIV created a fear that gay sex is not only bad but equals death. People with AIDS have been stereotyped as promiscuous and treated like lepers. The association of gay sex with fatal illness has had an extremely negative effect on gay liberation as a sexual freedom movement.

Gay men, especially those in large cities, struggled against sex-negative attitudes in themselves and in the often hostile heterosexual world. To reaffirm the dignity and value of their sexual lives took great courage as their friends and lovers died around them, an aspect of the AIDS epidemic ignored by the media. President Ronald Reagan's inaction on AIDS reinforced the folk belief that there was something wrong with gay sex. If there had been any rational or scientific basis for this belief, it would have been amply demonstrated during World War II, when army and navy psychiatrists had the opportunity to study thousands of homosexuals from diverse backgrounds. [4]

Nowhere is the distortion of gay sex more apparent than in the 1986 Bowers v. Hardwick Supreme Court decision. The court ruled five-to-four that sodomy laws do not violate the Constitution. To reach this conclusion, the justices accepted the traditional, Christian condemnation of gay sex. They did not of course acknowledge this bias; they cited the laws against homosexuality in the time of Henry VIII as evidence of a long legal tradition. These laws, however, were church laws, canon law, taken over into English civil law. Thus sixteenth-century religious prejudice against homosexuals became a justification for discrimination in the late twentieth century.

In essence, the 1986 ruling rested on arguments from authority rather than reason. It clearly violated the principle of church/state separation. The implication for a possible Supreme Court decision in the near future on gay people in the military is obvious: In the absence of scientific evidence to support its discriminatory treatment of gays and lesbians, the military must turn to arguments from authority to bolster its case.

Gay Liberation as a Political Movement

The contemporary gay rights movement has roots in Victorian England and particularly in Germany at the end of the nineteenth century. The concept that homosexuality is a normal human variant and the corollary that laws against it are oppressive first appeared at that time. Earlier, in America, Walt Whitman's poems celebrated love between male comrades, which he called "adhesiveness," equating it with male-female relationships. By the 1990s millions had accepted these ideas, which a hundred years earlier were espoused only by a few visionaries and reformers.

Many scholars believe that the category "homosexual," meaning a person as distinct from a behavior, is only a hundred years old. When nearly all persons who engaged in homosexual behavior remained hidden it was impossible to know how widespread it was. Thus, for most of the twentieth century homosexuality was perceived as marginal. The political success of the current gay rights movement has been to thrust it into a central place in American life. One of the most dramatic signs of this shift from the margin to the center is the debate over gay people in the military. Research by several scholars has demonstrated the importance of World War II in modern gay history.[5] Wartime experience proved to thousands of young gay men and lesbians that they were not alone, that it was possible to live a fulfilling gay life among a circle of gay friends, and that certain cities were havens for them. In the 1950s, the homophile movement ("love of same") encouraged homosexuals to link their private lives to a political agenda and to seek acceptance from mainstream America.[6]

In the spirit of the radical 1960s, acceptance seemed too modest a goal. Influenced by the civil rights movement and later by women's liberation, politically active homosexuals popularized the term *gay* to describe themselves, declaring that "gay is good." The goal was no longer gaining acceptance but transforming society. Thus the "experts" on homosexuality were no longer psychiatrists and the vice squad, but gay people themselves. This shift brought empowerment, visibility, and a sense of community to women and men who had been relatively isolated and closeted. The sheer numbers of people willing to identify as gay or lesbian created an environment of safety for many more people to come out, and this has been the main development of gay liberation for twenty-five years. So widespread was the coming out phenomenon that by the late 1980s openly gay people could be found in the small towns and rural areas of America as well as in the major cities.

A Greenwich Village riot in June 1969, in which gay people responded to a bar raid by attacking police, symbolized an end to victim status and a new political awareness embodied in the word *gay* itself. Before, homosexuals had acquiesced to police brutality; now, gay people fought back. The bar, named the Stonewall Inn, was frequented by Puerto Rican drag queens and working-class lesbians. Before the riot, which later acquired mythical status in the minds of many gay Americans, the stigma attached to homosexuality and the resulting fear of exposure had kept most homosexuals in line. Stigma and fear did not, of course, disappear, but after Stonewall the will to resist increased, as gay people found pride rather than shame in their identities. Thus "Gay Pride Day" is celebrated in many cities on the last Sunday in June to commemorate the Stonewall rebellion.

As gay people across the country heard accounts of Stonewall, they felt strengthened in their belief that they constitute a true minority. They are like an ethnic minority, although ethnic identity differs from sexual identity in that it is conferred at birth and passed on through the family. Also, those who take on a lesbian or gay identity already have various other identities—

ethnic, racial, class, gender, religion—that claim allegiance.[7] Furthermore, sexual preference differs from race and sex in that the appearance of a person does not make it obvious. Can a group, many of whose members are invisible, be a minority? Often the most visible gays are affluent white men to whom minority status seems wrongly applied. Nevertheless, lesbians and gay men rightly claim minority standing because they are discriminated against on the basis of their sexual orientation and because heterosexuality is promoted by the major institutions of society, including the military.

From a political perspective, the gay and lesbian liberation movement of the past quarter-century has made dramatic progress but at the same time has triggered a furious right-wing backlash. The necessity of fighting antigay ordinances has siphoned off money and energy that would otherwise be spent building gay institutions. To a certain extent, the gay community has been forced to react to its enemies rather than to pursue its own strategy. Repeal of sodomy laws is hard to focus on when extremists marshall their forces across America. On the other hand, in Oregon, for example, antigay initiatives have been opposed by a wide spectrum of traditional liberals as well as by gay people themselves. Even churches rallied behind Oregon lesbians and gay men, an indication that gay liberation is perceived by many as part of a larger social justice movement. A sense of justice denied prompts many who are not gay to oppose the military ban.

The lack of strong, centralized, national leadership of the gay movement was painfully apparent in the months between President Bill Clinton's inauguration and the July 1993 "compromise" on the military issue, when the debate was dominated by defenders of the status quo. In a movement characterized by fluidity, improvision, and an extremely diverse membership, strong national leadership may be an unrealistic expectation. Strong leaders have been mistrusted in the gay and lesbian community and, at times, even power itself has seemed suspect.

Compared to other movements claiming a national constituency, gay liberation has been marked by zaniness, playfulness, and anarchic zest. Its few Washington lobbyists do not represent its grass roots foundation. A national leader with the charisma and vision of Harvey Milk may never emerge. On the other hand, the potential organizing skill of the movement has been powerfully demonstrated by the response to AIDS: Gay men and lesbians have established the largest self-help movement in American history. The AIDS crisis has quickened and deepened the commitment many people feel to gay and lesbian rights. In the face of an often indifferent medical establishment, an insurance industry all too ready to cheat them, preachers calling their lives an abomination, and families disowning them, people with AIDS are often heroic in their struggle against injustice. AIDS has pulled out of the closet many who would not otherwise have joined in a political struggle.

Coming out made gay liberation possible. Those who came out in the

1970s found pieces of their lives forming a coherent pattern for the first time. The childhood and adolescent feelings for which there was no name, fantasies, marriage resistance or discomfort in marriage, attractions to certain movie stars, all bore meaning. Anyone who cannot remember a time when homosexuality was absolutely unmentionable may not fully understand the high spirits of the gay rights movement in its first decade. An intricate blend of the personal and the political, coming out was a different experience for those who risked being fired than for those with secure jobs. It was riskier for married homosexuals than for singles. Coming out was not the same for women and men. People of color found it an especially complex process because they needed to keep the allegiance of their families for protection in a white-ruled society. African- American gay people may feel torn between primary allegiance to the gay movement and to their birth community.[8] In general, greater economic privilege gave white gays more options when friends, families, or employers rejected them.

The euphoria of coming out and joining a new movement was channeled into much hard work, organizing, fund-raising, and consciousness-raising in the 1970s. Gay and lesbian groups were formed first in big cities. A major focus was passing laws protecting those who had come out from housing and job discrimination. Aside from addressing real problems, these laws had a strong symbolic significance because they equated gays with established, respected minorities. Gay liberation had a strong leftist tinge in its early days. Later on, as coming out became somewhat safer, the ranks broadened to include many who were comfortable in mainstream American society. People in both categories tended to believe, falsely, that gay liberation was a completely new movement. By the 1980s, scholars had begun to recover the nineteenth-century roots of the movement and to document the homophile movement in America in the 1950s.[9]

Gay Liberation as a Movement of Ideas

Among the important concepts that gay liberation established are (1) homophobia, (2) heterosexism, and (3) heterocentrism. A major accomplishment of gay and lesbian liberation has been to identify homophobia, rather than homosexuality itself, as a social problem. This shift represents consciousness-raising on a massive scale. A fairly new word in the vocabulary of mainstream America in the 1980s, *homophobia* is now widely used. Without the context that the word provides, the current debate over the military ban could be regarded simply as a job discrimination issue. In strenuously resisting social change, the military represents all the conservative forces in America for whom widespread homophobia is a desirable social control.

Homophobia arises in part from a need for scapegoats, especially in a time of rapid social change and economic dislocation. Its roots may be the cultural association of violence with masculinity. The Tailhook scandal suggests, for example, that rituals are needed to reinforce this connection. For some, homosexuality represents all hidden and forbidden sexual feelings. When it is not kept taboo, people are more likely to realize that sex is powerful, irrepressible, and sometimes hard to keep within fixed boundaries. Merely by existing, gay people prove that sex cannot be policed. Homophobia also results from rigid ideas about gender. "Gender bending," blurring the distinction between male and female or suggesting that these divisions are fluid, may provoke homophobic reactions from those who cannot tolerate challenges to the way they have always thought.

The notion that gay men or lesbians might threaten "good order and discipline" in the military rests on homophobia. It is an irrational fear that the unknown Other is a threat, not by acting in a certain way but simply by being. It also belies a fear that lesbians and gay men might not be as easily controlled as their heterosexual counterparts. Further, this misconception greatly exaggerates the significance of difference itself. Lesbians and gay men in the military focus on their work; they are more like than unlike their fellow soldiers and sailors. To acknowledge this, of course, would undercut the argument that they must be excluded from the military. Unfortunately for lesbians and gay men currently serving in the military, homophobia is like racism and sexism in that it cannot be eradicated by individual changes of heart but only by institutional change.

Gay liberation has also popularized the concept of heterosexism, which is prejudice or discrimination against gay people, analogous to racism and sexism. The notion of heterosexism challenges the dominant group's claim to superiority. Heterosexuality is more common than homosexuality, but it is not inherently better for that reason, any more than right-handedness is preferable to left-handedness. Lesbians and gay men reach that conclusion from their own experience. If homosexuality were a lesser form of being, millions of people would not choose to act on those feelings for a lifetime. No one would leave a socially sanctioned heterosexual marriage for a devalued same-sex relationship unless he or she found deeply fulfilling benefits from this change. Homosexuality has survived all attempts to stamp it out, including imprisonment and death. As soon as social prohibitions were slightly eased, it became the basis for a mass movement.

But the idea that a homosexuality is equal to heterosexuality is not yet a majority opinion in America and may not be for a long time. Since this idea is gaining more adherents, the effort to draw the line with the military is significant. If lesbians and gay men are judged unfit to serve their country, their second-class status is reemphasized. If, on the other hand, they are deemed acceptable, the rationale for stigmatizing them is greatly weakened.

Because heterosexism is deeply ingrained, a national policy change will not ensure just treatment for lesbians and gay men in the military, but it will symbolize defeat for those who regard gays as inherently flawed.

Besides outright prejudice against lesbians and gay men, a more subtle form of bias is *heterocentrism*, which is the often unconscious assumption that heterosexuality is the norm by which all human experience is measured. The whole weight of Western culture obviously supports heterocentrism, but the new field of gay and lesbian studies has been a healthy corrective to traditional assumptions. From that perspective, for example, it is clear that nearly all research in the humanities and the social sciences is heterocentric: It purports to be about humankind when in fact it is about heterosexuals. In addition, lesbians and gay men are almost completely missing from college textbooks.

From the viewpoint of gay academics, heterocentric thinking harms not only lesbians and gay men by excluding them from consideration but also harms all teachers and students because it offers a distorted, incomplete view of reality. Heterocentric teaching and research is conceptually flawed. Even worse, the blinders of heterocentrism prevent researchers from asking many interesting questions. Gerontologists believe that the family is the chief support of older persons, for example. But what happens when their life choices have alienated families or prompted them to move to large cities hundreds of miles away from their biological families? What do these facts mean for the aging patterns of homosexuals?

Right-wing critics of the multiculturalism now stirring on American campuses have so far been more vociferous in attacking women's studies than gay studies, probably because women's studies is a more visible target. But for some critics, nothing symbolizes the breakdown of Western civilization more dramatically than widespread homosexuality, and they fear that it might actually be promoted by colleges and universities. In fact the forces of multiculturalism on campus are not very potent; right-wing critics typically overestimate their power. In some cases, merely naming difference is the only power that gay campus groups wield. Those who wish to preserve white heterosexual male domination are easily threatened by any signs that campus life is becoming more diverse and that the curriculum is changing. But it is only beginning to reflect, in a very rudimentary way, the diversity of America.

In a sense, conservatives lost the battle for control over the college curriculum when the faculty began to lose its WASP male club identity in the 1960s as women, people of color, teachers from working-class backgrounds, and a few radicals joined the club. Thirty years later, some of these upstarts are in power positions from which they can nurture the seeds of multiculturalism on their campuses. Gay studies is thus part of a larger trend toward opening up the professoriate to groups formerly disenfranchised.

A recent development related to the ideas of gay liberation has been the attempt of some lesbian and gay teachers, including high school teachers, to introduce into their classes, especially social studies and literature, a few positive images of gay people, not to push a party line but simply to say: This is what the world looks like. Any inclusion of gay, positive material looks like advocacy to the Right, however, and thus this very modest and tentative curriculum reform has provoked furious debates over the appropriateness of including any gay material in the high school curriculum. Some school libraries have banned lesbian and gay books; those describing families headed by same-sex couples, such as *Heather Has Two Mommies*, seem to be the most upsetting to conservative parents. An Oregon group made up of gay and lesbian parents is called "Love Makes a Family," a slogan that marks the ongoing struggle to define family. From the viewpoint of conservatives, the notion that "gay is good" is bad enough; even more appalling to them is the idea that gay families are good families.

Conflicts within the Movement

As in other social change movements, conflicts and acrimonious debates among gay activists sometimes overshadow common goals. At times the clash is intergenerational, pitting reformers who have been through the fifties, sixties, and seventies against the recently radicalized young, who are often angry and confrontational. When a professor could not understand why a colleague would feud with another colleague who was also gay, she was reminded of the different outlooks of the NAACP and the radical African-Americans who launched the civil rights movement. When young activists in San Francisco chose "Year of the Queer" as the slogan for the 1993 Gay Pride Day, many older lesbians and gay men felt alienated because the word still has terrible connotations for them. Another clash involves differences between those leaders who envision a broad social movement of which gay rights should be a part and others, mistrustful of coalitions, who argue that gay liberation should be a single-issue movement.

At present the military issue creates tensions among gay liberationists because many veterans of antiwar work in the 1960s, as well as younger people holding pacifist beliefs, abhor the attention given to the military debate. To them, this is the wrong front for a gay battle: Inclusion in the war machine is not progress. Many lesbian feminists in the 1970s and 1980s who demonstrated at nuclear weapons plants saw a close connection between the oppression of militarism and male oppression in general. Some gay male activists, including those influenced by Quakers, Buddhists, or the neopagan group, the Radical Faeries, believe no gay person should be part of the military.

For others, however, the fight against the ban is extremely important both for its symbolic value and because the military has been and will continue to be the employer of many thousands of gay people. Furthermore, in their eyes, the so-called compromise of July 1993 legitimates discrimination and thus must be vigorously opposed. A class gulf may be apparent here, as well as a philosophical clash. Most middle-class gay men and lesbians, until the recent severe and prolonged recession, could expect to find jobs, whereas for many working-class gay people, the military is one of very few employers.

Other sources of tension pit lesbians against gay men. Some of the latter regard lesbian feminists as antisex and procensorship. Feminists have vigorously attacked sex involving children, for example, which some gay men regard as an acceptable form of sexual expression for them and beneficial to children. Feminists point to the power imbalance in such relationships. The antisex label stereotypes lesbians as polemical and puritanical. In fact, the early days of lesbian feminism in the 1970s were a time of much sexual experimentation and the rhetoric of sexual freedom was all pervasive. Today some sexually explicit films about lesbian life and some erotic material are produced by lesbians who consider themselves feminists.

Conflicts about depictions of sex occur not only between women and men in the gay community but also within the ranks of lesbians. On the question of censoring pornography, lesbians are sharply divided. Some support the Mackinnon/Dworkin position that pornography violates the civil rights of all women and must be attacked as a form of sex discrimination having the power to destroy women.[10] Others hold that the First Amendment free speech clause protects pornography, however loathsome it may be. Acknowledging the harm that pornography does women, they fear that the machinery needed to suppress it could easily be turned to the suppression of all lesbian and gay publications.

Other conflicts center on "outing," people of color, and marriage and family issues. Is outing an acceptable political action, especially useful against closeted people in high places who obstruct the movement, or is it an unethical invasion of privacy? Why is it that people of color remain largely invisible in the gay and lesbian community? The media portrays gay liberation as a whites-only movement, a distortion apparent to gay people. However, sometimes their own newspapers and organizations seem incapable of including people of color in significant ways.

In the Mission District of San Francisco, for example, a flourishing gay Latino culture exists, but people in that neighborhood are not asked for their opinion on gay issues by the national press. The San Francisco papers report tensions between the gay community and the African-American community as if no African-Americans were gay. Many white lesbians and gay men have probably never met a gay Native American. Observers of a recent Gay Freedom Day parade who saw the sign "Arab Lesbians" had perhaps never thought of those two words together.

Finally, marriage and family issues crop up because many gay people regard marriage as an oppressive institution that rebels like themselves should not help to prop up. Others wish to be married in formal, public ceremonies and to have their bond recognized by the state. Some believe that child rearing is a good choice for gay people to help them become more assimilated into the mainstream, while others believe that gay people are better off as outcasts and nonconformists.

Conclusion

Gay liberation is a current manifestation of the ancient and continuing battle between the forces of repression, exemplified in our society by organized religion and the military, and the forces of individual freedom. From Thoreau, Walt Whitman, and Emily Dickinson to the present day, lovers of their own sex have rebelled against authoritarian control of their bodies and minds. Like feminists and pacifists, gay liberation adherents stand in fundamental opposition to the military. The *New York Times* disclosure in August 1993 that fake tests were used to justify Star Wars only deepened their distrust.

In the 1990s, reason and evidence are slowly eroding discrimination against lesbians and gay men, but institutions like the military must rely on authority rather than evidence to maintain themselves. Thus the military disregards Pentagon studies concluding that the ban against gay service people has no rational basis. As long as arguments from authority against gay people, which are essentially religious arguments, prevail over reason and evidence, no compromise is possible between the military and the gay liberation movement.

For the foreseeable future gay people will have a keen sense of their social difference. Lingering prejudice in the dominant culture will make identification with the gay subculture inevitable. In America today it is possible for lesbians and gay men to organize their lives so that they interact with heterosexuals only at work, and sometimes all of their co-workers are gay too. This life pattern was inconceivable before gay liberation. Even those who are less immersed in the gay world celebrate their sexuality in a way that was impossible before many thousands of people, from all walks of life, came out of the closet. When an Episcopal bishop came out recently, it seemed only a matter of time before a gay general would come out, or have his sexual preference revealed by others.

To the dismay of some gay and lesbian activists, the military issue has turned out to be a major battleground for gay rights in the early 1990s, a development that would have astounded former marine Harvey Milk, the nationally known gay leader who was assassinated in San Francisco in 1978.

The stakes are high in the conflict with the military. Acceptance of openly gay people as fit for military duty would call into question the rationale for excluding gays from any occupation. If a conservative, authoritarian empire like the military is forced to abandon its discriminatory treatment of lesbians and gay men, then in time religions will be the only remaining social force aligned against gay people. The military gave up segregation before some Christian churches did; it may be that the military will also be slightly ahead of the churches in accepting another stigmatized group of American citizens.

Notes

1. This essay is drawn from Margaret Cruikshank, *The Gay and Lesbian Liberation Movement* (New York: Routledge, Chapman & Hall, 1992).

2. Randy Shilts, *Conduct Unbecoming: Lesbians and Gays in the U.S. Military, Vietnam to the Persian Gulf* (New York: St. Martin's, 1993).

3. Dennis Altman, *The Homosexualization of America* (Boston: Beacon, 1982), 93.

4. For a thorough and fascinating account of military psychiatrists in World War II and their treatment of homosexuals see Allen Berube, *Coming Out Under Fire: The History of Gay Men and Women in World War Two* (New York: Free Press, 1990).

5. See, in addition to Berube, Lillian Faderman, *Odd Girls and Twilight Lovers: A History of Lesbian Life in Twentieth Century America* (New York: Columbia University Press, 1991) and John D'Emilio and Estelle Freedman, *Intimate Matters: A History of Sexuality in America* (New York: Harper and Row, 1988).

6. The best account of the homophile movement is John D'Emilio, *Sexual Politics, Sexual Communities: The Making of a Homosexual Minority in the United States, 1940–1970* (Chicago: University of Chicago Press, 1983). Lesbian activists Del Martin and Phyllis Lyon have given many speeches about their role in the founding of the Daughters of Bilitis in San Francisco, one of the major homophile groups.

7. Steven Epstein, "Gay Politics, Ethnic Identity: the Limits of Social Constructionism," *Socialist Review* 17 (1987): 35.

8. Lisa Keen, "Beyond Stonewall." Part Four. *Washington Blade*, 27 October 1989, 25.

9. For the nineteenth century, see Martha Vicinus, *Independent Women: Work and Community for Single Women, 1850–1920* (Chicago: University of Chicago Press, 1985) and Lillian Faderman, *Surpassing the Love of Men: Romantic Friendship and Love between Women from the Renaissance to the Present* (New York: Morrow, 1981). For the twentieth century, see D'Emilio, *Sexual Politics*, and the collection of essays on gay history edited by Martin Doberman, Martha Vicinus, and George Chauncey, *Hidden From History, Reclaiming the Gay and Lesbian Past* (New York: New American Library, 1989). See also the account of the Buffalo lesbian community in the 1950s by Elizabeth Kennedy and Madeline Davis, *Boots of Leather, Slippers of Gold* (New York: Routledge, 1993).

10. These are the central points of Andrea Dworkin's *Letter from a War Zone* (New York: Dutton, 1988).

Chapter 2

An Overview of the Debate on Homosexuals in the U.S. Military*

DAVID F. BURRELLI

This paper considers the political controversy over the issue of allowing homosexuals to serve openly in the military. It briefly reviews the history of the these policies, discusses the issue as it arose during the 1992 presidential campaign, and considers the unfolding of the debate. In addition, the paper reviews and analyzes efforts by the Clinton administration and Congress to seek a resolution. Finally, it considers the effects of current and possible future court challenges.

History

The history of the military policy on homosexuality follows two tracks: legal restrictions and administrative directives or regulations. Considering the legal question first, U.S. military law prior to World War I did not specifically address homosexuality. Although commanders had great discretion in the control and disciplining of their troops, specific laws, regulations, or policies addressing homosexuality did not exist. The Articles of War of 1916 (effective March 1, 1917) restricted consideration of sodomy to cases of assault with the "intent to commit" sodomy.[1] Following the end of World War I, Congress enacted the Articles of War of 1920 (June 4, 1920), which first named sodomy (Article 93) as a specific offense. The 1921 Manual for Courts-Martial addressed the issue of consent as it pertained to the sodomy laws enacted by Congress (para. 443, sec. XI): "Both parties are liable as principals if each is adult and consents." This language pertained to both homosexuals and heterosexuals.

*This paper expands the report, "Homosexuals and U.S. Military Personnel Policy," (David F. Burrelli, Congressional Research Service, CRS Report No. 93-52F, January 14, 1993). The views are those of the author only, and should not be construed as representing the opinions of the Congressional Research Service or any other agency of the United States Government.

Some have erroneously concluded that the lack of specific language concerning homosexuality prior to this period meant that homosexuality, if not accepted, was at least a "nonissue." However, the social norms and taboos of the day meant that homosexuality was kept private or "in the closet." Indeed, there are instances in which public officials attempted to enforce moral standards concerning homosexuality and the military. For example, in 1920, Franklin D. Roosevelt, then-assistant secretary of the navy, was involved in the Newport, Rhode Island scandal in which the navy used service personnel in compromising ways to investigate homosexual behavior.[2]

In 1950, the Uniform Code of Military Justice (UCMJ) was enacted into law, replacing previous military judicial statutes. The UCMJ included Article 125, which specifically bans acts of sodomy (between members of the same or opposite sex). Cases of assault with the intent to commit sodomy were charged under Article 134, known as the General Article, which prohibits "all disorders and neglects to the prejudice of good order and discipline in the armed forces." Violations of either of these articles, which remain in effect, can result in a dishonorable or bad conduct discharge and/or other punishments as a court-martial might direct.

Military regulations (as differentiated from military law) pertaining to homosexuality (or other issues involving sexuality in general) can be traced to early attempts to treat sexuality from a medical perspective. In the 1860s, under the *Manual of Instruction for Military Surgeons*, the reasons cited for rejection of enlistment and removal from the ranks included "Habitual and confirmed intemperance, or solitary vice."[3] In 1921, following a medical model of treating homosexuality as a personality disorder, the army "issued expanded psychiatric screening standards that remained in effect until the eve of World War II."[4] In World War II, the regulations on homosexuality became more routinized. Under the Roosevelt Administration, psychiatrists made numerous efforts to identify and "treat" homosexuals in uniform.

The policies concerning homosexuality shifted gradually from the 1940s to the 1970s. Early policies were based on a treatment and retention model. Later policies continued to accept treatment but moved increasingly toward separation (and, in certain cases, punishment) of known homosexuals. Flexibility was maintained to the extent that certain homosexuals could be retained in situations involving "heroic service." Nevertheless, until the mid-1970s, efforts to address the issue remained under a medical model of illness, treatment, and integration into or, later, exclusion/separation from the services.

In the late 1970s, the Carter administration revised the policy once more. This revision included the statement, "Homosexuality is incompatible with military service," and recommended that cases involving homosexual tendencies or homosexual acts between consenting adults result in an honorable discharge. Created in a period of legal remands and challenges to its policies on homosexuality, this language became the basis of the Department of

Defense (DoD) policy.[5] This policy was promulgated on January 16, 1981—
five days before the Reagan Inauguration—by W. Graham Claytor, deputy
secretary of defense.[6] The directive on Enlisted Administrative Separations
(discharges) established the DoD policy for these that remained in effect
until 1993. It is therefore the most often cited and disputed statement of this
policy:

> Homosexuality is incompatible with military service. The presence in the
> military environment of persons who engage in homosexual conduct or who,
> by their statements, demonstrate a propensity to engage in homosexual con-
> duct, seriously impairs the accomplishment of the military mission. The pres-
> ence of such members adversely affects the ability of the Military Services to
> maintain discipline, good order, and morale; to foster mutual trust and confi-
> dence among servicemembers; to ensure the integrity of the system of rank
> and command; to facilitate assignment and worldwide deployment of ser-
> vicemembers who frequently must live and work under close conditions afford-
> ing minimal privacy; to recruit and retain members of the Military Services; to
> maintain the public acceptability of military service; and to prevent breaches of
> security.[7]

This directive addressed homosexual administrative discharges from a behavioral or "behavioral intent" perspective. In short, "persons who engage in
homosexual conduct or who, by their statements, demonstrate a propensity
to engage in homosexual conduct" are considered eligible for separation.
Statements that acknowledge an individual's homosexuality are considered
reasonable grounds of intention, but may not be sufficient to warrant a
discharge: A person may be suspected of using statements of homosexuality
to avoid service. To this end, an investigation is required. Thus, the admission of being a homosexual is not treated, ipso facto, as a propensity to
engage in homosexual behavior. Rather it is considered a reasonable cause
for conducting an investigation.

Generally speaking, when an individual was administratively discharged
for homosexuality alone, an honorable or general discharge was issued. The
type of discharge is based on the nature of the individual's service (i.e.,
behavior) while on duty. The directive listed those instances in which certain
homosexual behaviors would result in a discharge "Under Other Than Honorable" conditions. These conditions included the use of force, homosexual
acts with a minor, and fraternization deemed sufficiently disruptive to good
order. In other words, sexual "orientation" alone is insufficient grounds for a
general or lesser discharge.[8]

It is important to note that an individual could not receive a dishonorable
or bad conduct discharge under these administrative regulations. These
discharges can be affixed only by a court-martial and must be based on a
finding of criminal acts. During the 1980s, most individuals separated under

these provisions received honorable discharges. While the above pertains to enlisted personnel, officers may also be separated.[9]

Under another directive (Physical Standards for Enlistment, Appointment, and Induction),[10] prospective service members were denied entry into the service for homosexual activity. During the screening process, individuals were asked if they were homosexual. An affirmative answer, technically, was sufficient grounds to deny entry into the service. Thus, a recruit who stated that he/she was a homosexual was reasoned to have been engaged in, or to have intended to engage in, homosexual behavior.

From 1981 to 1993, the separation policy remained unchanged. Numerous court decisions considering the policy on due process, equal protection, free speech, and privacy grounds upheld the policy.[11]

1992 Presidential Election

Early in the 1992 presidential campaign, then-candidate Bill Clinton commented that, if elected, he would "lift the ban" on gays serving in the military. The issue drew heated debate among policymakers and the public at large. The amount of attention and opposition to the president's "proposal" resulted in an interim compromise that allowed the Department of Defense an opportunity to study the issue and report a "draft executive order" that would end discrimination on the basis of sexual "orientation." This interim compromise (announced January 29, 1993) also provided Congress additional time to more fully exercise its authority, including the consideration of legislation and the holding of hearings.[12] Interestingly, this compromise also prevented Congress from enacting the then-current policy into law.[13] At the time, it appeared that Congress was willing to attach language to the Family Leave Act that would have instituted into law the current policy. Senate Armed Services Committee (SASC) chairman Sam Nunn's (D-Ga.) agreement to hold hearings and his willingness to negotiate with the Clinton administration served to delay the enactment of this amendment.

The interim policy stated that DoD officials would cease asking recruits questions on homosexuality, but that anyone who announced his or her homosexuality would be placed in the nonactive duty, nonpay status of standby reserve. During this interim period, the secretary of defense was instructed to study the issue and to draft an Executive Order for presidential consideration by July 15, 1993.[14] (In addition to the DoD's study of the issue, the Rand Corporation was also instructed by the secretary of defense to conduct a study on this issue.)[15]

While the Pentagon studied the issue, research attempts by those outside the Pentagon were blocked by the administration. Professor Charles Moskos testified that the administration was preventing others outside the Pentagon from access, for research purposes, to troops or DoD sources.[16] In addition, although many in uniform felt it was not in their best interest to step forward in a political debate between the White House and the Congress, those who did, did so at risk of reprimand.[17] These findings lead some to believe that the administration, by controlling access to information, intended to block others with differing opinions from being able to present credible arguments.

Although nearly all legal challenges upheld the DoD policy during the 1980s (if not at the district level, then at least on appeal), one case in particular complicated the political issues. In Meinhold v. United States Department of Defense, Judge Terry Hatter of the U.S. District Court permanently enjoined the Department of Defense from discharging or denying enlistment to any person based on "sexual orientation."[18] Not only did this decision depart from a large body of judicial precedents but its release, some claim, was timed to coincide with the announcement of the president's interim policy and was based upon political considerations made from the bench.[19] Although the judge noted that sexual "orientation" is the issue, he ignored evidence that Meinhold had behaved improperly and that his readmission back into the navy had proven disruptive. (It is important to note that the DoD's 1981 policy addressed behavior or intent, not "orientation.") Although the decision seemed to bolster the president's position, it ultimately proved to further complicate the debate since some viewed it as being in conflict with the presidential-congressional compromise.

An appeals court failed to overturn the decision to readmit Meinhold into the navy. Nevertheless, the administration continued to press for Meinhold's discharge. On September 30, 1993, Judge Hatter stated that his ruling applied to all military personnel, not just Meinhold (despite the fact that Meinhold had not filed a class action suit). On October 30, 1993, the Supreme Court, without comment or dissent, lifted Hatter's order as it applied to the military in general, and allowed Meinhold's appeal to continue.

During the interim period, the SASC held extensive hearings on this issue. The House Armed Services Committee (HASC) also held hearings. By May 1993, a congressional consensus appeared to emerge over what SASC chairman Nunn described as a "don't ask, don't tell" position. Under this approach, the department would not ask questions concerning sexuality, and individuals would be required to keep their sexuality to themselves. Reports from the Department of Defense study group also suggested a "don't ask, don't shout" approach, in which individuals could admit their sexuality, but would be required to act discreetly to limit any disruptions. Representative Barney Frank (D-Mass.), a proponent for "lifting the ban," then advocated a "don't ask, not in uniform" compromise in which individuals could live a homosexual life-style provided that they did so off base and off duty. Finally, homosexual rights advocates argued for a "don't ask, don't investigate" policy. Placed on a theoretical continuum, the Senate approach would have, in large part, reinstated the 1981 policy restricting behavior or conduct, while the homosexual rights approach would have lifted the policy and also severely limited the DoD's ability to enforce the law under the UCMJ.

The Debate Continues

The media, particularly large city newspapers, were quick to take an editorial position. Once a position was taken, either for or against changing the policy, reporting and coverage of the issue tended to follow the editorial leadership. Reports and stories favorable to the paper's position often were reported prominently and unquestioningly.[20] Information damaging to the paper's position was either ignored, refuted, or placed inconspicuously in the back pages.

While many small circulation papers and national reporting services generally did a balanced job of covering the debate, many papers, including the *Washington Post*, *New York Times*, *Atlanta Constitution*, and *Washington Times*, appeared unable to maintain a semblance of balance. Rather than informing the public and reporting the news objectively, fairly, and with customary skepticism, these papers approached the issue as something of a crusade invested with such moral substance as to overwhelm the relevance of normal journalistic standards. The result was editorialized and selective reporting, including the reporting of false information or statements.[21] Many of these papers uncritically cited advocates' claims that the military utilized "witch-hunts" as a means of separating homosexuals.[22] Many papers also erroneously presumed that the policy was the creation of the Reagan administration thereby adding political "spin" that the exclusion policy was part of a "right wing or fundamentalist" agenda that "should be rejected by mainstream America." Had these reports made clear the origins of this policy, i.e., from the Roosevelt and, more recently, the Carter administrations, the public's generally negative response to the Clinton "pledge," as registered to members of Congress, would not have been so confounding. The credibility of these news organizations among policymakers and those familiar with the issues can only have suffered. Nevertheless, a number of papers managed to maintain high standards of balance and accuracy.

Several organizations sponsored or conducted public opinion polls about the issue. These surveys produced inconsistent findings. In some cases, the results reflect the political or editorial stance of those who commissioned them. These results were achieved by varying the group sampled, the method and type of questions asked, and the context in which these questions were asked. Despite several polls showing results consistent with the agenda of those who commissioned them, other polls—where the politics or editorial policies of the those conducting the polls cannot be ascertained—show that the country is divided over the issue with no clear majority on either side.

On April 25, 1993, homosexual rights groups conducted a march on Washington, seeking among other things, an end to the military's policy of excluding homosexuals. Although march organizers stated that over one million participants would and did attend, the National Park Service's count was just over three hundred thousand. The dispute over these numbers proved distracting and brought into question both groups' credibility. Although the march proved to be a major rally for homosexual rights, the effect of the march and other activities on the political process is questionable.[23]

Seeking Resolution

Two issues need to be considered in seeking a resolution to the debate: the compromise and the basis of the policy. The compromise acts as a guide for those in uniform, e.g., "don't ask," "don't tell," "don't shout." The basis, however, addresses how such guidelines should be framed. There are three possibilities: (1) Military concerns are paramount, (2) a balance between military concerns and civil rights concerns is maintained, or (3) Civil rights concerns are paramount. As the July 15, 1993, deadline neared, several compromises were being advocated. It was generally expected that the services would continue to refrain from asking recruits questions about their sexuality. "Don't ask," therefore, was a component of all suggested compromises. In this analysis, however, it is treated separately in considering possible outcomes.

"Don't ask" suspended only the policy of "asking" recruits. However, it may at times be necessary, as a result of criminal investigations or HIV epidemiological assessments,[24] for example, that individuals be asked. A strict limit on asking could inadvertently affect matters beyond the scope of the current exclusion policy. Hypothetically, it may be necessary to add the provision that individuals may not be asked questions concerning their sexuality except for medical, legal, or other purposes deemed necessary in maintaining good order and discipline, i.e., in cases where military or medical necessity supersedes personal privacy issues. Such language could discourage investigations except in those cases where there is reason to believe that violations of the sodomy or other UCMJ articles are involved. In addition, some instances disruptive to discipline, though not criminal violations, may require that questions be asked.

Turning to other options, a "don't tell" policy would be consistent with the 1981 Directive on Administrative Separations and the Ben-Shalom v. Marsh or Pruitt v. Cheney case.[25] Under this language, individuals who state that they are homosexual may be subject to possible investigation and/or discharge. In other words, homosexuals will be permitted to serve only so long as they stay in the closet. Arguably, such a compromise would create a dual standard between heterosexuals, who can announce their sexuality and have recognized relationships officially sanctioned via benefits, and homosexuals, who would be forced to keep their sexuality a nonissue or face possible discharge.

Alternatively, under a "don't shout" provision, individuals would be allowed to state that they are homosexual but would be required to prevent their homosexuality from becoming an issue in the military setting. In other words, should their behavior prove disruptive, such individuals could be separated. Arguably, saying "I am homosexual" to relatives or friends in the privacy of one's own home would not result in a discharge. However, statements made to the national media can be viewed as shouting since the statement is being used for political purposes unrelated to military duties or privacy issues.

Such a distinction, however, raises questions concerning the abridgment of speech made for political purposes. Indeed, any attempt to force the military to further recognize homosexuality could be used as a reason for discharge. Although this may raise freedom of speech questions, it also leads to a twist of the Ben-Shalom decision. Under that decision, individuals could argue against the military policy provided they did not say they were homosexual. Under the "don't shout" compromise, an individual may say that he/she is homosexual but would then be prevented from making any statements that could be viewed as challenging the military policy (i.e., shouting). In other words, only those who did not admit to being homosexual could safely argue against the policy.

Such a policy also would leave acknowledged homosexuals open to blackmail since it is, to some extent, the reactions of others that determine whether or not they will be subject to discharge. Indeed, homosexuals would still be forced into the closet under fear that any activities, such as attending a gay church or bar, could be viewed as flaunting or shouting. The limits of such a policy would likely be tested daily, with commanders varying in their decisions as to what is and is not allowed.

The "don't tell, not on duty" proposal is another possible alternative. Under this compromise, service members would be expected to maintain military professionalism and decorum while in uniform or on base, but would be free to exercise individual "lifestyles" off base or off duty, even if this violated UCMJ sodomy provisions. Such a scenario could lead to a situation similar that in Newport involving Franklin D. Roosevelt. In Newport, military personnel did not state their homosexuality on base but used local civilian facilities to gather and solicit sex. In essence, local communities would have to deal with such behavior. However, such language contradicts the legal contention that those in the military serve twenty-four hours a day and are always subject to the UCMJ.

The basis of these compromises is important since it is likely to frame the issue for those in uniform and for courts in considering potential legal challenges to any policy. A basis that regards military concerns as paramount would place a greater burden on those challenging the policy on civil rights grounds. Conversely, a civil rights basis lays a greater burden on the military services in any action that provides differential treatment based on sexuality.

Consider first a compromise that holds military concerns to be paramount. An example is the 1981 DoD directive cited earlier which begins, "Homosexuality is incompatible with military service." Under its language, individuals seeking relief in the courts have generally been required to prove that equal protection, free speech, privacy, or due process considerations outweigh rational government interests in maintaining a strong defense. Although certain courts have recently required the military to prove that homosexuality would prove disruptive, these remain a part of a growing minority of decisions.

Next, consider language that would seek to balance the military and civil rights concerns:

> It is hereby declared to be the policy of the President that there shall be equality of treatment and opportunity for all persons in the armed service without regard to race, color, religion, national origin or sexual orientation. This policy shall be put into effect as rapidly as possible, having due regard to the time required to effectuate any necessary changes without impairing efficiency or morale.[26]

The burden of proof in this case would be shared by the competing interests of the military and homosexuals asserting their democratic rights.

Finally, the following policy basis would give precedence to civil rights:

> No member of the Armed Forces, or person seeking to become a member of the Armed Forces, may be discriminated against by the Armed Forces on the basis of sexual orientation. The Armed Forces are not required to modify any rule or policy regarding sexual misconduct or otherwise to sanction or condone sexual misconduct, but such rules and policies may not be applied in a manner that discriminates on the basis of sexual orientation.[27]

Under this language, any treatment of homosexuals that is perceived as being different from that of heterosexuals will be viewed as discriminatory regardless of any government rationale. Under this language, the military would be forced to argue in legal cases either that discrimination did not occur or that such discrimination is necessary for a fundamental purpose that could not be achieved through other means.

All of the above possible compromises can be considered under each of these bases. Considered together, Table 1 provides a heuristic model of these compromises and these bases. "Don't ask, don't tell" would be in

Table 1.   Heuristic Model

Compromise/ Basis	"Don't ask, don't tell"	"Don't ask, don't shout"	"Don't ask, not on duty"
Military paramount	A		
Balancing of concerns		B	
Civil rights paramount			C

keeping with the military's need to maintain discipline and cohesion above all else, while a "don't ask, not on duty" compromise would allow individuals to live a homosexual lifestyle so long as it did not encroach on military duties.

Unlettered cells represent areas in which the compromise and the basis would be in potential conflict and thereby prove difficult to implement and likely to be successfully challenged in the courts. For example, a "don't ask, don't tell" compromise would be inconsistent with a civil rights basis which seeks to protect individuals from discrimination. Conversely, a "don't ask, not on duty" compromise that is based on military concerns may create a double standard that calls into question the military's need for such a restrictive policy. Lacking critical political support from the Joint Chiefs of Staff, the administration appeared to seek a compromise that would allow it to maintain control of the issue via a presidential-congressional agreement incorporated into a DoD directive, rather than tempt Congress into enacting legislation that would codify the interim policy (or some modified version of it).[28]

President's Announced Compromise

On July 19, 1993, President Clinton announced his compromise: "don't ask, don't tell, don't pursue." The inclusion of the "don't pursue" (akin to a "don't investigate" stance advocated by homosexual rights groups) seemingly creates contradictions in the president's policy. On the one hand, it notes military necessity via a "don't ask, don't tell" approach, and then appears to defeat efforts to maintain discipline and good order by limiting the military's efforts to enforce rules: "Don't pursue." In other words, the military would be blocked from questioning individuals about their sexuality but would be allowed to discharge individuals should investigations so warrant (although a "don't pursue" policy seems to argue against, or require a higher standard of cause for, commencing investigations). These problems were brought to the surface in congressional hearings. Secretary of Defense Les Aspin indicated at one moment that individuals could not be forced to admit their homosexuality; later, he said that such statements are not credible grounds for investigating but could be credible grounds for discharge proceedings. Ultimately the secretary agreed that statements are grounds for discharge.

The president's policy was also based on sexual "orientation," a term that seems to defy definition.[29] This proposal also suggested that statements of homosexuality created a "rebuttable presumption" that the individual is or has been involved in homosexual acts or has an intention or propensity to engage in such acts. Such language places the service member in a (perhaps impossible) position of presenting evidence that he or she does not have such a propensity or intention to engage in homosexual acts. (A difficulty arises in that individuals may need to prove a negative.)

Hearings held by Congress raised numerous questions as to what behavior, if any, would justify the commencement of an investigation, and what grounds would need to be argued to justify an administrative discharge. Since commanders and noncommissioned officers are not trained lawyers, many members of Congress argued that such rules created legal technicalities that would prove dysfunctional in a military setting and thus lead to an expansion of unpredictable court remedies.[30]

Congress Acts

The HASC and SASC reports on the fiscal year 1994 National Defense Authorization Act were filed shortly after these hearings.[31] Both recognized the constitutional authority granted solely to Congress for making rules and regulations for the military, and the Senate report noted at length the traditional deference granted by the courts to Congress in the control of the military. Both recognized the unique needs and demands of military life and the necessity for maintaining order, discipline, and unit cohesion. The House language included a reiteration of the statement that homosexuality is incompatible with military service. In other words, both reports held as their basis that military necessity is paramount.

On November 30, 1993, the Defense Authorization Act was signed into law by President Clinton (P.L. 103-160). In many ways, this law represented a reiteration of the 1981 policy. Viewing homosexuals in the ranks as an "unacceptable risk . . . to morale, good order, and discipline," this law codifies the grounds for discharge: 1) the member has engaged in, attempted to engage in, or solicited another to engage in a homosexual act or acts (as defined), 2) the member states that he or she is homosexual or bisexual, or 3) the member has married or attempted to marry someone of the same sex. This law also states that DoD will brief new entrants (accessions) and members on a regular basis concerning these laws and regulations. Finally, the law instructs that asking questions concerning sexuality may be done on a discretionary basis. As such, this law represents a "discretionary don't ask, definitely don't tell" policy.

Update

On December 22, 1993, Secretary of Defense Aspin released the new military regulations.[32] It appeared that the administration was trying to incorporate both the restrictions in the law, as signed by the president, and the president's desire to open the military to those who have a homosexual "orientation." However, with Aspin's resignation and the confirmation of William Perry as the new secretary of defense in February 1994, DoD accepted the recommendation of certain senators to delete from DoD regulations the phrase, "homosexual orientation . . . is not a bar to military service."[33] In its place, DoD inserted the statement:

> A person's sexual orientation is considered a personal and private matter and is not a bar to service unless manifested by homosexual conduct.[34]

Current regulations are based on conduct, including statements. Since sexual "orientation" is "private and personal," DoD is not to ask and personnel are not to tell. Should an individual choose to make his or her homosexual "orientation" public—i.e., no longer private or personal—an investigation or discharge are likely to result. So long as the services don't ask and the service member does not tell, the issue of sexual "orientation" is moot.

While challenges to the old regulations continue to work their way through the courts,[35] new challenges must address the law as enacted by Congress and signed by the President. Although courts would continue to consider the constitutionality of military laws and regulations, their role is markedly circumspect in matters constitutionally under legislative and executive jurisdiction—the control and discipline of the military.[36]

Acknowledgments

I am grateful for the comments of Robert Goldich and James Robinson on a draft of this paper.

Notes

1.   Major Jeffrey S. Davis, "Military Policy toward Homosexuals: Scientific, Historical, and Legal Perspectives," *Military Law Review*, 131 (Winter 1991):115.

2.   U.S. Congress. Senate. Committee on Naval Affairs, Alleged Immoral Conditions At Newport (R.I.) Naval Training Station, 66th Cong., 1st Sess., 1921:5,[citing the Dunn court] "Therefore this court is of the opinion that it was unfortunate and

ill-advised that Franklin D. Roosevelt, Assistant Secretary of the Navy either directed or permitted the use of enlisted personnel to investigate perversion." "Lay Navy Scandal to F.D. Roosevelt," *New York Times*, 20 July 1921.

3.   John Ordronaux, in Ira M. Rutkow (ed.), *On the Examinations of Recruits and Discharge of Soldiers* (San Francisco: Norton, 1990), 212, 223–224.

4.   Allan Berube, *Coming Out Under Fire: The History of Gay Men and Women in World War Two*, (New York: Penguin, 1991), 13–14.

5.   William P. Snyder and Kenneth L. Nyberg, "Policy Paper Gays and the Military: An Emerging Policy Issue," *Journal of Political and Military Sociology* 8 (Spring 1980).

6.   U.S. Department of Defense, the Deputy Secretary of Defense, Memorandum, January 16, 1981: "I am promulgating today a change to DoD Directive 1332.14 (Enlisted Administrative Separations), including a completely new Enclosure 8 on Homosexuality. The revision contains no change in policy. It reaffirms that homosexuality is incompatible with military service." Although these changes were put into place under the Carter administration, the directive on Enlisted Administrative Separations was again revised in 1982. This later revision did not affect the policy on homosexuality. Nevertheless, the 1982 date has caused some to erroneously attribute this language to the Reagan administration.

7.   U.S. Department of Defense, Directive No. 1332.14, Enlisted Administrative Separations, 28 January 1982:1-9–1-13.

8.   Under DoD regulations and the UCMJ, a person cannot be prosecuted for merely being homosexual. Although a person can be administratively discharged, with an honorable or general discharge for making statements confirming that he or she is homosexual, such statements are viewed as acts (see Ben-Shalom v. Marsh, 881 F.2d 454, 462 (7th Cir. 1989) as discussed in the Appendix of Burrelli, CRS Report). Merely making a statement, however, is likely to lead to an investigation under the policy. (See H. G. Reza, "Sailor at Odds with the Navy's Anti-Gay Policy," *Los Angeles Times* (Washington, D.C.), 1 April 1992, B-2).

9.   U.S. Department of Defense, Office of the Assistant Secretary of Defense, Directive No. 1332.30, Separation of Regular Commissioned Officers for Cause, 12 February 1986, section 2:2-1, 2-2.

10.   U.S. Department of Defense, Office of the Assistant Secretary of Defense (HA), Directive No. 6130.3, Physical Standards for Enlistment, Appointment, and Induction, 31 March 1986: See XVI. Mental Disorders, para. 2-34. Psychosexual Conditions, p. 1-36. The other two subsections cite as reasons for rejection: (b) Transsexualism and Other Gender Identity Disorders, and, (c) Exhibitionism, Transvestism, Voyeurism and Other Paraphilias.

11.   Burrelli, CRS Report.

12.   U.S. Constitution, Article 1, Section 8, provides Congress with the power to "make rules for the Government and Regulation of the land and naval Forces." Under Article H, Section 2, the Constitution states "The President shall be Commander in Chief of the Army and Navy of the United States, and of the Militia of the several States, when called into the actual Service of the United States."

13.   See *Congressional Record*, 139(14), 4 February 1993:S1263–S1339.

14.   *Congressional Quarterly,* January 30, 1993:235.

15.   Bill McAllister, "Aspin Orders Outside Study on Gays Issue," *Washington*

Post, 26 March 1993. A press report of the Rand study (which was released in October 1993), suggested that Rand advised the services to take a "disinterest in service member's sexual orientation and place the military's focus on the member's conduct." Grant Willis, "Study's Advice on Gays: Turn a Blind Eye," *Navy Times*, 21 June 1993:18. It is important to note that the Rand Corp. was instructed to study how to implement an order ending discrimination against homosexuals. Rand was not asked to study whether or not such a policy change should be made. Some have erroneously viewed the Rand study as providing support for the argument that the "ban should be lifted."

16.   U.S. Congress. Senate. Committee on Armed Services, Hearings on the Military Policy Concerning the Service of Gays and Lesbians in the Armed Forces, 29 April 1993. (Hearings have not yet been published; I was in attendance.)

17.   Rowan Scarborough, "Aspin Aide Upbraids Major Whose Book Supports Gay Ban," *Washington Times*, 15 April 1993.

18.   Meinhold v. United States, 808 F. Supp. 1455 (C.D. Calif. 1993).

19.   "[P]erhaps Judge Hatter was not concerned about possible appellate review because of a very simple fact: At the time he issued his opinion he could have made a calculated guess that the Clinton administration would not be appealing his decision, however broad and unconventional." Sanford Levinson, "Presidential Power and Gays in the Military," *Wall Street Journal*, 3 February 1993.

20.   For example, on 26 May 1993, the *Washington Post* published an article on the front page concerning an alleged "gay bashing" case entitled "Sailor's Killer 'Disgusted' by Gays, Court Is Told Defendant in Vicious Beating Said 'I'd Do It Again.'" Such hyperbole was tailor-made for the slogan used by homosexual rights advocates "Don't let hate win." The next day, the same paper wrote on page A37, "Sailor Denies Murder Was Gay-Bashing, 'Temper' Outburst Blamed in Slaying of Shipmate." The article also notes that both the prosecution and the defense "played down the gay issue."

21.   For instance, the *Philadelphia Inquirer* reported that while congressional committees "heard from dozens of uniformed personnel and Pentagon lawyers, not a single gay person testified" (Mark Thompson, "Confusion by policy on gays in military," *Philadelphia Inquirer*, 25 July 1993). Thompson fails to report that numerous self-acknowledged homosexuals testified, including Tanya Domi (before HASC), Tracy Thorne, and Greta Cammermeyer (before SASC). Likewise, the *Wall Street Journal* reported that prior to the Persian Gulf deployment, a "Commander's Handbook" barred the discharge of homosexuals after an alert notification was made. No such handbook has been found nor has their been any documentation that any such bars existed (Wade Lambert, "U.S. Military Moves to Discharge Some Gay Veterans of Gulf War," *Wall Street Journal*, 30 July 1991).

22.   While I do not doubt that certain individuals were separated under harassing conditions, the data on the number and type of discharges do not support the notion of "witch-hunts" as a general operating policy. See Burrelli, CRS Report.

23.   Barney Frank, "however, said the battle already has been lost. 'I don't think the campaigning [by those in favor of overturning the policy] has been productive,' said Frank, who described the recent gay rights march on Washington as a political failure." John Lancaster, "Rep. Frank Urges Deal on Gay Ban," *Washington Post*, 19 May 1993.

24. See David F. Burrelli, "HIV-l/AIDS and U.S. Military Manpower Policy," *Armed Forces and Society,* 18 (Summer 1992):452–75.

25. Ben-Shalom, see note 9; Pruitt v. Cheney, 963 F.2d 1160 (9th Cir. 1992), cert. denied 61 U.S.L.W. 3414 (S.Ct. 12-8-92). For a more complete discussion of the legal history, see Charles V. Dale in Burrelli, CRS Report, 56–62.

26. This language is a modified version of a section of President Truman's Executive Order 9981, July 26, 1948, integrating the armed forces.

27. This language is from H.R. 5208, Rep. Patricia Schroeder, May 19, 1992; S. 3084, Sen. Howard Metzenbaum, July 28, 1992.

28. U.S. Department of Defense, Office of the Secretary of Defense, (unsigned) Memorandum, Policy On Homosexuals in The Armed Forces, (undated), cited in Rowan Scarborough, "Aspin Policy Follows 'Don't Ask, Don't Tell,'" *Washington Times,* 22 June 1993, and Rowan Scarborough, "Gay-Ban Memo Called Trial Balloon," *Washington Times,* 23 June 1993. See also Rowan Scarborough, "White House Short on Votes to Lift Gay Ban," *Washington Times,* 24 June 1993.

29. Congress, the courts, homosexual rights groups, academic researchers, and others have used this term to indicate homosexuality as a status, even if such a status includes behavior. As such, the term has proven to be a source of obfuscation.

30. "[I]t is difficult to conceive of an area of governmental activity in which the courts have less competence. The complex, subtle, and professional decision as to the composition, training, equipping, and control of the military force are essentially professional military judgments, subject always to civilian control of the Legislative and Executive Branches." Gilligan v. Morgan, 413 U.S. 1, 10 (1973). "[C]ourts are 'ill-equipped to determine the impact upon discipline that any particular intrusion upon military authority might have.'" Chappell v. Wallace, 462 U.S. 296, 305 (quoting Chief Justice Earl Warren, "The Bill of Rights and the Military," 37 N.Y.U.L. Rev. 181, 187 (1962).

31. U.S. Congress. Senate. Committee on Armed Services, National Defense Authorization Act for Fiscal Year 1994, 103d Cong., S. 1298, 1st Sess., S. Rept. 103-112: 263-322. House of Representative's language is cited in unpublished form.

32. U.S. Department of Defense, Office of the Assistant Secretary of Defense (Public Affairs), "Secretary Aspin Releases New Regulations on Homosexual Conduct in the Armed Forces," December 22, 1993.

33. Rowan Scarborough, "White House Cuts Phrase Restricting Gay Discharges," *Washington Times,* 10 February 1994.

34. "Defense Policy on Gays Takes Effect," *Washington Post,* 2 March 1994.

35. Eric Schmitt, "Appeals Court to Reconsider a Right to Bar Gay Troops," *New York Times,* 8 January 1994.

36. Legislation effectively providing an administratively implemented "Don't ask, Don't tell" policy on a statutory basis reflects a national consensus on the subject and vests it with all the sovereign power of the United States. See Justice Jackson's concurring opinion in the landmark Steel Seizure Case, Youngstown Co. v. Sawyer, 343 U.S. 579, 634, 635-636 (1952).

Chapter 3

Social Science Research on Homosexuals in the Military[1]

DAVID R. SEGAL, PAUL A. GADE,
and EDGAR M. JOHNSON

In providing a social science perspective on sexual orientation and U.S. military services, Herek recommended that social scientists focus their empirical research on three areas:[2] collecting of descriptive data on the attitudes and stereotypes of military personnel concerning homosexuals; studying the experiences of other organizations with openly gay and lesbian personnel—including military services in foreign countries; and examining the U.S. military experiences surrounding the integration of women and minorities. The wisdom of these recommendations became manifest in the course of hearings on policies regarding homosexuality in the armed forces held by the armed services committees of both the Senate and the House of Representatives in the spring of 1993.

Questions reflecting Herek's proposed research agenda were repeatedly asked of social science witnesses who were testifying before both congressional committees.[3] At the time of the hearings, the information that could be offered with regard to each of the above questions was, for different reasons, incomplete, and consensus was absent among the social scientists testifying. Nonetheless, since these questions are within the purview of social science and since the issue of homosexuals in the military has not reached its formal resolution, it seems reasonable to document the state of knowledge as we understand it today. Our focus in this paper is on the experience in other militaries and on surveys of civilians and military personnel. Several other papers in this volume, notably the one by Horner and Anderson, address comparisons with the integration of blacks and women in the U.S. military.

The Cross-National Experience

Policy regarding the integration of homosexuals in the military is not a uniquely American issue. In recent years there has been both growing awareness and growing tolerance of homosexuality in Western industrial democratic societies. This has been reflected in decisions by medical and psychological associations to cease regarding homosexuality as a mental illness and, in some jurisdictions, in decriminalization of homosexual acts between consenting adults, and in making homosexuals legally eligible for "partnership" benefits that previously were restricted to legally married heterosexual couples.

Policies regarding homosexuals in the military seem to reflect but lag behind the policies in their host societies. However, the social sciences have neither a long research tradition nor a rich database on the policies and practices that exist cross-nationally that might be used to inform the policy debate. Social scientists in the international community have begun to turn their attention to this issue, largely in response to American concerns, and papers that describe policies and practices in individual nations have recently been given at professional conferences.[4]

There are two general patterns that are noteworthy. First, there are at least five dimensions that are important in describing sexual orientation integration in military forces. The first two are defined by the temporal difference between military accession and conditions of subsequent service, and by potential differences between policy and practice. The position of any given nation on each of these four dimensions may range from exclusion of homosexuals, through laissez-faire, to complete tolerance and support. However, in any given nation, there may be considerable difference among the four dimensions. Beyond the point of accession, policies and practices regarding conditions of service also frequently differ from each other and from policies and practices regarding accession as well.[5] The last of the five dimensions deals with the distinction between conscripted and volunteer soldiers who, as we will note below, may serve under different policies. Table 1 summarizes the differences in these five dimensions in seven European nations.

The second general pattern we note is that, in many of the nations we discuss, policy on sexual orientation has been related to policy on racial, ethnic, and gender integration. This speaks to the third issue raised by Herek. We do not want to prejudge the appropriateness of this linkage, but we do want to note that the United States is not the only nation in which this association has been raised. In Canada, Australia, and the Netherlands in particular, sexual orientation integration has been seen explicitly as a civil rights or human rights issue.

Most nations with which we are familiar do not categorically exclude homosexuals. Some of those which in the past have excluded homosexuals have changed their policies in recent years. We know of no nation that in the past has admitted homosexuals and has recently moved to exclude them. Thus, the number of nations that exclude homosexuals from military service has been declining.

The Anglo-American Nations

The major group of nations that in recent history has been concerned with homosexuals in the military is composed of the Anglo-American nations: the United States, Great Britain, Canada, Australia, New Zealand, and Northern Ireland. These nations share a more-or-less common cultural heritage.

Reporting on Australia and New Zealand at the 1991 conference in Baltimore, Dr. Cathy Downes, an analyst in the Office of the Chief of Defense Staff of New Zealand, reported the following:

> Arguments challenging the exclusion of homosexuals from armed forces have been raised. These flow from changes in the parent societies of these armed forces. For example, the change between early and late Cold War periods is also the time period in which there is a significant shift in societal attitudes toward tolerance of homosexuality. . . . If the relationship between social change and military response holds true, the gradual normalization of homosexuality in larger societies, which is a 1980s phenomenon, is likely to be increasingly refracted in military forces of the 1990s.[6]

Dr. Downes was prescient. Late in 1992, Australia set aside its exclusion. New Zealand began to move toward a policy change after our presidential election, but seems to have delayed further consideration until the direction that the United States will take is clear.

At the same conference, Col. Franklin Pinch, who holds a Ph.D. in sociology and who at the time was the ranking behavioral scientist in the Canadian Forces, reported:

> The Canadian Forces are preparing a defense involving homosexuality which is before the courts. While these outcomes cannot be prejudged, two points are relevant: first, the tribunal on the employment of women did not accept the argument that cohesion and morale would be impaired by the introduction of women, since it was based largely on "customer preference" (i.e., that men would not accept women), and it is unlikely to be accepted for other issues; second, the Canadian public, and especially opinion leaders, are generally not supportive of such exclusions . . . [homo- and hetero-] sexual behavior that is disruptive may well supplant concerns regarding sexual orientation.[7]

Table 1

Country	Accessions		Conditions of Service	
	Policy	*Practice*	*Policy*	*Practice*
United Kingdom (volunteer)	Since June 1992 enlistees have not been asked about sexual orientation. Homosexuality is considered incompatible with military service.	Recruits are rejected if they volunteer that they are homosexual.	Sexual Offences Act of 1967 legalized homosexuality for those over 21.	Administrative discharge for homosexuals.
Germany (conscription)	Homosexual men are considered fit for military service.	Sexual orientation is asked in medical exam. Homosexuals are almost never admitted to military service.	Homosexual may not command or instruct troops; homosexuality not reason for discharge.	Administrative discharge for homosexuals.

Belgium (conscription)	No difference between civilian and military law in employment rights. Sexual orientation is not asked.	Homosexuals permitted to serve.	No discharge for homosexuality.	Transfers from unit or service for open displays of homosexual behavior.
Denmark (Scan.) (conscription)	Homosexuals serve on equal terms with others.	Can self-eliminate by declaring homosexual status.	No discharge for homosexuality.	Very little "coming out"
Netherlands (conscription)	Homosexuals serve on equal terms with others.	Can self-eliminate by declaring homosexual status.	Homosexual emancipation and integration. Published leaflets welcome homosexuals.	Emancipation and integration less than full.
France (conscription)	No specific policy regarding homosexuality.	Homosexuality seen as behavioral disorder. Can self-eliminate by declaring homosexual status.	No specific policy.	Open homosexuality sanctioned informally.
Italy (conscription)	No specific policy. Homosexuality considered a behavioral anomaly not a pathology.	Homosexuals accepted as draftees but not as volunteers.	No specific policy for officers. NCOs under different rules.	Homosexual draftees released, junior officers and NCOs discharged, senior officers and NCOs transferred.

Sources: Presentations at the Conferences on Comparative International Military Personnel Policies, Beverly, U.K., April 2–4 and July 9–12, 1993.

Again, the statement was prescient. Canada has set aside its exclusion, as one part of a more general human rights movement. Dr. Pinch is now retired from the Canadian Forces and is doing research on the impact of their policy change. He recently indicated that there has been no impact of the policy change on recruitment or retention, nor have there been incidents of harassment of homosexuals. Homosexuals, for their part, have not made declarations of their sexual orientations.[8] The Australian experience is reported to have been similar.

The United Kingdom is a particularly interesting case, because it highlights the direction of social change, reflects a frequently found divergence between official policy and actual practice, and exemplifies a commonly found pattern: that of limited tolerance. In terms of official policy, when most homosexual acts were decriminalized in the 1967 Sexual Offenses Act, the British military was exempted from decriminalization. In May 1991, a parliamentary Select Committee on the Armed Forces recommended decriminalization in the armed forces as well, and in June 1992 the government accepted this recommendation. While decriminalized, homosexuality is still regarded as incompatible with military service and is grounds for denial of enlistment or instant dismissal.[9] Thus, the official policy is one of exclusion. However, as indicated in Table 1, military personnel are not asked about their sexual orientations. The practice is to not act unless they call attention to themselves. Indeed, if their orientation becomes known but they are not openly engaged in homosexual behavior, they might be counseled and warned against misconduct, rather than discharged. If they are discharged, in the great majority of cases the action is administrative rather than disciplinary.

Most of our other NATO allies do not exclude homosexuals in terms of policy. The exceptions are Turkey, where homosexuals are explicitly prohibited from serving openly but soldiers are not asked their sexual orientation,[10] and Greece, where homosexuality is regarded as a mental illness.[11] Belgium, Denmark, France, Italy, Luxembourg, Norway, Portugal, and Spain all to varying degrees regard sexual orientation as irrelevant to military service.[12]

Latin Europe

A common pattern, found widely in Latin Europe, might be labeled laissez-faire. A revision of the military service laws in Portugal in 1989 set aside regulations prohibiting homosexuals from serving in the armed forces.[13] Spain decriminalized homosexuality in the military in 1984, making sexual orientation simply a matter of personal choice.[14] France takes a similar position.

Two of France's foremost military sociologists, Professors Bernard Boene, head of the sociology program at the French Military Academy, and Michel Martin, of the University of Toulouse, reported the following at the 1991 Baltimore conference:

> As [a] Catholic [country, France] . . . tolerated deviant behavior . . . because the possibility of forgiveness is current. This explains why one finds great military figures with known homosexual tendencies, or why homosexuality was proverbial among colonial troops. . . . Today the issue is rarely mentioned in the military, though the recognition of homosexuality in the civilian sphere has become a fact. In the military, it is shrouded in a kind of silence that does not express embarrassment, but a complete lack of interest. The clue may be that most homosexuals are screened out or self-selected out. It should be noted that in France, the gay movement as well as the feminist movement, from the 1960s until today has had a strong anti-militarist tradition.[15]

More recently, Robert and Fabre have confirmed that the issue of homosexuality is not a preoccupation of the French armed forces, and have contrasted the tolerance and the reserve of the French position with the acrimony of the American debate. Unless there are behavioral problems, sexuality is regarded as a private matter by the French military, and in fact homosexuality per se is not grounds for avoiding conscription, although behavioral problems associated with homosexuality may preclude military service.[16]

In Italy, until 1985, homosexuality was a basis for exemption from conscription. It is no longer a categorical reason for exclusion, and, as in most European societies, conscripts are not routinely asked their sexual orientation. Individual conscripts may declare themselves as homosexual as a means of trying to avoid military service, but to achieve this they must in addition convince the Military Medical Psychological Unit that there are behavioral problems associated with their sexual orientations. Among career military personnel, homosexuals are unlikely to reveal their sexual orientations, and if they are discovered, they are likely to be encouraged to resign, discharged, or transferred.[17]

Belgium, which is in the north but is close to Latin Europe and has a significant francophone population, likewise holds a laissez-faire position. There are no laws, rules, or regulations discriminating against homosexuals in the military, as long as they separate their personal and professional lives. Indeed, homosexuals have equal employment rights in both the civilian and military arenas.[18] In this sense, Belgium is more explicitly tolerant than other laissez-faire countries and is closer to the dominant northern European pattern. In the past, homosexuals were not allowed to serve in the Paracommando regiment, but this seems to have been a function of the commander's preference rather than service policy. Soldiers whose sexual behavior is abusive of peers, i.e,. harassment, or disruptive of the unit are subject to reassignment or medical discharge.

A similar lack of interest is noted in Switzerland, which has significant Francophone and Italian-speaking populations, but which is not a member of NATO. Sociologist Karl Haltiner reported in 1991:

> Homosexuality itself has never been a reason for military exclusion. If, as a result of homosexual behavior, social or psychological problems occur, an inspection for leave in the psychiatric-medical manner is possible but not compulsory. The highest [Swiss] military lawyer laconically remarked in 1985: "The problem of homosexuality does not exist in the Swiss army."[19]

Northern Europe

Just as the restrictive positions of Turkey and Greece contrast with the laissez-faire policies of the Latin nations in southern Europe, so is there a range of positions in the north. Germany is an especially interesting case because, like Great Britain, it manifests a major difference between policy and practice, but in the opposite direction, and because it lies at one end of the range of patterns. It is also an extremely complex case, because its armed forces are composed of both conscripts and volunteers, who, as in the Italian case, serve under different policies, and because there are civilian service alternatives to conscription for conscientious objectors. In practice, as reflected in Table 1, Germany is the most exclusionary country we have studied.

Currently, like most European countries, officially Germany does not regard sexual orientation as a relevant criterion for conscripted military service. However, homosexual volunteers cannot be inducted,[20] and career personnel who are discovered to be homosexual are limited in the nature of their service,[21] not officially because of homosexuality per se, but because of its presumed impact on their military aptitude and leadership ability.[22] In practice very few homosexuals seem to serve. Unlike most nations, German doctors ask conscripts and volunteers about their sexual orientation during the accession process, as noted in Table 1, although this is not an official policy.

Many homosexual young men appear to opt for alternative civilian service rather than serving conscripted military service. Those who are conscripted, if they reveal their sexual orientation during in-processing, are likely to be rejected as "mentally unfit for service," thereby avoiding both military service and alternative civilian service. Official policy states that regular servicemen and volunteers are not rendered unfit for military service by homosexuality nor can they be discharged for a homosexual orientation. If they are discovered to be homosexual and have served for more than four years, they are not discharged before their term of service is completed. However, in practice, as noted in Table 1, if their orientation becomes known, homosexuals will not be allowed to assume supervisory positions nor to serve as instructors. They may be restricted from high-security assignments as well. Junior officers within three years of commission may be discharged on grounds that they are unfit for a career as an officer.

Homosexuality has been decriminalized in German society, and homosexual behavior by military personnel off duty is not prosecuted. However, the German courts have affirmed the right of the *Bundeswehr* to prosecute soldiers for homosexual acts while on duty. Molesting a subordinate is grounds for discharge. Less serious offenses may be punished by demotion, ban on promotions, or salary cuts.

In contrast, a few nations currently treat homosexuals as a privileged minority, at least in the military accession process. In the Scandinavian countries, for example, homosexuality was initially ignored by the armed forces in the post–World War II years. Then, until the late 1970s draftees were asked about their sexual orientations, and homosexuals were registered and in some cases forced out. However, draftees are no longer asked about sexual orientation nor are homosexuals registered. Homosexual draftees can avoid military service, with varying degrees of difficulty among countries, by claiming that their sexual orientation is psychologically incompatible with military service. Thus, control over whether the homosexual draftee serves is in his hands.[23]

The Netherlands probably represent the most tolerant position regarding homosexuals in the military. Dutch sociologist Jan van der Meulen reported at the 1991 conference:

> The acceptance and integration of women, ethnic minorities, and homosexuals in the armed forces was initiated as principle and policy before the end of the Cold War. . . . This does not mean that women, ethnic minorities, and homosexuals nowadays meet no discrimination any longer, nor that all three integration processes are concurrent.[24]

More recently, Marion Andersen-Boers and van der Meulen have elaborated the Dutch position, and emphasized that sexual orientation has been ruled out as a selection criterion for both conscript and career personnel and that where problems occur, they are seen not as a consequence of homosexual orientation, but rather of homophobic reaction.[25]

Because the Netherlands are probably the most open and tolerant of nations with regard to homosexuality in the military, it has been in a position to openly undertake policy initiatives to make integration work, and to conduct research on problems of integration. Given the view that problems are primarily a result of homophobia rather than of homosexuality per se, the

Dutch military has instituted a training program to familiarize personnel with the range of homosexual life-styles and to attempt to dispel incorrect stereotypes.[26] This position and the findings of a major survey of Dutch military personnel are detailed in the paper by Andersen-Boers and van der Meulen in this volume.[27] The Dutch Defense Ministry has established a Commission for Advice and Coordination on Homosexuality in the Armed Forces, and homosexuals in the service have their own union, financed in part by the Defense Ministry.

Eastern Europe

While homosexuality was anathema to Soviet communism, laissez-faire was characteristic of at least one of the countries of the old Warsaw Pact as well. Jerzy Wiatr, the foremost Polish military sociologist, and now a member of parliament, reported in 1991:

> In the Polish armed forces there are no laws discriminating against homosexuals. I have also not found instances of extra-legal discrimination. . . . In Poland, because of the intensity of conformity in publicly accepted norms of sexual behavior, homosexuality remains taboo. People do not reveal their homosexuality, not because of laws, but because of informal social control. . . . The fact that the armed forces do not discriminate against homosexuals does not mean that they are accepted. Rather it can be said that as far as the military structure is concerned, they simply do not exist.[28]

General Patterns

There is consensus within the international community of social scientists that some individuals with homosexual orientations have managed to serve undetected in the military forces of virtually all Western nations. There is also consensus that most homosexuals in the military do not come out, but rather keep their sexual orientation a private matter, even where policy and practice allow them to serve. There is still a stigma attached to being homosexual even in the most liberal societies and there may be career costs associated with such declarations. Thus, the number of military personnel in Western nations who publicly identify themselves as homosexual is very small. Even in those countries with nonexclusionary policies, practices are such that open homosexuals may find themselves referred for psychiatric counseling and excluded from combat units and from certain assignments.

The sociohistorical context of a country's military service is very important in determining its policies and practices toward homosexuals. The more liberal countries seem to have had a long history of struggles with homosexual issues, and the liberalization of attitudes toward homosexuals in the military has evolved slowly, lagging behind more general social attitudes. Gay and lesbian activist groups, although they are usually antimilitary, have often served as the catalyst for changing policies and practices concerning homosexuals in the military services of more tolerant countries.

Most countries seem to be more conservative in practice than they are in policy. Even in countries where no questions are asked about sexual orientation at accession or during military service, the practice of not asking may be more an act of active omission designed to avoid addressing potentially more complex issues, such as partnership benefits, than it is an act of passive acceptance of homosexuality. Potential issues are thus "silenced" by not asking about sexual orientation. In fact, the most common pattern cross-nationally seems to be that military forces do not ask about sexual orientation, even when they have exclusionary policies.

Policies and practices about homosexuals in the military seem to follow national social norms. Heterosexuality is clearly the dominant norm in Western societies. Even in the most liberal societies, homosexuals in the military do not flaunt their life-style; in fact they often choose not to openly identify themselves as homosexuals at all.

Perhaps because heterosexuality is the dominant norm, few data are available on homosexuals and no country, no matter how liberal, seems to know the precise percentage of its military that is homosexual. Neither does any of the countries we have studied seem to know what percentage of its general population is homosexual, although there are estimates, ranging from one to ten percent.

Exclusion of one's sexuality and gender altogether from the workplace are emerging norms in Western societies that will, in all likelihood, eventually serve to regulate homosexual as well as heterosexual behavior. However, the process is far from complete and the path to resolution is likely to be a difficult one.

Public and Military Opinion Regarding Homosexuality

In discussions of whether or not the integration of homosexuals in military forces is a civil rights issue, no analyst has argued that the historical experiences of minority racial or ethnic groups, women, and homosexuals have been the same. Rather, the argument has been that there have been parallels in societal reactions to groups whose participation in military forces and other citizenship roles has been precluded or limited.

In recent years, questions regarding homosexuals as a social group and homosexuality as a pattern of behavior have been asked of both civilian and military respondents in a number of European countries and in the United States. While the questions and samples vary from nation to nation, sufficient data are available to begin to describe existing patterns, as well as dominant and changing social norms.

The European Case

Fleckenstein has assembled data from 1990 for ten European countries (Belgium, France, West Germany, Great Britain, Northern Ireland, Republic of Ireland, Italy, Netherlands, Portugal, Spain) on their tolerance for homosexuality.[29] Data were also collected on tolerance for two forms of sexual misconduct: married men or women having an affair, and sex under the legal age of consent. The general picture for most of these nations (with the exception of the Netherlands), is that while homosexuality is devalued, it is more tolerable, on average, than sexual misconduct. The Dutch are more tolerant of homosexuality than are citizens of other nations, but the former express similar negative views of marital infidelity.

In the German case, Fleckenstein also presented, as a measure of social distance, the willingness of respondents in a 1992 survey to have people from a variety of social, ethnic, and religious groups (including homosexuals) as neighbors.[30] By a considerable margin, homosexuals were found more desirable as neighbors than left-wing or right-wing extremists, drug addicts, alcoholics, and gypsies. They were relatively close in acceptability to people with criminal convictions, people with mental disorders, people with AIDS, and Muslims. They were less acceptable than Hindus, foreigners, people with a different skin color, large families, and Jews (who were seen as the least undesirable neighbors). Data from German conscripts in 1992, by contrast, reveal that they found homosexuality less acceptable than unmarried cohabitation, prostitution, and abortion.

The data on Belgium presented by Fleckenstein—showing homosexuality to be unjustified but less so than marital infidelity—is complemented by Manigart, whose 1993 data on 1,000 civilians aged fifteen to twenty-five showed that 58 percent of the respondents disagree with the statement that "Homosexuals should not be allowed to serve in the Belgian military." Twenty-seven percent of the sample agreed, the rest having no opinion.[31] Manigart notes a parallel between this distribution and the fact that a previous survey had found 67 percent of the Belgian public to agree that women as well as men should be in the military, highlighting the similarity in reactions to excluded groups.

Manigart also reports on a first step toward gauging attitudes toward homosexuals among Belgian military personnel. In May 1993, two groups of soldiers (officers, NCOs and volunteers) undergoing human resource management training at the Military Training Center were asked: "Should gay men or lesbians be kicked out of the military?" The groups consisted of about thirty individuals each. Across the two groups, only one person, who had had a negative personal work experience with a colleague, thought that homosexuals should not be allowed to serve. Although these groups were not chosen to be statistically representative of the Belgian armed forces, Manigart infers tolerance within the armed forces from these data.

Fleckenstein's data did not include the Scandinavian countries, where on the basis of the policies described earlier, one would expect to find a higher level of tolerance. Sorensen reports differences among the Scandinavian countries, as well as change over time, with regard to the extreme issue of whether homosexuals should be allowed to marry. In Sweden, in 1993, 48 percent of survey respondents felt they should be allowed to marry. In Denmark, which appears the most tolerant of the Scandinavian countries, the percentage increased from 35 percent in 1970 to 64 percent in 1989. In Norway it increased from 16 percent in 1983 to 22 percent in 1988. While the dominant Scandinavian view still seems to oppose homosexual marriage, there is support for homosexuals being accepted for military service: 50 percent in Denmark in 1985, and 73 percent in Norway in 1983.[32]

The largest database in Europe on this issue is from the Netherlands, which was the outlier nation in Fleckenstein's data. There, due to the openness of the system, there has been both an ability to do research, and a desire on the part of decision-makers to have it done. Andersen-Boers and van der Meulen provide a summary of these data in this volume.[33]

The American Case

Public Opinion. The pattern of American public opinion toward homosexuality is similar to the one that seems to prevail in most other Western nations: aversion toward homosexual behavior, but respect for the rights of homosexuals. Mueller, for example, using data from the General Social Survey from 1973 to 1980, found that a majority of Americans thought that it was wrong for adults of the same sex to have sexual relations. About 20 percent thought it was never wrong or almost never wrong.[34] However, slowly increasing majorities of the same respondents felt that homosexuals had the right to teach in colleges and universities, to have books advocating homosexuality in local public libraries, and to speak in public. The gradient shows up particularly strongly with regard to employment rights. In 1977, 56 percent of Americans felt that homosexuals should have equal rights in terms of job opportunities. By April 1993, the figure had reached 80 percent.[35]

This equality did not extend to the military. Here the population was more evenly divided. In January 1993, 50 percent of Americans disapproved of ending the ban on homosexuals in the military, while 43 percent approved.[36]

Military Attitudes. Three survey efforts that assessed the attitudes of service members toward homosexuals serving in the miliary services were undertaken in 1992 and 1993. Since the paper by Miller later in this book also covers these surveys,[37] we will discuss each only briefly and then draw three conclusions based on these survey efforts.

Unfortunately, all three survey efforts have flaws. The first, and most reliable, of these surveys was a random telephone survey of service member personnel conducted by the air force.[38] The results are probably generalizable to personnel within the air force who have telephones, but may exclude some junior enlisted members, who frequently do not have telephones, and are not necessarily generalizable to the other services.

This survey showed that service personnel, especially younger, lower-ranking males, were decidedly against openly admitting homosexuals into the military services. They felt that open homosexuals serving would be disruptive and an invasion of their privacy. Senior officers and females tended to be more liberal in their attitudes about the service of homosexuals and seemed less threatened by the privacy issue. Those officers in direct combat jobs were more likely to say they were against the integration of homosexuals into the service than were those in support positions.

Although none of the other services was able to execute a similar large-scale survey investigating the homosexual issue in detail, Miller and Moskos were able to conduct a quota sample survey of army personnel in December 1992 and again in June 1993.[39] Because the sample was not randomly selected and because only a few army installations participated in the survey, the results may not be generalizable to the army as a whole. Nevertheless, the results are strikingly similar to those of the air force survey in that male combat soldiers at the lower ranks were most likely to express strong negative opinions about homosexuals openly serving in the military services.

Similar to the air force survey findings, women and senior officers were likely to be more positive about homosexuals serving in the Army. Forty-five percent of the junior enlisted men and 21 percent of the junior enlisted women said they would definitely leave the Army if the ban on homosexuals was lifted. For male NCOs and officers the figures were lower, at 25 and 23 percent respectively. The percentages were also lower for female NCOs (17 percent) and officers (11 percent).[40]

Finally, a February 1993 *Los Angeles Times* survey of a convenience sample of enlisted military personnel of all military services from thirty-eight different installations showed results similar to those of the air force telephone survey and the Miller and Moskos surveys. All service members generally disapproved of lifting the ban on homosexuals. Again, as in the previous two surveys, males, those in the junior ranks, and those who were in combat jobs were most likely to disapprove of homosexuals serving in the military. This survey also showed that African-Americans were more approving of lifting the ban on homosexuals in the military services than were whites or Hispanics, and older service members were likely to be more favorable as well.

This survey, like the Miller and Moskos survey, tried to assess the impact of lifting the ban on homosexuals on reenlistment intentions. However, contrary to the Miller and Moskos survey, the *Los Angles Times* survey showed that the potential negative impact on reenlistment intentions would be small if the ban were lifted, being largest for men (15 percent), younger military members (17 percent), those in combat jobs (14 percent), those lower in rank (14 percent), and for whites (11 percent) and Latinos (12 percent).

Of the three surveys, only the *Los Angles Times* survey tried to assess the issue of lifting the ban in the context of other major issues facing the military services. Respondents were asked to indicate what they thought the top two problems facing the U.S. military were. For men, the top two problems were troop cuts/downsizing and possible lifting of the ban on homosexuals; low morale was their third top problem. The top two problems for women were downsizing and low morale, with the possible lifting of the ban on homosexuals ranked third.

Although all three recent surveys of service members suffer from problems of reliability and generalizability, we think some general conclusions can safely be drawn about several of the relationships found in each of the survey efforts. Because some of the relationships in these three surveys, such as more positive attitudes toward homosexuals among females, have been found in other surveys with civilian populations, we are inclined to accept similar relationships here as well.[41] We are also inclined to accept relationships that are consistent across the three surveys.

What then can we conclude from these surveys of military personnel about the potential effects of integrating homosexuals into the military services? It is clear that lower-ranking (who are probably younger as well) men in combat jobs would be most negatively affected and the most negative toward such integration. Although retention intentions would be diminished by allowing homosexuals to serve, the magnitude of this effect on actual retention behavior is impossible to assess at this time for at least three reasons.

First, the magnitude of the effect on retention intention behavior measured was quite different in all three surveys. Furthermore, none of the surveys is a good representation of the population to which we would wish to generalize.

Second, the relationship between retention intention and actual retention behavior in normal circumstances is imperfect. Under conditions where no special emotional conditions apply, we estimate that the correlation between retention intention and retention behavior to be approximately .60.[42] With an emotionally charged issue such as this, we suspect the correlation between intention and action would be much lower.

Finally, previous research by Orthner and others has clearly shown that attitudes of spouses and significant others influence the retention process of service members as much as do their own attitudes, yet no data have been collected from these key influencers of the retention decision process.[43] Most service members are men and, as we have seen, men tend to be more negative when asked about their retention intentions if homosexuals were allowed to serve. However, because most military spouses are women, and because women in general tend to be more positive about homosexuals serving in the military, the wives and significant others of male service members are likely to be less negative about their husbands and future husbands remaining in the service. Spouse/significant-other attitudes toward remaining in the service if homosexuals were allowed to serve openly is obviously a critical missing variable in the retention equation.

Summary and Conclusions

In this paper, we briefly summarized the state of knowledge in two of the social science research domains suggested by Herek—studying foreign militaries and assessing the attitudes of civilians and military personnel—and rendered several conclusions and generalizations within these areas. Despite shortfalls in the evidence, social scientists still have much to contribute to the formation and implementation of policy concerning homosexuals in the U.S. military services.

The most useful current information on homosexuals and military service, and our most promising laboratories for the future, come from the experiences of other Western nations. We have found that the general trend among Western cultures seems to be moving toward removing most discrimination, including lifting restrictions on military service, toward people because of their sexual orientation. Tolerance for homosexuality, rather than active integration, appears to be the cultural norm for most countries. The notable exception to this is the Netherlands, which has taken an active role toward integrating homosexuals into society in general, and the military in particular.

In most Western countries, including the Netherlands, homosexuals who serve in the military services do so without revealing their sexual preferences. Heterosexuality is still the norm for the vast majority of those in Western nations and as a result homosexuality in the military as well as other walks of life is likely to remain a shunned life-style. As a result, homosexual "bashing" may be a particular problem for military services, especially in countries where bans against homosexuals in military service have only recently been removed. It is imperative that social scientists continue to study countries that have recently removed restrictions on homosexuals serving in the military to derive lessons learned from the problems and solutions that flow from those changes.

Although public opinion in the United States seems to be becoming more tolerant of homosexuals, the vast majority of men in the military services are strongly opposed to homosexuals serving in the military. We know from surveys of racial and gender attitudes of men in the military that they tend to be more conservative on these issues than is the American public generally. We also know, however, that their attitudes change over time as a function of experience working with the previously excluded group. Women and African-Americans in uniform are less strongly opposed to sexual orientation integration than male soldiers, although they are more strongly opposed than their civilian counterparts.

We know from the surveys of U.S. military personnel that there is the potential for violence and disruption if homosexuals serve openly. Social science research needs to address these issues before they become problems for the military services, rather than wait for policy changes that are likely to come about as a result of court actions.

Notes

1. The views expressed in this paper are those of the authors and do not necessarily reflect those of the Army Research Institute, the Department of the Army, or the Department of Defense.

2. Gregory M. Herek, "Sexual Orientation and Military Service." *American Psychologist* 48 (May 1993): 538–49.

3. The question most frequently asked of social scientists during the hearings was what impact sexual orientation integration in the military would have on cohesion and unit effectiveness. We do not address this issue here both because there are no data that might support an empirical answer, and because the issue itself does not have comparative relevance. It has not emerged as an issue in any country except the United States.

4. The first panel convened at the Inter-University Seminar (IUS)/Olin Foundation Conference on Armed Forces in a Warless Society, Baltimore, October 10–11, 1991, and a second at the Conference on Comparative International Military Personnel Policies, Beverly, United Kingdom, July 1993.

5. The General Accounting Office concludes that no major discrepancies exist between policy and practice in foreign nations. We believe that their data support our position. See United States General Accounting Office (GAO), *Homosexuals in the Military: Policies and Practices of Foreign Countries*, Report #GAO/NSIAD-93-215 (Washington, DC: U.S. Government Printing Office, 1993).

6. Cathy Downes, "Australian and New Zealand Armed Forces and Society after the Cold War." Paper presented at the IUS/Olin Foundation Conference.

7. Franklin C. Pinch, "Canada's Post-Cold War Military." Paper presented at the IUS/Olin Foundation Conference.

8.   Franklin C. Pinch, *Perspectives on Organizational Change in the Canadian Forces* (Alexandria, Va.: U.S. Army Research Institute for the Behavioral and Social Sciences, 1993).

9.   Christopher Dandeker, "Homosexuality and the British Armed Forces: Official Policy in Recent Years," in *Comparative International Military Personnel Policies*, Research Note 93-17, Gwyn Harries-Jenkins, ed. (Alexandria, Va.: U.S. Army Research Institute for the Behavioral and Social Sciences, 1993), 21–28.

10.   See David F. Burrelli, *Homosexuals and U.S. Military Personnel Policy*— Report 93-52 F (Washington, D.C.: Congressional Research Service, January 14, 1993), 68.

11.   Dimitrios Smokovitis, "Greece." Paper presented at the IUS/Olin Foundation Conference.

12.   Burrelli, *Homosexuals and U.S. Military*, 66–67.

13.   GAO, *Homosexuals in the Military*, 22.

14.   Burrelli, *Homosexuals and U.S. Military*, 67.

15.   Bernard Boene and Michel Martin, "The French Military in a 'Warless' Society." Paper presented at the IUS/Olin Foundation Conference.

16.   Gilles Robert and Louis Michael Fabre, "Armee et Homosexualite." Paper presented at the Conference on Military Policies.

17.   Marina Nuciari, "Homosexuality and Armed Forces in Italy." Paper presented at the Conference on Military Policies.

18.   Philippe Manigart, "Homosexuality and the Belgian Military," Harries-Jenkins, *Comparative International Policies*, 45–55.

19.   Karl W. Haltiner, "Switzerland: Paradigm of a Warless Society." Paper presented at the IUS/Olin Foundation Conference.

20.   GAO, *Homosexuals in the Military*, 35.

21.   Burrelli, *Homosexuals and U.S. Military*, 66.

22.   Bernhard Fleckenstein, "Homosexuality and the Military: the German Standpoint," Harries-Jenkins, *Comparative International Policies*, 29–44.

23.   Henning Sorensen, "Homosexuals in the Armed Forces in Scandinavia," Harries-Jenkins, *Comparative International Policies*, 57–73.

24.   Jan van der Meulen, "The Netherlands." Paper presented at the IUS/Olin Foundation Conference.

25.   Marion Andersen-Boers and Jan van der Meulen, "Homosexuality and Armed Forces in the Netherlands," Harries-Jenkins, *Comparative International Policies*, 75–87. An interesting discussion of the etiology of homophobia among military personnel appears in Thomas Spence Smith, "Violence as a Disintegration Process: Counterphobic Reenactments of Dissociated Traumatic Events in Individual and Group Life." Paper presented at the 100th Anniversary Conference of the International Institute of Sociology, Paris, June 21–25, 1993.

26.   Henk van den Boogard, "Training Courses on Homosexuality for Armed Forces Personnel." Paper presented at the Conference on Military Policies.

27.   See Marion Andersen-Boers and Jan van der Meulen, "Gays in the Military in the Netherlands," this volume.

28.   Jerzy J. Wiatr, "Armed Forces in Eastern Europe after the Cold War." Paper presented at the IUS/Olin Foundation Conference.

29.   Bernhard Fleckenstein, "Homosexuality and the Military: The German Posi-- tion." Paper presented at the Conference on Military Policies.

30.   Much of the data brought to bear on the debate on homosexuals in the military has been concerned with social distance. A long research tradition has demonstrated that expressed attitudes regarding social distancing from members of minority groups are poor predictors of actual behavior when confronted by members of that group. Behavior tends to be more tolerant than expressed attitudes. See Richard T. LaPierre, "Attitude vs. Action," *Social Forces* 13 (1934): 230–237, and, more generally, Allen E. Liska, *The Consistency Controversy* (New York: Wiley, 1975).

31.   Philippe Manigart, "Homosexuals in the Belgian Military." Paper presented at the Conference on Military Policies.

32.   Henning Sorensen, "Homosexuals in the Armed Forces in Scandinavia." Paper presented at the Conference on Military Policies.

33.   Andersen-Boers and van der Meulen, "Gays in the Military in the Netherlands," this volume.

34.   Carol Mueller, "In Search of a Constituency for the 'New Religious Right.'" *Public Opinion Quarterly* 47 (1983): 216.

35.   David W. Moore, "Public Polarized on Gay Issue," *Gallup Poll Monthly* 331 (April 1993): 30.

36.   Lydia Saad and Leslie McAneny, "Americans Deeply Split over Ban on Gays in the Military," *Gallup Poll Monthly* 329 (February 1993): 6.

37.   Laura L. Miller, "Fighting for a Just Cause: Soldiers' Views on Gays in the Military," this volume.

38.   Ibid.

39.   Ibid.

40.   Percentages are based only on the December survey at two army installations.

41.   Rand National Defense Research Institute, *Sexual Orientation and U.S. Military Personnel Policy: Options and Assessment* (Santa Monica: Rand, 1993), 436–462.

42.   Hyder Lakhani and Paul A. Gade, "Career Decisions of Dual Military Career Couples: A Multidisciplinary Analysis of the U.S. Army," *Journal of Economic Psychology* 13 (1993): 153–166.

43.   Dennis K. Orthner, *Family Impacts on Retention of Military Personnel*, Research Report 1556/NTIS No. AD A225 084 (Alexandria, Va.: U.S. Army Research Institute for the Behavioral and Social Sciences, 1990). Also see: Rose M. Ethridge, *Family Factors Affecting Retention: A Review of the Literature*, Research Report 151 1/ NTIS No. AD A210 506 (Alexandria, Va.: U.S. Army Research Institute for the Behavioral and Social Sciences, 1989); and B. L. Seboda and R. Szoc, *Family Factors Critical to the Retention of Naval Personnel: The Link between Retention Intention and Retention Behavior*, Technical Report NTIS No. AD A144 492 (Washington, DC: Office of Naval Research, 1984).

Chapter 4

From Citizens' Army to Social Laboratory*

CHARLES MOSKOS, JR.[1]

These are uncertain times for the armed forces of the United States. How could they not be? With the cold war over, the very foundations of our thinking about national security have undergone profound changes. Short of a terrible accident, the likelihood of a nuclear war between major powers is slim. Indeed, wars among any major powers appear unlikely, though terrorism and internal wars triggered by ethnic and religious animosities will be with us for some time, if not forever. More to the point, nonmilitary threats—economic competitiveness, environmental pollution, and crime—have now moved to the fore of our national-security preoccupations.

Of course, no serious observer sees the imminent end of warfare. Clausewitz's dictum about war being the extension of politics by other means remains in the back of any thinking person's mind. Nevertheless, we are witnessing the dawn of an era in which war between major powers is rejected as the principal, much less inevitable means of resolving conflict. At the same time, the citizens of the United States, like those of other advanced industrial nations, are increasingly reluctant to become engaged in uncertain, protracted wars in parts of the world where no vital interests appear to be at stake. In the absence of traditional threats, political support for military spending has slowly given way to expectations of a "peace dividend" for domestic social expenditures—a phenomenon that is as pronounced in Moscow as it is in Washington.

In this most unprecedented of historical epochs, we are also seeing important changes in the relations between the military and American society, changes that have been under way for at least two decades but that are now being accelerated by the end of the cold war. Among these, perhaps the most consequential is the demise of military service as a widely shared coming-of-age experience for American males. Another change, more diffuse in shape and possible consequences, is a redefinition of the military's role in society. Once thought of as the institution through which citizens—at least male citizens—discharged their basic civic obligation, the military is now coming to be seen as a large and potent laboratory for social experimentation. Such changes and others are part of a larger movement, a trend toward what I call the postmodern military.

Postmodernism is not one of those words that tend to win friends or influence people, at least outside the academy. Indeed, its overuse by the tenured classes makes it seem, variously, pretentious, empty, or imprecise. That said, the concept has its uses. From its humble origins as the name of an architectural style blending whimsy, pastiche, and playful historical allusion, it has been generalized into an all-embracing theory of society. Simply put, this theory posits a world in which the old verities are thrown into question, social institutions become weak or permeable, and uncertainty everywhere reigns.

In matters military as well as cultural, the adjective *postmodern* implies a modern precursor. In America, as in most of the Western world, the military acquired its distinctively modern form with the rise of the nation-state in the late eighteenth and early nineteenth centuries, reaching a kind of zenith during the two world wars of this century. The modern military was distinguished by two conditions. The first was sharp, clear distinctions between military and civilian structures. The second was universal male conscription. Both conditions allowed military leaders to stress the more traditional martial virtues, the virtues of combat. Some fraying of the modern military occurred during the last decades of the cold war with the rise of a military establishment driven as much by technical and information imperatives as by those of the trenches. Still, the modern military remained recognizable, in form and mission, right up to collapse of the Soviet Union.

Since then—and particularly since the end of the Persian Gulf War in March 1991—American armed forces have been deployed in more than twenty different operations, few of which had traditional military objectives. The list includes two operations related to the Gulf War: the multinational Operation Provide Comfort in Kurdistan and Operation Southern Watch in southern Iraq. The American military has taken part in Operation Sea Angel for flood relief in Bangladesh, in the rescue of citizens following the volcano eruptions of Mount Pinatubo in the Philippines and of Mount Etna in Italy, in drug interdiction along U.S. borders as well as in Latin America, in domestic mission to restore order after the Los Angeles riot, and in disaster relief following hurricanes in Florida and Hawaii. The United States has also joined other nations in rescuing foreign nationals in Zaire and until recently was spearheading relief efforts Somalia. To the success of most of these operations, administrative and logistical skills, not to mention health-care and social-work skills, were far more important than tactical insight, marksmanship, or courage under fire.

To be sure, Western militaries have performed nonmilitary roles in times past, but what is different about these post–cold war missions is their frequency and multinational character. Although it may be hard to imagine a U.S. soldier becoming misty-eyed about duty served under the aegis of the United Nations or the Conference on Security and Cooperation in Europe, the move toward multinational forces will gain momentum. The next step may well be the formation of a genuinely international army with its own recruitment and promotion systems, as outlined in the 1991 "Agenda for Peace" written by United Nations Secretary General Boutros Boutros-Ghali.

In the postmodern setting, the legitimacy of conscription has progressively weakened. The draft has either been abolished—as it was in the United States in 1973 and ten years earlier in the United Kingdom—or severely cut back, as in various European countries during the last fifteen years. The political forces pushing for an end to conscription, though unlikely bedfellows, constitute a formidable bloc. They include traditional peace organizations, assorted religious groups, political radicals who dislike the military establishment, libertarian conservatives, policy specialists who seek to transfer military spending to social programs, young people imbued with individualism and materialism, and even some military leaders.

In America specifically, the abandonment of conscription jeopardizes the nation's dual-military tradition, one-half of which—and truly its heart—is the citizen soldiery. This institution antedates the Revolutionary War. The first colonists came to the shore of the New World anticipating conflict, and they prepared for it. Each colony formed its own militia on the principle that fundamental liberties entailed individual responsibilities. The militia, it must be stressed, was not a voluntary force. Every able-bodied man was obliged to possess arms and to train periodically. And every such man was subject to call-up when military needs dictated.

The military requirements of the Revolutionary War led to the creation of America's first professional army. This force remained small because of Americans' deep distrust of a standing army, but it marked the beginning of America's dual-military tradition. Henceforth, a citizen soldiery of varying sizes was balanced by a permanent and professional force. Large forces consisting of short-term volunteers, draftees, or draft-induced volunteers came into being during the Civil War and World War I. But it was World War II that shaped our most recent understanding of military service.

In 1939, 340,000 men were serving in the U.S. military. By June 1941—six months before Pearl Harbor—American mobilization was well under way. America's first peacetime draft raised U.S. military strength to 1.8 million men. Shortly after it entered the war, the United States raised the largest military force in the nation's history. At war's end, more than 12 million people were in uniform.

By 1946, the number of servicemen had shrunk to 3 million. The draft was suspended in 1947, and the number of active-duty military personnel fell to 1.5 million. The draft was resumed in 1948, as the cold war heated up, and though the Korean War never resulted in total mobilization, there were some 3.7 million Americans in uniform in 1952. During the ensuing decade, America's military posture was based on "nuclear deterrence" and large troop deployments abroad, notably in Europe and Korea. Between 1955 and 1965, the number of people in uniform hovered around 2.5 million, more than during any other peacetime period in American history.

A clear conception of the place of military service in American society survived from early in World War II right up to the beginning of the Vietnam War. According to this view, service in the military, and particularly the army, was almost a rite of passage for most American males. Eight out of ten age-eligible men served during World War II, the highest ratio in U.S. history. From the Korean War through the early 1960s, about half of all men coming of age served in the armed forces. But the proportion began to fall— to roughly four out of ten—during the Vietnam War, as the children of privilege found ways to avoid service in an unpopular and ill-defined military quagmire. Since the suspension of the draft in 1973, only about one in five eligible males has been entering the military. And when the post–cold war "drawdown" to the projected base force of 1.6 million is reached in 1995 (though it will likely be smaller), the proportion of young men serving will be down to one in ten, if that.

The changing social composition of the military—evident first in the Vietnam War—became even more obvious during the first decade of the all-volunteer force, when the military began to draw disproportionately from among minorities, particularly blacks and Hispanics, and from lower socioeconomic groups. By 1979, 40 percent of army recruits were members of minorities, and half of the white entrants were high-school dropouts. This shift in social makeup corresponded with a tendency on the part of Defense Department policymakers to redefine military service as an attractive career option rather than the fulfillment of a citizen's obligations. Perhaps the best example of the loosening hold of the military experience in the United States is seen in the changing background of America's political leaders. For at least the first three decades after World War II, military service (or at least a very good reason for having missed it) was practically a requirement for elective office. The unpopularity of the Vietnam War and the termination of the draft both chipped away at this attitude. In 1982 the proportion of veterans fell below half in Congress for the first time since before Pearl Harbor. And as the Vietnam War generation replaced the World War II cohort, it brought with it a highly ambivalent view of military service. Not surprisingly, this view reflected the electorate's changed attitude toward the importance of military experience to service in elective office. In 1988, the nomination of Senator Dan Quayle as a candidate for vice president created a stir because of his avoidance of active duty in the Vietnam War. In 1992, Governor Bill Clinton, who not only avoided all forms of duty but protested against the war, was elected to the nation's highest office.

The changed composition of the military and new attitudes toward military service raise the inevitable question: What has been lost? The answer is simple. Universal military service was the one way in which a significant number of Americans discharged a civic obligation to their nation. If this fact is obvious, its significance has been obscured by a political culture that ignores the importance of individual obligations while virtually enshrining individual rights—possibly to the detriment of our civic health. Universal military service did something else: It brought together millions of Americans who otherwise would have lived their lives in relative social and geographic isolation. No other institution has accomplished such an intermingling of diverse classes, races, and ethnic groups.

The racial dimension of this social intermingling—the integration of the armed forces and the impressive record of African-Americans in the services—is often cited as the great success story of the American military. Unfortunately, many people forget that this success came only at the end of what is in fact a rather ugly story, one that too faithfully reflects the larger national tragedy of racism. Until relatively recent years, African-Americans were a group resolutely excluded from equal participation in the armed forces. Even though they have taken part in all of America's wars, from colonial times to the present, they have usually done so under unfavorable and often humiliating circumstances, typically serving in all-black units with white commanders. And though they have served bravely, they often received less than glowing reviews from condescending, unsympathetic white officers. (By contrast, black units that served directly under the French in World War I received high praise from their commanders.)

The plight of blacks in uniform did not even begin to change until World War II. On the eve of that global struggle, there were only five black officers in the entire American military, and three of them were chaplains. Black soldiers during the war continued to serve in segregated units, performing mainly menial labor. Strife between black and white soldiers was common. Despite these conditions, blacks proved themselves when given the chance—none more so than the all-black 99th Fighter Squadron, whose performance in combat over Italy won the highest plaudits of the previously skeptical commander of U.S. tactical air forces.

In December 1944, during the Battle of the Bulge, African-American soldiers were finally given the chance to prove that segregation was not only unjust but militarily inefficient. Desperately short of combat troops, Lt. Gen. John C. H. Lee, General Eisenhower's deputy for logistics, asked for black volunteers to fill the thinned-out ranks of white combat units. The soldiers who stepped forward performed exceptionally well in battle, gaining the respect of the white soldiers they fought next to and the high regard of the white officers under whom they served. Notably, there was none of the hostility that usually existed between white officers and black soldiers in the all-black units and none of the fighting that often broke out between whites and blacks in segregated units.

The unqualified success of this small experiment in racial integration was cited after the war to support arguments for integrating the military. Those arguments prevailed in 1948, when President Harry S. Truman abolished segregation in the military. Little happened at first, but when the Korean War erupted manpower requirements in the field led to many instances of ad hoc integration. By 1955, two years after the end of the Korean War, the last remnants of military Jim Crow were gone.

Integration alone did not bring an end to the problem of race in the military. Between the wars in Korea and Vietnam, African-Americans made up about 11 percent of the enlisted ranks but less than 3 percent of the officer grades. Racial tensions mounted dangerously during the Vietnam War, the outcome of both real and perceived discrimination in the military and of spillover from the racial and political turmoil in society at large. Even after the war and the termination of the draft, there were frequent outbursts of hostility between blacks and whites in the all-volunteer force.

Thanks to decisions made by the military leadership in that "time of troubles," things have changed markedly for the better. Today, in terms of black achievement and a general level of interracial harmony, few civilian institutions approach the army. In 1992, blacks made up 30 percent of the enlisted force, over a third of the senior noncommissioned officers, 12 percent of the officer corps, and 6 percent of the generals. General Colin L. Powell became chairman of the Joint Chiefs of Staff in 1989, the first African-American to head the American military. The army is still no racial utopia. Beneath the cross-race bantering, an edge of tension often lurks. Still, the races do get along remarkably well. Under the grueling conditions of the Gulf War, for example, not one racial incident was brought to the attention of the military police. Certainly the racial climate is more positive than that found on most college campuses today.

What has made the military in so many ways the vanguard of racial progress? I suggest three factors. The first is a level playing field, dramatized most starkly by basic training. For many black youths from impoverished backgrounds, basic training is the first test at which they can outshine Americans coming from more advantaged backgrounds.

The second factor is the absolute commitment of the military leadership to nondiscrimination, regardless of race. One sign of this commitment is the use of an "equal-opportunity box" in officer evaluation reports. While such a box may not eradicate deep prejudices, it alters outward behavior, for any noted display of racism will prevent an officer's promotion. Just as effective have been guidelines for promotion boards—"goals" that are supposed to approximate the minority representation in the eligible pool. If this looks like a quota by another name, one should note that the number of blacks promoted from captain to major, a virtual prerequisite for a full military career, is usually below goal. (The most plausible explanation for this is that about half of all black officers are products of historically black colleges, where a disproportionate number of more recent graduates fail to acquire the writing or communication skills necessary for promotion to staff jobs.) By contrast, promotions through colonel and general ranks come far closer to meeting goals. Significantly, the military has avoided the adoption of two promotion lists, one for blacks and one for whites. While the army's system satisfies neither the pro- nor anti-quota viewpoints, it works.

Third, the armed forces developed an equal-opportunity educational program of unparalleled excellence. Courses with specially trained instructors were established throughout the training system during the time of racial troubles in the 1970s, and these courses stressed not who was at fault but what could be done. Mandatory race-relations courses sent a strong signal to black soldiers that the military was serious about equal opportunity.

The attractions of the military to African-Americans are worth pondering. To begin with, blacks find that there are enough other African-Americans in the military to provide a sense of social comfort and professional support. Just as important, though, they know that they are not in a "black-only" institution. They appreciate the fact that the military provides uplift in the form of discipline, direction, and fairly meted out rewards—and does so without the stigma of a social uplift program. The justification of the military remains—at least to date—national defense, not welfare or social engineering.

One cannot exaggerate the importance of this last point in evaluating the lessons of recent black success in the military. For the driving force behind formal and actual integration of the armed forces was not social improvement or racial benevolence but necessity (notably manpower shortages in World War II and the Korean War) and the belated recognition of the military superiority of an integrated force to a segregated one. Put another way, it was the imperative of military effectiveness that led to equal opportunity, not the imperative of equal opportunity that led to greater military effectiveness. Overlooking this fact, political leaders and scholars have come to think of the military as a social laboratory, in which charged debates over gender roles and homosexuality and national service can not only be addressed but possibly resolved. This lack of clarity about the military's primary function is indeed a cardinal characteristic of the postmodern military. It is also potentially harmful to the long-term security interests of the nation.

The issue of women in the military—and particularly in fighting roles—is important. Recent history sets the stage of the current controversy.

When World War II broke out, the only women in the armed services were nurses. By the end of World War II, some 350,000 women had served in the various female auxiliary corps of the armed forces, performing duties that ranged from shuttling aircraft across the Atlantic to breaking enemy secret codes. Following the war, a 2 percent ceiling on the number of women in the military was set, and most women served in administrative, clerical, and health-care jobs. This situation remained basically unchanged until the advent of the all-volunteer force in 1973. Finding it difficult to recruit more than a few good men, the military allowed good women to fill the ranks. Today, women make up about 12 percent of the total armed forces.

Both before and after the draft was abolished, a number of important gender barriers within the military began to fall. Women entered the Reserve Officer Training Corps on civilian college campuses in 1972. Female cadets were accepted by the service academies in 1976. (Today, about one in seven academy entrants is a woman.) Congress abolished the separate women's auxiliary corps in 1978, and women were given virtually all assignments except direct combat roles. This meant that they were excluded from infantry, armored, and artillery units on land, from warships at sea, and from bombers and fighter planes in the air.

The combat exclusion rule, already opposed by feminist leaders and many women officers, came under renewed attack in the wake of the Gulf War. The performance of the some thirty-five thousand women who served in that conflict received high praise from both the media and Pentagon officials. But surveys of soldiers who served in the Persian Gulf yield a murkier picture. Forty-five percent of those who were in mixed-gender units reported that "sexual activity had a negative impact" on unit morale. Over half rated women's performance as fair or poor, while only 3 percent gave such ratings to men. Nevertheless, almost as a direct result of the Gulf War, Congress lifted the ban on women in combat planes, even though service regulations effectively kept the ban in place.

The usual response to a thorny social impasse is a presidential commission, and, true to form, one was established late in 1991: the President's Commission on the Assignment of Women in the Military. The fifteen-member panel (on which I served) took up three areas of consideration. The first was primarily factual. What, for example, were women's physical capabilities, and what would be the cost of modifying equipment or quarters to accommodate a woman's size or need for privacy?

A trickier area concerned questions of how mixed-gender groups would perform in combat. Here definitive answers are harder to come by, because apart from the defense of the homeland, no military force has ever used women in combat roles. Just as difficult to determine were matters related to the last area of concern: culture and values.

In addition to hearing opposing arguments, the commission sponsored a poll to determine whether the American public was willing to accept women in combat roles for the sake of equal opportunity. The answer that the Roper Organization came up with was a qualified yes. Three findings deserve mention. First, the public was split pretty much down the middle on the question of whether the combat-exclusion rule should be lifted. A large minority favored giving women the option to volunteer for combat arms, as long as no woman was ever compelled to assume a combat role. Second, most people believed that women already served in combat roles. Third, most respondents were more concerned with family status than with gender limitations. Three-quarters opposed mothers serving in combat; 43 percent felt the same way about fathers doing so.

By contrast with the general public, army women are much more wary about women in combat roles. One 1992 survey found that only 4 percent of enlisted women and 11 percent of female officers said they would volunteer for combat. But like the larger population, most military women favored a voluntary option.

The same survey disclosed that almost all army women—by a margin of fifteen to one—opposed the adoption of uniform physical standards for men and women. Ironically, it was in support of such standards that two opposed groups within the policy community were rapidly coming to a consensus. Feminists supported it because of its egalitarian purity. Conservatives liked it because they believed it would reduce the number of women in the military across the board. Focusing on a strength definition of capability, both groups scanted the social and psychological problems that would likely arise with men and women fighting together in life-or-death situations.

Feminists and female senior officers do come together on the question of the categorical exclusion of women from direct combat roles. They believe that such exclusion is a limit on full citizenship. More recently, opponents of the exclusion rule, notably Representative Patricia Schroeder (D-Colo.) of the House Armed Services Committee, have argued that if women were included in combat roles, sexual harassment would decline. But according to the 1992 survey of army women cited above, most respondents think the opposite is true—that sexual harassment would increase if women served in combat units. And, in fact, sexual harassment is far more common in the Coast Guard, the only service with no gender restrictions, than in any of the other services, at least as measured by reported incidents at the respective service academies.

Less dogmatic opponents of the exclusion rule favor trial programs, which on the surface sounds reasonable. Trial programs are not the same as combat, but they would tell us more than we now know. Yet even the most carefully prepared trials would not address the biggest question: Should every woman soldier be made to take on the same combat liability that every male soldier does?

If the need arises, any male soldier, whether clerk-typist or mechanic, may be assigned to combat. True equality should mean that women soldiers incur the same liability. To allow women, but not men, the option of entering or not entering combat is not a realistic policy. As well as causing resentment among men, it would be hard to defend in a court of law. To allow both sexes to choose whether or not to go into combat would be the end of an effective military. Honesty requires that anti-ban advocates state openly that they want to put all female soldiers at the same combat risk—or that they do not.

By a one-vote margin last November, the presidential commission arrived at a surprisingly conservative recommendation: While approving of women's service on most warships (except submarines and amphibious vessels), it advised keeping women out of combat planes and ground combat units. President Bill Clinton has said that he will take the recommendation under consideration, but debate will surely continue before the matter is settled.

The vexed issue of homosexuals in the armed forces draws the postmodern military into another heated social controversy. And some of the solutions proposed would present just as great a problem to the military's combat effectiveness as do those proposed in the gender arena.

Again, some historical background. Up to World War II, the military treated homosexuality as a criminal act, punishable by imprisonment. During the war, however, service leaders came to adopt a psychiatric explanation of homosexuality: Discovered gays were either "treated" in hospitals or given discharges "without honor." From the 1950s through the 1970s, gays—defined almost always as people who had engaged in homosexual activity—were discharged under less than honorable circumstances. In 1982, in an effort to bring about a more uniform policy, the Department of Defense issued new guidelines that for all practical purposes made stated sexual orientation, rather than behavior (unless it was overt) the defining quality of homosexuality. The policy stipulated that a service member who declared that he or she was gay would receive an honorable discharge if his or her record was otherwise unsullied. However, if a gay service member was caught in a compromising situation, he or she might receive a less than honorable discharge.

The exclusion of homosexuals from the military has come under intense criticism not only from gay-rights groups but from civil libertarians and champions of equal opportunity. The 1992 Democratic platform pledged to remove the gay ban. And a threshold was crossed when the 102nd Congress introduced House Resolution 271, which called for the Department of Defense to rescind the ban. Editorials in the national press and sympathetic television accounts of gays in the military have added pressure to abolish the restriction.

Public-opinion polls show that the number of Americans favoring the admission of gays into the armed forces has been creeping upward. By 1992, about two-thirds of those surveyed favored abolishing the ban. Support for repeal is strongest among women and whites, and weakest among males and minorities. Without question, the growing support for ending the ban reflects a generally more tolerant attitude among the general public, but it may also be a sign of how distant most of the citizenry has become from the realities of military service.

Certainly, some of the reasons for excluding gays do not stand up to scrutiny. The argument that homosexuals are susceptible to blackmail is illogical. (If there were no ban, a gay service member could not be manipulated by the threat of exposure.) No evidence exists that homosexuals, under present rules, have been greater security risks than anyone else. Furthermore, no one can prove that homosexuals are any less effective than heterosexuals as soldiers, sailors, airmen, or marines.

What is at issue today, however, is whether or not declared gays should be allowed to serve in the military. This is different from the question of tolerating the service of discreet homosexuals in uniform (though with some one thousand gays being discharged each year, it is clear that not all are discreet). To condone discreet homosexuality in the services while opposing the official acceptance of declared homosexuals is to set oneself up for the charge of hypocrisy. And it probably does no good to say that a little hypocrisy may be the only thing that allows imperfect institutions to function in an imperfect world.

Whatever is done, policymakers should think twice before they invoke a misleading analogy between the dynamics of racial integration in the military and the proposed acceptance of overt homosexuality. Racial integration increased military efficiency; the acceptance of declared homosexuals will likely have the opposite effect, at least for a time. In a letter to General Powell last year, Representative Schroeder invoked the race analogy. His response was direct:

> Skin color is a benign, nonbehavioral characteristic. Sexual orientation is perhaps the most profound of human behavioral characteristics. Comparison of the two is a convenient but invalid argument. I believe the privacy rights of all Americans in uniform have to be considered, especially since those rights are often infringed upon by conditions of military service.

At the very least, the lifting of the ban will create a controversy over the issue of privacy, which in turn could make recruitment (particularly among minorities) even more difficult than it is today. Just as most men and women dislike being stripped of all privacy before the opposite sex, so most heterosexual men and women dislike being exposed to homosexuals of their own sex. The solution of creating separate living quarters would be not only impractical but an invitation to derision, abuse, and deep division within the ranks.

There is also the problem of morale and group cohesion. Voicing the conservative position, David Hackworth, a highly decorated veteran who writes on military affairs for *Newsweek*, acknowledges that equal rights arguments are eloquent and theoretically persuasive. The only problem, he insists, is that the military is like no other institution: "One doesn't need to be a field marshal to understand that sex between service members undermines those critical factors that produce discipline, military orders, spirit, and combat effectiveness."

Foes of the ban point to the acceptance of homosexuals in the armed forces of such countries as the Netherlands, Sweden, Denmark, and Israel. In the Netherlands, an alleged 10 percent of the military is gay (though nine out of ten, studies say, remain undeclared), and a four-day seminar stressing sensitivity toward minorities, including gays, is mandatory in all Dutch services. Harmony is said to reign throughout the tolerant ranks of the Dutch army.

Those who object to the validity of national comparisons charge that the Dutch and Scandinavian cultures are far more progressive and tolerant than is mainstream American culture. Furthermore, they say, neither the Dutch nor Scandinavian armies have been in the thick of combat in recent decades. These objections are partially invalidated by the example of Israel's military, which inducts declared homosexuals. Israel is a conservative society, and its troops are among the most combat-seasoned in the world. Yet while it is true that gays in Israel are expected to fulfill their military obligation, it is also true that they receive de facto special treatment. For example, gays are excluded from elite combat units, and most sleep at their own homes rather than in barracks.

It is likely that the United States will soon follow the example of these and other nations and rescind the gay ban, despite widespread resistance within the U.S. military. One can, of course, argue that the United States now has such a decisive strategic advantage over any potential enemy that it can well afford to advance the cause of equal opportunity at possible cost to military effectiveness. Still, such a risk must be acknowledged.

Because we live at a time when the combat mission of the armed forces appears to be of secondary importance, it is easy for citizens and their leaders to assume that the military can function like any other private or public organization. But we must face certain realities if we accept this assumption. We must decide, for one, whether we will be willing to restore compulsory national service if dropping the gay ban makes recruitment even more difficult than it now is. (Most nationals without such a ban do have obligatory national service, the military being an option in many cases.) Unless such realities are faced, we can only hope that our postmodern military never has to face the uncivil reality of war.

Note

1.   This essay originally appeared in early 1993 as the controversy erupted over President Clinton's intention to lift the ban on gays in the U.S. military. It represents one of my efforts at the time to assist policymakers and inform the debate.

PART II

Homosexuality and the U.S. Military:
A Clash of Worldviews

Chapter 5

Fighting for a Just Cause: Soldiers' Views on Gays in the Military

LAURA L. MILLER

Two value systems collide head-on in the campaign to allow gays and lesbians to serve openly in the military.[1] Both camps see themselves as moral defenders in a just war. On the one hand, soldiers opposing the ban stand on the principle that gays are a minority group whose civil rights should not be violated. They contend that the ban creates an unwarranted climate of fear and intimidation for gays and lesbians in the military. In contrast, soldiers who support the ban believe that the initiative undermines basic moral values on which this country was founded. They view homosexuality as sinful behavior that cannot be condoned. The two sides show little inclination to compromise: the anti-ban soldiers share only pro-ban sentiments concerning privacy, while pro-ban soldiers dismiss anti-ban arguments altogether.

This paper uses survey and interview data from active-duty army soldiers to analyze these themes and the underlying principles that guide them. It also examines why men, who comprise 88 percent of army personnel, are more strongly opposed to allowing open gays in the military than are women. The findings show that women more easily identify with gays and lesbians as a fellow minority and, further, some servicewomen feel this debate has advanced their own concerns about sexual harassment and women in combat roles. Most servicemen, however, are unwilling to relinquish the assumption of universal heterosexuality as the guide for everyday interaction and are especially opposed to having gay men in the military.

The Research

The research was carried out from February 1992 to June 1993. I spoke with hundreds of U.S. Army soldiers in formal interviews and discussion groups, and held informal conversations in barracks and dining halls, and

during field exercises. I traveled to eight stateside posts, two national training centers, and several sites in Somalia during Operation Restore Hope.
Questionnaires were distributed to over 2,000 men and 1,700 women.

For this nonrandom, stratified sample, I aggressively sought to include a
cross section of race, rank, and occupational specialties proportionate to
their numbers in the army. Women, who now comprise 12 percent of the
army population, were oversampled because of the questions on gender
issues. Higher-ranking officers were undersampled in the formal written
surveys but were extensively interviewed. Additionally, I targeted posts
where I would find Desert Storm and Restore Hope participants. The questionnaires covered a range of issues, but each contained an item about lifting
the ban on gays in the military. However, my last two surveys, administered
to 892 men and 569 women in December 1992 and June 1993, incorporated
a several questions about the possibility of openly gay soldiers in the military.

Table 1 presents responses by gender to the question about the policy on

Table 1.   Attitudes of Military Personnel on Gays in the Military: Results from Three
Surveys (in percent)

Author's U.S. Army Surveys, 1992–1993: "Gays and lesbians should be allowed to
enter and remain in the military"

	Strongly agree or agree	Not sure	Strongly disagree or disagree	N
Servicemen	16	8	75	1,943
Servicewomen	43	13	43	1,606

Los Angeles Times Survey, February 1993: "How do you feel about lifting the ban
on homosexuals in the armed forces of the United States?"[a]

	Approve	Don't know	Disapprove
By gender			
Servicemen	16	8	76
Servicewomen	35	10	55
By service			
Army	15	11	74
Navy	22	9	69
Marines	10	4	86
Air Force	21	5	74

Air Force Telephone Survey, January 1993: "How do you feel about the current
policy of separating known homosexuals or discharging people who state
they are homosexuals?"[b]

	Disagree	Undecided	Agree
Servicemen	19	14	67
Servicewomen	32	25	43

[a]N = 2,346 enlisted personnel. Weighting procedures used to conform with DoD
demographics. Gender breakdown by service not reported.
[b]N = approximately 800 (N by gender not available).

gays in the military. Seventy-five percent of the male soldiers disagreed or strongly disagreed with the proposal to lift the ban, while 43 percent of the women did so.[2] Soldiers' responses were consistent from post to post (regardless of size or location), and across the seventeen-month period in which the issue moved from virtual obscurity to the center of public controversy.[3] Most soldiers appear to have remained steadfast and unswayed by the public arguments of their opponents.

The *Los Angeles Times* and the air force reported strikingly similar findings in their surveys asking the same question. The former survey found that 76 percent of male soldiers from all forces disapprove of the proposal to lift the ban, while 55 percent of the women do. The air force survey found that 67 percent of airmen and 43 percent of airwomen believe that gays and lesbians should be dismissed from the military. These data demonstrate that there is strong objection to gays in the military in all branches of the service, though the *Los Angeles Times* survey suggests navy and air force personnel may be slightly less opposed than the battlefield branches.

The qualitative data presented in this paper come from interviews and discussion groups conducted by me during the entire period of the research. I also draw from the questionnaires, which encouraged soldiers to add written comments when they felt their concerns were not covered adequately by survey options.

Black males of all ranks are underrepresented in the qualitative data, though they are present in representative numbers in the quantitative data. This imbalance was not fully realized until after the data were collected and I had read all the comments on questionnaires and analyzed my field notes. The reasons behind this discrepancy still need to be explored.[4]

Soldiers Who Oppose the Ban

Sixteen percent of the men and 43 percent of the women surveyed oppose the military ban on gays and lesbians. Qualitative data reveal that the primary reasons for objecting to the ban are: (1) the ban discriminates against a minority group, (2) sexuality does not detract from job performance, and (3) the ban has been ineffective in keeping gays and lesbians from entering the military.

The Ban Is Discriminatory

Soldiers who oppose the ban often refer to gays and lesbians as a minority group facing discrimination. They see sexual orientation as a status, akin to the ascribed attributes of race, ethnicity, or gender. Given the heterosexual organization of society and the hostility toward gays, no one, they argue, would simply "decide" to be gay if given a choice. They stress that race, gender, and sexual orientation should not have an impact on employment opportunities. Since the United States strives for equality based on other statuses, they believe it should do the same for the gay status. An "other"-race, male noncommissioned officer (NCO) observed:

> I believe the issue of gays in the military is way out of proportion. We already have gays and it hasn't harmed the system. The system needs to be improved, not this one issue. We are the army for the country that claims the most freedoms in the world. However we have the worst discrimination. When blacks and women tried to do the same, they met the same resistance. We have forgotten what we are fighting for. The issue is worn out and it's not even resolved yet.

Nevertheless, some anti-ban soldiers disapprove of homosexuality: 45 percent of the men and 44 percent of the women who oppose the ban agree that "homosexuality is a sin." Additionally, 50 percent of the men and 21 percent of the women agree that "homosexuality is abnormal and perverted." But in preferring to lift the ban, they have adopted a relativist or tolerant attitude, giving priority to minority status over their feelings about homosexuality itself. A black female, rank not given, wrote, "My opinion isn't law. . . . I'm no one to openly judge another, I can only live my life," and a white female officer asserted:

> About moral choices, let's not let people who have had premarital sex or an affair be in the army either!!! Then there would be no one protecting our country. And the bible bashers need to reread the section that says he without guilt should cast the first stone!

Among soldiers who oppose the ban, however, many do have reservations about privacy issues when rooming or showering with gay personnel. Sixty-three percent of these servicemen and 35 percent of the servicewomen agree they would be "uncomfortable having to share my room with a homosexual." They suggest that bathrooms and showers should have individual stalls or curtains and that, like college students in a dorm, soldiers in the barracks should be able to change rooms or roommates.

How should the army deal with homophobia? About 50 percent of these men and women agree with the survey item that "lifting the ban would increase soldiers' acceptance of gays and lesbians." Also, 67 percent of the women feel that "the army needs sensitivity courses on accepting gays and lesbians," although the men are split on this proposal. To extend the principle of equality beyond voluntary military service, the overwhelming majority of anti-ban men (75 percent) and women (93 percent) agree that "in the event of a draft, gay men should be drafted the same as straight men."

Finally, some soldiers argue that the problems from gay integration will not be as acute as pro-ban soldiers threaten. A black enlisted female wrote: "The majority of soldiers already have a live and let live attitude. I don't think the problems will be as big as people say." Soldiers point out that the army is an institution with rules, regulations, and a chain of command, and already has regulations in place to deal with sexual harassment, public displays of affection, and disorderly conduct. A white male officer claimed:

> Gays should be held to exactly the same standards of propriety and public behavior as everyone else—public or indiscreet sexual behavior ought to be discouraged, whether participants are gay or straight.

In sum, anti-ban soldiers do not feel that those who wish to discriminate against gays should be allowed to do so, regardless of how loudly they protest or what negative consequences they predict.

Sexuality and Job Performance Are Separate Issues

Anti-ban soldiers also argue that homosexuality is a private matter between consenting adults that has no bearing on soldiers' abilities to perform their jobs. For 89 percent of the anti-ban servicemen and 97 percent of the servicewomen, what people do in their private sex lives "is no business of mine." One white female NCO stated:

> I feel that as long as they can perform the jobs required of them they should be allowed in the military. What goes on behind closed doors is none of the military's business. As long as gays and lesbians keep their private lives out of the workplace, I foresee no problems.

And a enlisted servicewoman, race not reported, stated:

> I feel if you follow the army regulations this would never happen in the first place. And what they do on their personal time is their business, just as I feel [it should be for] straight soldiers.

A black female officer suggested that dismissing highly competent soldiers because they are gay is more detrimental to military effectiveness than open integration would be:

> This army would be far more technically and tactically proficient if people were judged solely on their job performance and not on the color of their skin, their gender, or their sexual preference.

Another thought that all people should have the chance to benefit from military experience:

> How do you know who's gay and who's straight? You don't. So let everyone who wants to be in the service be in the service. It's a good experience for everyone—not just straight people—I'd fight for anyone as long as they'd fight for me (white enlisted servicewoman).

However, 68 percent of anti-ban men and 82 percent of the women agree that "allowing openly gay and lesbian soldiers in the army would cause some problems, but we could manage." Some of those problems, they argue, stem from resistance to any type of organizational change. More seriously though, 86 percent of these men and 89 percent of the women surveyed agree that "openly gay male soldiers would likely be subject to violence from fellow soldiers." Anticipated problems cause some soldiers to feel the ban should be lifted conditionally. A white enlisted serviceman observed: "I think that gays should be allowed and not asked whether or not they are. But they should not be allowed to flaunt it because it would cause problems between others."

The Ban Is Ineffective

Anti-ban soldiers typically argue that gays and lesbians are already in the military and have served with distinction. They believe that gays should no longer have to fear being exposed, and military resources should not be wasted trying to "discover" them. A white male NCO argued: "Gays and lesbians have always been in the military, and we've always known who they were. Their private life is theirs."

Most anti-ban servicemen and women have a positive image of gays and think that gays would be unlikely to pursue straight soldiers. A white female officer stated:

> Gays are already in the military, and they always have been. By dropping the ban on gays we will merely be reducing the stress that they already have [in performing] a difficult job. Sexual harassment problems will continue to be primarily a heterosexual problem. Most gays and lesbians just want to be left alone to do their jobs. My opinion is that most gays will remain in the closet long after the ban is lifted—they just don't want to continue living under threat.

Others echoed the doubt that many gays would come out in a hostile environment in which they would likely be harassed:

> Changing the policy will not bring career soldiers "out of the closet" because they will be afraid of harassment that will be placed on them, even though the army/military says [homosexuality] is "officially" allowed (white female NCO).

Finally, anti-ban soldiers generally feel that fears about the spread of AIDS by gays are misplaced. Over 70 percent of these men and women disagreed with the statement, "If gays were allowed in the military, I would be more hesitant to help a wounded soldier because I would be more afraid of getting AIDS." One white female officer wrote: "AIDS isn't a homosexual disease anymore!!!!" Anti-ban soldiers dismiss the topic as an illegitimate objection based on irrational fear.

In brief, anti-ban soldiers contend that gays and lesbians are not going to disappear because of any ban, and since their sexuality does not affect their performance as soldiers, they deserve protection from discrimination.

Soldiers Who Support the Ban

The 75 percent of servicemen and 43 percent of servicewomen who support the ban typically view the issue in moral terms. They object vehemently not only to gays in the military but to homosexuality itself. The servicemen's feelings about the ban are more intense than the servicewomen's, as demonstrated by their raised voices and red faces during interviews, time and energy spent discussing the matter with me, and emphatic comments written on their surveys. For example, one serviceman wrote on his questionnaire, "NOT NO, BUT HELL NO!!!," underlining *hell* four times.

Their comments reveal that the primary reasons for wanting to keep the ban are: (1) homosexuality is immoral, (2) homosexuality would reduce the army's cohesion, morale, effectiveness, and good discipline, and (3) fear of intimate situations with someone of the same sex who is sexually attracted to them.

Homosexuality Is Immoral

The first objection usually raised in interviews is that homosexuality violates personal, religious, and moral convictions. For these soldiers, homosexuality is not a "natural" status. A white enlisted servicewomen stated: "I can't say what homosexuality is, I don't know. But just by going on how our bodies are made I have to say that it's not the way we are supposed to act." They strongly resist any comparisons between homosexuality and ascribed statuses such as race or sex.

Most believe that homosexuality is an immoral choice. One white female enlisted respondent argued:

> I'm not afraid [of] or hate homosexuals. I have some dear friends who are, but I disagree with their life-style. It is a moral choice—people aren't born homosexual, they choose (though some can have tendencies—they can be cured). It is a sin. This isn't saying they aren't intelligent and nice, but it's an area of life that colors all they do.

They believe, therefore, that such a deviant choice has a price. A white male officer contended:

> Homosexuals have the right to choose that life-style, but if they make that choice, they should accept that they are shutting some doors on their career options—including military service. Women and minorities deserve protection under the law [against] discrimination—they were born the way they are. Homosexuals made a life-style choice and need to face the consequences of that choice. I believe the argument that homosexuality is genetic is a fallacy.

Supporters believe this choice may be reversed through willpower. A white male NCO stated: "I will give my life for my country. If a gay feels as strongly as I do then he/she can change his/her ways."

To others who support the ban, it is a disease that may need treatment to be remedied:

> Homosexuality is a sexual disease, not a sexual preference. If it is a sexual preference and we allow homosexuals in the military we should also allow pedophiles and necrophiliacs and other sexual deviants in the military as well. I believe homosexuals should be treated like other mentally ill people (white male officer).

Finally, 69 percent of the pro-ban men and 77 percent of the pro-ban women agree that "homosexuality is a sin" (compared to 44 and 45 percent among anti-ban soldiers) that society should not encourage or permit. An Hispanic male NCO stated:

> I believe that homosexuality is trained and not born. Gay men and women strongly believe themselves to be gay, and so practice their beliefs. The bible discourages it and even calls it wrong. What God calls wrong we should not call right. And we should not encourage gay men and women to practice a lifestyle that God considers immoral.

Supporters of the ban react very strongly to homosexuality and rule out the possibility of accepting gays as a persecuted minority. When asked if sexual orientation is relevant to job performance, one white male officer countered: "What about child molesters? If it doesn't affect their work?" A white female NCO argued:

> [T]he problem is not gays, but perverted sex lives. Would we tolerate incest? Sex with children? Rape? Adultery? These are [other] examples of depraved sex.

Because these soldiers object to homosexuality on moral grounds, they do not accept the accusations of homophobia or irrational fears of gays. To them, that would be equivalent of declaring that people who want to punish pedophiles, rapists, or thieves are merely "phobic."

Pro-ban soldiers contend that morals play more of a role in military employment than in civilian life. Unlike most employees in civilian occupations, soldiers, they say, are expected to adopt and follow a moral code, whether on- or off-duty, even if the behavior has no direct impact on their job performance. For example, though such policies may not be regularly enforced, soldiers can be dismissed for alcoholism, adultery, or spouse abuse. Pro-ban soldiers see the gay issue as falling under the same moral proscriptions.

These soldiers also complain that a vocal minority of gay activists seems to have the ear of policymakers and the military to lift the ban. A white male NCO stated:

> If gays and lesbians are allowed in the military, I would ask to be discharged. I feel it is a sin and would lead to the fall of the United States as a superpower. Why don't they let the soldiers decide these issues instead of fat cats in Washington?

They do not believe that the army should lead the way for social change or that those in the service should be asked to accept that which the larger society has not yet resolved. Supporters of the ban doubt that lifting the ban is intended to benefit the army or the country. A white male NCO stated:

> I am absolutely opposed to homosexuals in the military. Homosexual—"gay" is a euphemism the homosexuals came up with themselves—activists are salivating over the prospect of the ban being lifted. If our government and society allow open homosexualism in the military, they are both clearly morally bankrupt and their ultimate demise inevitable.

Homosexuality Undermines Military Effectiveness

Pro-ban soldiers bolster their moral arguments with concerns that open homosexuality will be detrimental to the effectiveness of the nation's defense. They point out that the army discriminates based on age, weight, mental ability, and other characteristics because these characteristics impact on a soldier's ability to carry out the mission. These soldiers overwhelmingly agree that discipline will be a major issue if the ban is lifted because, in the words of a white female officer, "so many soldiers would be upset. I'm presently in command and if the ban on homosexuality is lifted I anticipate a number of incidents (fights, etc.) to occur. It will be a challenge."

Of pro-ban soldiers, 73 percent do not think the army could manage the problems caused by lifting the ban, and 90 percent of the men and 81 percent of the women agree that it "would be very disruptive of discipline." Soldiers who have been in the army since the late 1960s often commented that the army is the best it has ever been and see lifting the ban as a major setback. Among those who are confident that the army can handle the change, some worry about the effect on readiness. A white male officer contended:

> Regardless of the decisions, I am confident the army can adapt—we always do. But while we're adapting, what will be the short-term effects on readiness? Does anyone know? If not, then why are we pressing ourselves into making hasty decisions? We're facing far more important issues concerning [the reduction in forces].

Loss of cohesion, an element crucial for the success of units in combat, is another fear expressed by pro-ban soldiers. A white male NCO commented that "cohesion is very important in small units and you won't have cohesion if other soldiers know an individual is gay or lesbian. There is no way it can be kept a secret in tight units." Likewise, living conditions during field exercises and deployments with gay soldiers jeopardize the sense of unity necessary for combat effectiveness, ban supporters say. The statements of a white male, rank not given, are typical:

> I think gays shouldn't be allowed in the military because in field duty and combat everything is done in groups in close quarters, such as sleeping, bathing, and using the latrine. And I myself feel it would make a lot of soldiers uncomfortable doing those things with gays present.

Pro-ban soldiers also use the issue of AIDS to turn sexuality into a matter of public regulation, just as anti-ban people use a rhetoric of equality and fairness to argue for public intervention against the ban. Sixty-five percent of pro-ban soldiers say that, with the ban lifted, they would "be more hesitant to help a wounded soldier because [they] would be more afraid of getting AIDS." Soldiers expressed concern over the impact fear and resentment about AIDS would have on the troops. A white male officer stated:

> [Gays] can do their job just the same as anyone else, sure. Everything's just the same except sexual preference. Sure, morale will go down some, but it will recover at least part way. The real problem that I have seen is the fear of AIDS. Everything from PT to CPR and combat lifesaving practice, to administering IVs to save lives (this happens a lot) will be affected. Bottom line—soldiers will suffer, especially emergency situations and training.

One medic doubted that fear of contracting AIDS would cause soldiers to sit back and watch fellow soldiers who are gay bleed to death in battle. He did feel, however, that straights would experience "incredible stress" after helping gays because of fear that, having done so, they would contract AIDS. Many soldiers report that the HIV testing of soldiers is too sporadic and unreliable to give them any sense of security, and that tests are unlikely to be administered regularly during wartime.

Lifting the Ban Will Violate Privacy and Gender Norms

Privacy is another concern of pro-ban soldiers. Civilians, they feel, do not understand the privacy issues that make having gay co-workers in the army more difficult than in most civilian jobs. Pro-ban servicemen and -women contend that sexual behavior in the military is not a matter of "what happens behind closed doors" because soldiers share living quarters and have no choice in the selection of roommates or tentmates. Soldiers often work together, shower together, and sleep in close quarters, while civilians typically can go home at the end of the day and, if they wish, avoid intimate contact with co-workers. Pro-ban soldiers also point to norms against forcing members of the opposite sex to room, undress, or shower with each other. Placing gays into the formula, supporters of the ban argue, undermines the assumptions and strategies already in place for managing sexual attraction.

Most pro-ban soldiers feel that straight soldiers should not be forced to room with gays and lesbians against their will. Ninety-six percent of pro-ban men and 88 percent of the women report they "would feel uncomfortable having to share my room with a homosexual" (compared to 63 and 35 percent for anti-ban men and women, respectively). If gays were allowed to enlist openly, pro-ban soldiers wonder, should the military discontinue segregation by sex, give everyone individual rooms and showers, or set up separate facilities for gays and lesbians?[5] Most soldiers agree the first proposal is morally unacceptable, and the latter two costly and impractical. Soldiers argue that it would be unfair or problematic for gay soldiers to be able to room with their boyfriends or girlfriends when straights are not allowed to do so. A white male NCO stated, "If two gay males were allowed to live in the same barracks and room then why not a male and a female? Because it causes conflict and we don't need more conflict in the military."

Male soldiers appear much more emotional over lifting the ban than women. Many women I talked with wonder "what's the big deal" with accepting gays in the military. Women generally made their points and then preferred to spend the rest of the discussion talking about harassment, child care, or job restrictions. In contrast, the issue consumed the interviews with pro-ban male soldiers. Some indicated they would be so offended by an infringement on their privacy that they would react with violence. A white serviceman warned:

> I totally disagree with homosexuality as a normal lifestyle. It goes against my values not to mention God. I can't change or want to change any of them. But if you place one in my room, bunker, tent, or showers, I'd bash his head in. Once in [the National Training Center] it was so cold, [infantrymen] shared [sleep-

ing] bags with each other. There is no way that trust and confidence would be
there. Only paranoia and anger.

Though most soldiers admitted they did not know much about gay culture
and practices, many straight servicemen guess that gays will think and act as
they do. Forty-four percent of both pro-ban men and women feel that "openly gay and lesbian soldiers will try to seduce straight soldiers." "Men and
women who are straight try to seduce men and women, so why wouldn't gays
try to seduce soldiers?" observed an Hispanic male NCO. Some soldiers,
however, say they are concerned with sexual harassment from gays because
they have already experienced it. A white enlisted female declared:

> This needs to be stopped now. It has happened. Allowing them to be in the
> army and be openly homosexual would encourage more behavior such as this
> because they would no longer feel threatened by the fear of being found out, as
> they do now.

Worse, soldiers expect that gay men will behave toward them as straight
men sometimes act toward women, i.e., they will use force or the suggestion
of force to pursue their sexual interests. Realizing that they—servicemen—
could be on the receiving end of such attention, several said that they now
understand more fully why unwanted stares, comments, and flirtation from
men bother women. The idea of being approached by gays, being perceived
as gay, or being overpowered by gays brings out violent reactions in many
male soldiers. The distress stems not only from unwanted advances, pro-ban
soldiers say, but also from having been perceived as open to an invitation. In
the words of a white serviceman, "I have to wonder why it is [a gay male]
thinks it's OK for him to come up to me." When asked if they would risk
being discharged from the military for reacting violently, some state that they
would feel they had no other choice and would take the consequences.
    Particularly for those in command roles, the potentially violent reactions
of straight male soldiers may be the deciding factor in supporting the ban. A
white female officer observed:

> Gays and lesbians would be fine in the army except for the stigma placed upon
> them by many soldiers. People are ignorant of the homosexual life-style and
> therefore afraid of it. Until the attitudes of those in the military change it would
> be unsafe to allow them to serve.

Reactions If the Ban Were Lifted

Pro-ban soldiers feel lifting the ban would have a profound effect on their
lives. What would they do if the ban were lifted? Of those who were undecided about career plans or who were planning to remain in the military, 59
percent of the men and 29 percent of the women said they would not remain

if the ban were lifted. This figure—a behavioral intention—may not be accurate predictor of behavior, but it does show the strength of the sentiment among pro-ban soldiers. A white male NCO claimed:

> Being an infantryman, I feel that the sense of camaraderie, responsibility, and morale would be severely disrupted if homosexuals were openly allowed in the military. This opinion is shared by just about every infantry soldier I know. If and when homosexuals are allowed, I will be forced to terminate my service as soon as the opportunity arises. I do not wish to leave the army, I truly love what I do for a living.

Likewise, a white male warrant officer wrote on his questionnaire, "If I didn't have my retirement paperwork in—this would make me do it," and a white serviceman wrote on his form, "I will do my best to be [discharged from] the military if homosexuals are allowed to join." Another white serviceman warned, "I'd go AWOL. I don't want fags staring at me while I shower or dress or anything." Finally, a black enlisted man said he simply "would move to another country that is neutral in case of war."

Several soldiers said they would use intimidation and violence, either to keep gays out of the military or "in the closet," if the ban were lifted. They said they would not respect gay commanders or follow them in combat. Common in the interviews and written comments from men were statements like: "It's not right. It's sick, it's despicable, nauseating and I'll kill them." One enlisted man, who indicated that religion is very important in his life, wrote: "Gays should be shot. Gays should all die." Since these soldiers believe everyone in their unit feels the same way, they do not anticipate serious personal repercussions for their behavior.

Pro-ban soldiers are unmoved by the argument that gays have always served and are already present. They generally do not dispute that gays are capable of doing their jobs as other soldiers. They feel gays should be excluded because of their own feelings about homosexuality.

Soldiers Who Are Undecided

Eight percent of the men and 13 percent of the women in this study are undecided on this issue. An examination of their thinking may illustrate which points have gained the most validity for each side of the debate. The undecided soldiers are torn between equal rights for minorities on one side versus their feelings about homosexuality and privacy on the other. Also, they do not want the added burden of managing increased sexual harassment or discipline problems among the troops.

Like anti-ban soldiers, the undecideds agree that gays and lesbians are a minority whose rights are being violated by not being allowed to serve in the armed forces. For women, this parallel holds special implications regarding their own status. For example, a white female officer observed:

> Once the army allows homosexuals to serve in combat roles without discrimination, what can be used as the excuse to prevent women who want to serve in combat roles from taking them?

Undecided soldiers have reservations about privacy, being "hit on" by members of the same sex, and violence that openly gay soldiers may face. Forty-five percent of the men and 60 percent of the women would not "be uncomfortable if there were some homosexuals in my unit." But when it comes to sharing a room, 80 percent of the undecided men and 64 percent of the women would feel uncomfortable. For some, this issue of practicality hampers the implementation of their egalitarian philosophy. A white female officer stated:

> [Gays] should be allowed to die for their country just like the rest of us, but I don't want to shower with one. That would be the same as showering with a man. I would feel very uncomfortable.

Privacy, therefore, may present the greatest obstacle to lifting the ban since it is the one concern shared among anti-ban, pro-ban and undecided soldiers.

Some undecided soldiers are uncertain how open gays would act toward straights, but they do not want to be seen as potential mates. Of the women, 40 percent agree and 40 percent are unsure that "openly gay and lesbian soldiers will 'hit on' straight soldiers they are attracted to." The men were split about the same way (42 percent agree, 25 percent disagree, and 34 percent are not sure).

For other undecided soldiers, the issue rests not on their own reaction to gays, but the reaction of others. Seventy-seven percent of the undecided men and 87 percent of the women agree that "openly gay male soldiers would likely be subject to violence from fellow soldiers." A white female officer stated, "I think that gays and lesbians have their own rights, but a lot of my mixed feelings are because I know the army system and soldiers, and it just isn't accepted." Likewise, a female servicewoman, race not listed, contended: "Gays are already in. But I feel if they let them in and people know [who is gay] lots of people will be either killed or hurt badly."

Discussion

Table 2 summarizes the competing arguments that fuel the soldiers' public views on gays in the military and reflect the values soldiers hold as sacred.

Table 2. Soldiers' Arguments for and against the Ban

	Against the ban	For the ban
1. Discrimination	Ban is a violation of civil rights	Military service is a privilege, not a right
2. Morality	Values of differing groups should be respected	Homosexuality is morally wrong and unacceptable
3. Privacy	Accommodations are possible	Accommodations are impractical if not impossible
4. Sexual harassment	Current regulations are sufficient	Fear sexual advances from gay males
5. Cohesion, morale, discipline	Use strategies from integration of blacks and women	Homosexual integration detrimental; no good strategy
6. Gays already in military	Gays have already served with distinction	Gays should be kept out or firmly in closet
7. AIDS	Not a homosexual disease; soldiers already screened routinely	Primarily a homosexual disease; exposes soldiers needlessly

Anti-ban soldiers see the moral choice as obvious: Equal rights should be guaranteed to everyone regardless of race, gender, ethnicity, or sexual orientation. They see the issue here as discrimination and feel that personal judgments should have no place in the military's decision. To them, homosexuality is an alternative that falls within the limits of individual freedom and arguments advanced to support the ban are too similar to those used to justify racism and sexism. Freedom, equality, and justice—indisputable American principles—are on their side.

For pro-ban soldiers, the only moral choice is one that upholds heterosexuality as the norm. To them, homosexuality is unacceptable behavior that violates biology, human nature, and God's will. They consider it a mental illness, a violation of criminal statutes, or both. The rights of homosexuals, therefore, are not an issue. God's will and morality—also American principles—are on their side.

Why do most soldiers object so strongly to allowing gays in the military? Parallels can be drawn between this debate and the highly charged abortion issue. Sociologist Kristin Luker, who interviewed activists on both sides of the issue, found that participants see themselves as "defending a world view . . . [i.e., the] parts of life we take for granted, never imagine questioning, and cannot envision decent, moral people not sharing."[6] In such controversies, each side defines the issue in absolutes, leaving one moral choice on which there is no compromise. In the abortion debate, the sacredness of motherhood is a matter of dispute; here, heterosexuality, masculinity, and the rules governing gender interaction are at stake. Cultural warfare of this sort therefore entails a struggle for cultural dominance. Compromise is unacceptable and losing outright is unthinkable. Winning is crucial because the worldview extends beyond the issue at hand and gives meaning to the entire structure of people's lives.

Why are men so much more concerned about gays in the military than women? Sociologist Arthur Stinchcombe, commenting on the significance of moral disputes, argues that "moral categories form a catch basin for generalizing tendencies of beliefs, emotions, and moral injunctions."[7] Following Stinchcombe, a close look at the male-female and gay-straight categories should reveal differences in the emotional responses of men and women. Servicewomen are more likely to draw parallels between their own minority status in the military and that of gays. Women in the army must be prepared to deal with harassment and to find ways to make separate accommodations (when not provided) during field exercises and deployment. Therefore, for women, these issues are not new nor limited to straight women dealing with homosexuality. Adapting to lesbian co-workers may be a less difficult adjustment for straight women who have already devised strategies for coping with straight men.[8]

Further, many servicewomen feel sympathetic toward gays and lesbians because they know the feeling of being an outsider in a "real man's" army. Finally, servicewomen may have benefited when the category "woman" decreased in importance as the category "gay" grew to monumental proportions. I noticed, for instance, when comparing my first and last interviews with men, that the rhetoric about having to work with women softened after the possibility of lifting the ban arose.

For these reasons, disrupting the rules about heterosexuality sends shock waves throughout the entire system of gender as a pervasive social and cultural distinction. Fundamental beliefs about human identity and interaction are not easily shaken and are not abandoned on the basis of a single public policy. As Stinchcombe notes, "the close relation of pervasive [moral] categories to identity, to the confidence that both you and others know who you are, renders all change of basic moral categories a soul-wrenching experience."[9] Hence, both sides will continue to fight hard to protect the worldviews around which they have constructed their lives. Both sides will continue to fight passionately to win this "just war."

Notes

1.   There are political implications in use of the terms *gays and lesbians*, *homosexuals*, and *gays* when referring to gay men and women. I have used the terms as they were used by the soldiers surveyed.

2.   It would have been inappropriate and probably unreliable to ask active-duty

soldiers their sexual orientation, especially since they were usually seated close to fellow soldiers while filling out the questionnaire. The experiences of gay and lesbian soldiers coping with and confronting the ban have been documented in several recent publications: Allan Berube, *Coming Out Under Fire* (New York: Free Press, 1990); Mary Ann Humphrey, *My Country, My Right to Serve* (New York: Harper Collins, 1990); Randy Shilts, *Conduct Unbecoming* (New York: St. Martin's, 1993); and Joseph Steffan, *Honor Bound* (New York: Villard, 1992).

3.   Regression analysis of these data shows that male soldiers are more likely than servicewomen to support the ban ($p < .001$) but that race, rank, education, religiosity, marital status, and being a parent are unrelated to position on the ban. Also statistically insignificant are knowing a family member or someone in one's unit who is gay, region of the country in which raised, and rural/urban background. However, having gay friends is a significant correlate of opposing the ban ($p < .001$), and military occupational specialty is significantly related to soldiers' views ($p < .005$): Men and women in traditionally masculine specialties—mostly men—support the ban more than those in traditionally female jobs (comprised mostly of women). Within each specialty, however, a greater percentage of men support the ban compared to the women.

4.   Perhaps black servicemen are less concerned with the topic, or find other survey topics about their mission, race relations, or women in the military more worthy of comment, or are uncomfortable talking or writing about their opinions on gays in the military. Pro-ban soldiers in particular might be reluctant to put forth arguments that others often parallel with racist sentiments. Race was not significant in determining which side soldiers took in the debate (see previous note).

5.   An individual housing policy would also address the issue of bisexuals, whose existence was rarely mentioned. When asked specifically about bisexuals, most pro-ban soldiers were silent or declared "there's no such thing." Others said they "didn't even want to think about it" because they would have to admit the possibility that they might have unknowingly been involved with bisexuals.

6.   Kristin Luker, *Abortion and the Politics of Motherhood* (Berkeley: University of California Press, 1984), 7, 158.

7.   Arthur L. Stinchcombe, "The Deep Structure of Moral Categories," in *Structural Sociology*, ed. Ino Rossi (New York: Columbia University Press, 1982): 68, 79.

8.   For an analysis of the interactions of gender identity, soldier identity, sexuality, and success in the military, see Melissa S. Herbert, "Amazons and Butterflies: Gendered Attributes and the Construction of Sexuality as Mediators in the Participation of Women in the Military" (unpublished paper, University of Arizona, Tucson, 1993).

9.   Stinchcombe, "Moral Categories," 80.

Chapter 6

Lifting the Ban on Homosexuals in the Military: The Subversion of a Moral Principle[1]

COLONEL RONALD D. RAY (USMCR)

It is still true: Americans overwhelmingly consider homosexuality a grave disorder and wrong. Yet, since President Clinton announced his intention to lift the ban on homosexuals serving in the military, our national leadership has virtually ignored grass roots views and avoided the simple right-and-wrong thinking born of American common sense. How have America's founding principles and the will of the majority been thwarted by the federal government?

To have been a witness to the intense debate and the inner workings of the political process of our national government during 1993 has been most instructive and deeply disturbing. As a military historian acting as a regular citizen in no official capacity, I had the rare opportunity to observe the public and private handling of this issue within America's most powerful institutions. For months I met and worked with retired and active duty generals, admirals, senators, congressmen and their key staff members on this issue, as well as members of the Joint Chiefs of Staff. This included a meeting with Gen. Colin Powell, who told me on July 30, 1992, even before the election of Bill Clinton, that homosexual's serving openly in the military "was inevitable."

It is not surprising that Americans increasingly speak of their leaders as an "elite class" unresponsive to ordinary citizens and their values. Our governmental leaders, the media, and other elite institutions now construct public debates on a materialist dialectic that permits the accommodation of extreme and radical demands and always yields a compromise. This is unacceptable when the issue involves America's pure unyielding first principles and morality. The judgments of the elite are made upon values that are relative. In the Washington political process, nothing is fixed or absolute.

In 1993, the dialectic process began with a presidential thesis: as citizens, self-identified homosexuals should not be discriminated against and thus should have a right to serve in the military; followed by a military antithesis: homosexuals are disqualified and should not serve because homosexuality is incompatible with military service. This dialectic or bipolar approach sets up a clash of opposites that always gives way to a synthesis or compromise.

In contrast, "middle" Americans seek liberty with order. This delicate balance in government of checks and balances and limited, separated powers has been perverted today·by the elimination of absolutes and morals. In the politically-correct process of the elite, the central facts of American history— (1) limiting the coercive power of government and (2) liberty dependent upon Christian morality reflecting the will of the majority of hard-working Americans[2]—are disqualified early in the process.

Well before January 29, 1993, the stage was set to overturn the existing order and bring forward a new definition of freedom. Presented here are the confluence of events and the deeper underlying forces at work.

The Homosexual Moment: President Clinton's Election

For the first time in American history, a candidate was elected president who strongly and publicly supported homosexuality and gay rights,[3] although he rarely mentioned his support for homosexual rights on the stump.[4] News reports carried the gay leadership's characterization of Bill Clinton's election as "a historic moment in the history of gay politics" and "a rite of passage for the gay and lesbian movement."[5] After the election, Clinton said, in regard to the military, he wanted "to come up with an appropriate response that will focus sharply on the fact that we do have people who are homosexuals who have served our country with distinction. The issue ought to be conduct."

Sound bites on the evening news, elite newspapers and magazines, and the talking heads of the well-educated repeated the homosexual movement's own carefully selected public relations themes: Homosexuals should be allowed to serve openly in the military as a matter of "fairness" and "ending discrimination"; homosexuals are normal and are already serving; homosexuals have a right to serve. Clinton hastily swept away all deliberate efforts to address any serious moral, military, and medical consequences this decision would have upon the great majority of servicemen and -women and the negative long-term effects on the military institution, the national security, and our American way of life.

There was an overwhelming firestorm and well-attended protest from across America after Clinton's directive to the secretary of defense, which presumed that the ban should be lifted to "end discrimination" against homosexuals.[6] There were some who suspected the military was only a stop along the way to a homosexualized America. Largely, Americans are not interested in hurting or discriminating against homosexuals or "gay bashing," but rather in preserving laws to safeguard their children and their children's future.

The Joint Chiefs' Moment: January 29, 1993

The service chiefs, it was reported, were never consulted on whether this was a prudent action. Rather they were queried only on how to accomplish this tyrannical edict. However, the chiefs acquiesced despite existing congressional laws making sodomy and attempted sodomy felonies in the military and a 1956 statute rooted in America's founding. The Chairman of the Joint Chiefs of Staff, Colin Powell, advised U.S. Naval Academy midshipmen how an officer morally opposed to homosexuality could react if the ban were lifted:

> If after those decisions are made, you still find it completely unacceptable and it strikes to the heart of your moral beliefs, then I think you have to resign.[7]

Though General Powell publicly opposed lifting the ban in late January 1993, he would be a major factor in delivering the Joint Chiefs on this issue. Delivering the chiefs was crucial. Legally they would need to acquiesce to major changes to make way for the legal footing necessary to overturn 375 years of law, policy, and military order in the courts. The administration revealed its awareness of their tenuous position, their exposure to risk, and their strategy for succeeding in the military and changing the law order.

Rather sadly, America's "elite" leaders and "enlightened" representatives were focused ultimately on pragmatism rather than principle, and the ultimate result boiled down to a compromise that was most politically expedient. General Powell repeatedly acknowledged that he was only trying to "reconcile" and protect all of the competing interests.[8] His attorney, a marine colonel, told this writer that the military leadership is "realistic and pragmatic men who must operate in a political environment" where there is no place for moral judgments. Further, he admonished me by saying that I had done the joint chiefs no favor by making the moral argument in my book, *Military Necessity and Homosexuality*, and made their job of "reconciling" interests more difficult.[9]

Meanwhile General Powell was "engaged in a tense internal struggle with Pentagon colleagues over the approaching decision on how to handle homosexuals in the military."[10] A report from this period is very revealing about the Washington elite's compromise of an absolute moral principle:

> Mr. Aspin met with General Colin Powell . . . and five other chiefs. . . .
> Pentagon officials say some discussions have been heated. . . . Why all the

anger: "Because [General] Sullivan believes he is being told what he should do." Sources said *General Powell and his vice chairman, Adm. David Jeremiah, have acted as facilitators, searching for a consensus. . . . The chiefs adamantly insisted that any policy state that homosexuality is incompatible with military service. Mr. Aspin's aides have suggested a compromise, such as stating that "homosexual conduct," not homosexuality itself, is incompatible.*[11] [emphasis added]

On to the Courts

These concessions on the part of the chiefs, which included allowing openly homosexual servicemen and -women to return to duty as ordered by lower federal courts, form critically important parts of the gay rights legal position as they now enter the courts.

To understand where we were at the close of 1993, it is necessary to understand American history in general, and in particular the Supreme Court doctrine known as *military necessity*.[12] This concept denotes the Supreme Court's long-standing deference to military and executive leadership in areas of war, defense, and matters of a military nature. In the past, the Court has always supported the proposition to grant whatever America's military leadership has deemed necessary to defend America against its "enemies foreign and domestic." This concept has always embraced everything necessary to maintain good order and discipline within the ranks— even when the military standard has been at variance with constitutional rights afforded to citizens in wider society.

The lower federal court decisions since Colin Powell's retirement on September 30, 1993, have reinstated open homosexuals into the military and have ignored military necessity in favor of ending discrimination against homosexuals and their alleged right to serve. Under this faulty and deceptive legal reasoning, equal opportunity is emphasized over military necessity and constitutes a revolutionary departure from settled constitutional standards.

Fifty lawsuits have already been filed by gay rights advocates to overturn the pre-Clinton ban, including several recent cases attacking President Clinton's directive even as Congress was trying to tighten the law. In the first of these post-compromise legal challenges, the ACLU and Lambda Legal Defense and Education Fund filed suit in U.S. District Court, styled Doe v. Aspin, on behalf of seven gay servicemen and -women, contending that the new Clinton policy deprived them of their constitutional rights. These arguments are essentially legal abstractions to provide cover for a revolutionary change in American law, policy, and morals.

Reinstatement began after a September 30, 1993, court order from Federal Judge Hatter in Los Angeles barred the Department of Defense from enforcing the ban on gays in the military. Pentagon spokesperson, Kathleen deLaski, said, "We have to live with it." Dixon Osbourn, codirector of the homosexual advocacy group, Service Members Legal Defense Network, rightly said:

> It will undoubtedly be argued that openly gay service members served without incident which negates much of the opposition toward lifting the ban on gays in the military.

One gay service member's attorney said that there were "no conditions placed on his client's reinstatement." He can continue to be openly gay without consequence. This window of service for open homosexuals, which according to the homosexual press is ongoing, would not have been possible without the joint chiefs' endorsement of the questionable order and their support of the Clinton/Aspin compromise. The gay rights forces have thus made significant gains in their legal position since January 29, 1993, with the abetting of civilian and military leaders.

Not surprisingly for those who understand the Washington process, on July 30, 1993, the Clinton administration also announced the filing of briefs in the U.S. Courts of Appeals in Washington and San Francisco, respectively in the Steffan and Meinhold cases. Both navy men publicly announced their homosexuality and were ordered out of the service under the pre-Clinton policy. These cases pose a greater legal threat to the ban than does the new "political" suit filed in Washington. The Clinton/Reno Justice Department attorneys have argued in the appeals court that the military has discretion in these matters,[13] which was only acknowledged after they obtained the support of the joint chiefs. Said support, therefore, has been central to and critical for the Clinton strategy for removing the ban.

With the appointments of a respected member of the elite—distinguished feminist and American Civil Liberties Union lawyer, Judge Ruth Bader Ginsberg—to the Supreme Court and other liberal-leaning, pro-homosexual judges to the federal courts, it is very likely that the ban will be lifted without overturning the long-standing doctrine of military necessity. In deferring to and accommodating the president's homosexual policy, the chiefs' military judgments in such matters are now on record. The chiefs have knowingly or unwittingly through total loyalty to the Clinton administration agreed to a lifting of the ban. But even without the chiefs' acquiescence, the support of Justice Ginsberg may eventually make the military necessity doctrine vulnerable to legal challenge.

The erosion of the incompatibility principle has already occurred and the Clinton federal courts may be willing to make new law through the judicial process as in Steffan. This legal phenomenon happened often during the Carter years and came to be known as the "sweetheart" lawsuit. It was used as a lawmaking process and it is the primary method whereby the will of an

elite few overrules the majority values and effectively undermines representative democracy, which some have referred to as "judicial tyranny."[14] The
elite few dictate to the majority of Americans, who strongly oppose such
changes in the fundamental moral and legal order.

The fact remains that the compromise means that homosexuals are now
allowed to serve openly in the military, despite the fact that no military
reason for removing the ban exists or was ever raised by homosexual advocates. Strangely, many supporters of the ban are claiming the congressional
compromise as a "victory." Ten months ago, however, gay rights activists
declared that it was virtually impossible to open up military service to homosexuals through the courts. Today the gay rights public position is dramatically different primarily because the services, including the joint chiefs,
were willing to accommodate Clinton and Aspin.

The Moral Principle Has Been Removed

Regardless of the final court decision, one must conclude that much has in
fact been lost. The most important loss to this writer is morality, something
that was never a serious factor or consideration inside the Washington Belt-
way. It probably is no exaggeration to say that moral principle may never
again be decisive in a public debate. For America, the fact that our civilian
and military leaders avoided moral absolutes in the discussion of this issue is
sad and glaring. The last traditional institution in America, the military, now
makes judgments on military service based upon politically correct or equal
opportunity attitudes rather than moral principle or military necessity—
principles still contained in existing law.

The pre-Clinton defense policy said that homosexuality was incompatible
with military service. That principle had been enforced in America since the
Mayflower Compact. The compromise, engineered by questionable social
science, moral relativism, and mere abstractions—such as accepting the
theory that homosexual orientation or status can be separated from conduct
or behavior—has been substituted for moral principle as a standard for
judgment. Military lawyers for the chiefs of staff have unequivocally asserted
that the issue was not to be decided on moral considerations, in spite of the
fact that the ban on homosexuals in the military has been legally and traditionally in place since 1775 and has been the policy since World War II. With
epidemic levels of AIDS and other homosexually transmitted diseases,
caused primarily and spread most efficiently by sodomy and promiscuous
homosexual activity, this is no time to abandon moral principle.

It is simply not possible to compromise a moral principle. Moral principle
is fixed, unyielding, and not relative as to time or circumstances. It exists
externally, and when it falls into relativism, making each man a law unto

himself, the ultimate result is anarchy.[15] Absolute moral principles formed the foundation of our nation and became the animating spirit of the American armed forces. They sprang long ago from the pen of future president John Adams, father of the U.S. Navy. Adams, with the approval of the Continental Congress on November 28, 1775, established virtue and morality as America's first military principles and as prerequisites for commanding officers in the Naval Service with the warning "to guard against and suppress all immoral and dissolute behavior." His first principles for the navy have guided our armed services as law, policy, and custom since 1775, and were reaffirmed and enacted into law as recently as 1956.

The 1956 congressional mandate, when coupled with the felony sodomy provisions of the Uniform Code of Military Justice (UCMJ), obviously requires that the military screen out all homosexuals at entry level and also through subsequent investigation. When homosexuality is found, separation is to be prompt. The Congress, under its plenary constitutional authority "to make Rules for the Government and regulation of the land and naval forces," requires naval officers, as Adams wrote, to "guard against and suppress all dissolute and immoral practices . . . and to take all necessary and proper measures . . . to safeguard [those] under their command."[16] Homosexuality was clearly determined as immoral and dissolute then, and it is still viewed as such today.[17]

Furthering the Homosexual Agenda

Citizens must make an effort to understand how the elite—the executive branch of our government, the socially progressive legislative process, and the increasingly politicized courts—are working together to establish an entirely new morality, the morality of the New World Order. The new morality seeks to "free" people, including our children, from any moral limits or commonsense right and wrong. Good and decent people must see that the opening up of the military to homosexuals (right on the heels of allowing women to serve in combat) is simply the latest step in an agenda that has as its end the complete transformation of the nation's moral and spiritual being.

Such events require a watchman to shout the same warning recorded in Ezekiel 33 and 34 and Jeremiah 5: America, wake up, the sword is coming upon our land! Homosexuality is not about life but death. It is not benign, but both subversive and predatory in nature. As the gay rights movement wins more ground in its struggle to infiltrate and subvert our military, it also moves to take over our schools and indoctrinate our children, thereby threatening the very foundations of our future beliefs and values.

This is no grim and farfetched prediction—all these things are happening.

Homosexuals are currently serving openly in our armed forces. Some public schools blatantly offer courses that teach children to respect and experiment with homosexual behavior and to regard it as equal in value to traditional marriage. There is even a National Gay Teachers Association that publishes a newsletter debating such issues as whether it is ethical to have sex with students. If the military officially deems homosexuality as an acceptable status, then the push will begin to bring all public institutions—and particularly our schools—into lockstep with our armed forces.

The push by gay rights advocates began in 1948 and was apparently innocuous enough until 1972, when the gay rights movement began an orchestrated effort mindful of the wisdom in beginning slowly. Today, we are faced with scientists who attempt to find a genetic cause for homosexuality, and homosexual advocates who are already prepared to use such information, no matter how unreliable, in their quest for legitimacy through force, politics, scientific sanction, and civil rights protection. As one homosexual activist summarized the homosexual agenda: "When the [gay rights] bill passes, there will be something else. There will always be something else."[18]

In case anyone doubts this claim, homosexuals are now aggressively petitioning for same-sex marriage rights, and pedophiles are knocking on the cultural door, asking for the decriminalization of the age of consent laws so that they can have sex with our children and not go to jail.[19] For example, on January 24, 1993, the *New York Times Book Review* published a favorable review of a book by James Kincaid that praised adult-child sexual relations. In his book, Kincaid asserted that "the pathological condition called pedophilia . . . leads to very few crimes" and that "pedophiles, such as may exist, are gentle and unaggressive."[20] However, in a powerful rebuttal, Lynn Hecht Schafran, director of the National Judicial Education Program of the NOW Legal Defense and Education Fund, cited a "meticulously designed study" by Dr. Gene Abel of Emory University, which reported that, of 561 nonincarcerated male sex offenders, 377 were nonincestuous pedophiles; 224 of them targeted female children and assaulted 4,435 girls, and the 153 who targeted male children assaulted 22,981 boys.[21]

Given the recent successes of the gay rights movement, it is imperative that ordinary Americans become involved in the struggle—people who have up until now have been preoccupied with their own legitimate responsibilities and consequently have watched from the sidelines while our politicians and military leaders have capitulated to homosexual demands.

"Status/Orientation" Has Been Separated from "Behavior"

In a draft of the January 18, 1993, memorandum to the president that was leaked to the press, Defense Secretary Aspin stated that the goal of the new policy would be to "end discrimination on the basis of orientation." Under the policy, recruits would continue not being asked if they are homosexual as an orientation or a status, but only homosexual conduct, if discovered in an approved investigation, would still be grounds for separation from the military services. In another important concession to homosexual rights advocates, Clinton asserted that there will be a "decent regard" for privacy rights.

In so doing, Aspin and Clinton furthered a primary goal of the gay rights agenda, which, under cover of deception and through a lie, has been aggressively pushed by the homosexual movement and echoed by our elite institutions: that homosexuals are a "cultural minority" or a special class of people, that homosexuality is a "status" that is somehow separate from the conduct of sodomy and other homosexual behaviors. This occurred despite the fact that, in the absence of homosexual behaviors, there is nothing else immutable to distinguish a homosexual as such from other persons. Separation of homosexual status from homosexual behavior is a word game, an abstraction with no basis in reality or fact.

Activists have in effect argued that persons who practice sodomy and who think of themselves as homosexual, are able, in their own minds, to separate their status or orientation from their conduct. This distinction is a cornerstone to their progress, particularly after Bowers v. Hardwick in 1986. If there is no constitutional right of privacy to commit sodomy, then homosexual activists must strive to separate in the law homosexual orientation or status from homosexual conduct or behavior.[22]

Recent published scientific studies have attempted to provide a genetic explanation for at least some homosexuality.[23] The results are still not conclusive and can be explained in a variety of ways. The gay rights movement is looking to gain acceptability and credibility for homosexuality through politically correct social science. There are as many scientific researchers who find no genetic cause but instead point to environmental factors, especially early childhood sexual abuse by adults that often causes boys to think they are homosexual. Sexually victimized boys are seven times more likely to identify themselves as homosexual.[24] Significantly, the scientific results of the genetic studies fail to explain all homosexuality. As a result, behavior is still seen as intricately and inseparably linked with status, and environmental factors play a large role in shaping sexuality.

Deceit and Hypocrisy in Current Military Policy

In truth and fact and in existing law, homosexuality is indeed incompatible with military service. Given that, homosexuals must be screened out or disqualified along with many others with disqualifying characteristics, experience, or behavior patterns. Rather than setting up a screening process at the gate that will more assuredly deter homosexuals, the policy has now become in effect, "I get to serve and commit sodomy which is a felony under the UCMJ which is my identifying behavior, so long as I do not get caught."[25] Junior officers and NCOs already fear that any and every effort made to investigate or screen can and will be challenged as a "witch-hunt" leading to legal and public challenges and criticisms. Investigating or criticizing homosexuality will become as politically incorrect as pointing out the military significance of the many real differences between the sexes. The troops will get the message.

In a final tragic twist, the military committed a critical tactical error following President Clinton's order to stop screening for homosexuals on the basis of orientation. The Record of Military Processing form used by the Armed Forces of the United States, DD Form 1966, Jan. 89, question 27 (Character and Social Adjustment) reads: "a. Are you a homosexual or a bisexual?" The form defines homosexual and bisexual. Then it asks: "b. Do you intend to engage in homosexual acts (sexual relations with another person of the same sex)?" The Department of Defense Joint Staff eliminated both questions. Only one question had to be eliminated: question 27a. Question 27b related to conduct, which the military was still authorized to screen. This was either intentional or a grave oversight by the Pentagon Study Group led by Lt. Gen. Robert Minter Alexander, then deputy assistant secretary of military manpower and personnel policy. General Alexander is also charged with making the Clinton-Aspin pro-gay policy work and with putting women into combat and making sure that "it works."

The new Clinton policy creates a gray area around the definition of what is punishable homosexual behavior. This creates a confusing "rebuttable presumption" as to what constitutes activity sufficient to culminate in a dischargeable offense. Moreover, much of the responsibility for setting guidelines for enforcement of the proposed policy is left in the hands of a secretary of defense. Given Secretary Aspin's remarks, there is little confidence that guidelines, at least in the short term, will be carried out in the spirit and intent of the revised policy—to proscribe behavior that is deemed counterproductive to good order and discipline in the military.

The "rebuttable presumption" puts the onus on military commanders and junior military leaders rather than the persons who engage in homosexual behavior in violation of the policy. In prosecuting persons whose behavior is deemed disruptive and incompatible with good order and discipline, military commanders will be faced with the additional burden of proving that any investigation or discovery of homosexual behavior was proper and not malicious and subjective. Essentially, military commanders will now have to build an airtight case in order to prosecute with the confidence that inappropriate behavior will be rightfully punished and such prosecution will withstand any legal challenge. This will take time away from command and combat training, undermine authority in unsuccessful cases, and be a strong deterrence to rigorous enforcement.

In the courts, an indefensible legal contradiction will be created by gradually admitting homosexuals into the military under the pretense that the military can or should be policing sexual behavior. The July 9, 1993, *Washington Blade* reported that U.S. Attorney General Janet Reno sent "a terse letter" to the president saying the "don't ask, don't tell" proposal "could unleash a flood of litigation." The *Blade* also said Reno "was not going to pull her attorneys off of drug cases and crime (fighting) to cover the military's ass."[26]

Medical Risks under the Compromise

Removing the right of the military to inquire about one's sexual orientation during recruitment poses an unconscionable moral and medical risk to the sons and daughters of Americans serving within the military. Originally the directive to guard against and screen out those given to immorality was, as stated earlier, rooted in the nation's early first principles based on Christian morality.

Today the well-documented excesses and consequences of those in the homosexual life-style have resulted in the overwhelming majority of serious sexually transmitted diseases.[27] Notably, the deadly AIDS virus and various strains of hepatitis are a certain and sound medical reason scientifically supporting the wisdom of the moral principles for maintaining the ban at the point of entry. By denying the right and duty of the military to screen out homosexuals "at the door," President Clinton, the joint chiefs, and Congress allow a group of people who have a track record of very serious medical and public health problems and deadly diseases to fundamentally alter law and policy in order to enter into the ranks.

Particularly in the case of AIDS, the effect of nondetection could be devastating with regard to morale and combat readiness, if not life and health. Soldiers bleed in training and on the battlefield and are required to donate blood on the battlefield at any given moment.[28] As AIDS has a latency of three to six months (some evidence suggests years) before it can be detected by current testing methods, the possibility that it could be carried in a soldier's blood and either unwittingly or willfully be transmitted to another is greatly heightened if the military has no way of determining whether that soldier has had AIDS-efficient sex, the defining behavior of homosexuals. The homosexual movement also is demanding an end to HIV and AIDS testing as "discriminatory."[29]

Is it not logical that the best method to reduce the medical risk to a society is to guard against or screen out upon entry? By removing the ability to ask recruits or even enlisted personnel if they are homosexual or practice homosexuality, the military has lost its best hedge against an increased rate of sexually transmitted disease, particularly AIDS. This is unconscionable.

Conclusion

Today, the United States of America faces one of the greatest crises in its 217-year history. Battle lines are being drawn for a cultural war over the meaning of freedom between the forces advocating absolute freedom of subjective choice and those advocating the traditionally American freedom that springs from moral convictions. The proponents of absolute freedom of choice support a narcissistic liberation from all moral, political, and social responsibilities. These individuals deny any possibility of moral absolutes and believe that concepts of right and wrong are subjective, determined by the will of private persons.

The defenders of moral conviction mirror the thinking of America's Founding Fathers that government's function is to protect the God-granted inalienable rights of man, including the right to life, liberty, and property. Although these rights of man are most important in the scheme of America's self-evident freedoms, the constitutional freedom of religion is the pivotal liberty upon which all these rest. As the history of civilization has shown, when this liberty is threatened, all other liberties are weakened. And when this liberty is destroyed, a nation quickly succumbs to tyranny. No person describes the essential importance of religion in society better than the first president of the United States:

> Of all the dispositions and habits which lead to political prosperity, religion and morality are indispensable supports. . . . Whatever may be conceded to the influence of refined education on minds of peculiar structure, reason and experience both forbid us to expect that national morality can prevail in exclusion of religious principle . . . it is impossible to govern rightly without God and the Bible.[30]

No group marching under the banner of freedom of choice and dedicated to the subversion of religion and morality poses a more grievous threat to the freedom of religion than the militant relativists of the homosexual movement. By aggressively fighting for gay rights, homosexuals have become an incredibly powerful and well-organized political force in America. Seeking much more than a mere tolerance of their private life-style, these homosexual activists demand total public acceptance and glorification of their way of life by government, society, and traditional religion. This tyrannical demand for special rights directly threatens the constitutional rights of the majority of Americans who view this life-style to be aberrant and morally wicked.

Most Americans abide by the normative Old and New Testament principles upon which the United States was founded. Examples of these principles are clearly represented in the spiritual law of the Ten Commandments and the natural law teachings of the philosophical founders of Western democratic thought such as John Locke and the authors of the Federalist Papers. Our founders often looked to scripture and to history for guidance to light their path, and America might do well to do the same. After all, the homosexual act is "sodomy," a term drawn from Genesis.

God's actions against Sodom and Gomorrah were so striking and unforgettable that though Sodom was destroyed, its name lives on to describe the kind of spiritual iniquity and reprobate mind God will not in any way countenance. The Thompson's Chain Reference Bible carries a short summary on Sodom and Gomorrah by Dr. George Adam Smith. It is as follows:

> Here was laid the scene of the most terrible judgment on human sin. The glare of Sodom and Gomorrah is flung down the whole length of Scriptural history. It is the popular and standard judgment of sin. The story is told in Genesis; it is applied in Deuteronomy, by Amos, by Isaiah, by Jeremiah, by Ezekiel and Zephaniah, and in Lamentations. Our Lord employs it more than once as the figure of judgment He threatens upon sites where the word is preached in vain and we feel the flame scorch our own cheeks (Matt. 10:15; 11:24; Luke 10:12; 17:29). Paul, Peter, Jude make mention of it. In Revelation the city of sin is spiritual Sodom. Though the glare of this catastrophe burns still, the ruins it left have disappeared.[31]

Notes

1. The opinions and conclusions expressed herein are the personal views of the individual author and are not necessarily endorsed by nor necessarily reflect the official policy position of the Department of Defense, Department of the Navy, United States Marine Corps, or any other governmental agency.

2. Charles Francis Adams, *John Adams: The Works of John Adams, Second President of the United States*, Vol. IX (Boston: Little, Brown, 1854), 229.

3. Larry Whitham, "Clinton Lauded by Openly Homosexual Appointees," *Washington Times*, 3 November 1993.

4. J. Jennings Moss, "Clinton to Allow Gays in Military," *Washington Times*, 12 November 1992.

5. Jeffrey Schmalz, "Gay Areas Are Jubilant Over Clinton," *New York Times*, 4 November 1992.

6. Dr. Charles E. Rice, Professor of Constitutional Law at Notre Dame Law School, rendered an opinion on June 14, 1993, that the "don't ask" order would be an unlawful order in violation of the duty imposed in existing law; 10 U.S.C. 5947.

7.   Frank J. Murray, "Clinton Tells Top Brass Gay Ban Will Not Stand," *Washington Times*, 26 January 1993.

8.   John Marcos, "Gay Rights Protest Marks Powell's Speech at Harvard," *Courier Journal*, 11 June 1993.

9.   Meeting in the Office of the Chairman of the Joint Chiefs of Staff, July 31, 1992 and February 1993.

10.   Rowan Scarborough, "Gay-Bad Debate Divisive," *Washington Times*, 2 July 1993.

11.   Ibid.

12.   Ronald D. Ray, *Military Necessity and Homosexuality*. Second edition revised. (Louisville, Ky.: First Principles), 14–24.

13.   Lyle Denniston, *Courier Journal*, 31 July 1993.

14.   Carrol Kilgore, *Judicial Tyranny: An Inquiry into the Integrity of the Federal Judiciary* (Nashville: Thomas Nelson, 1977); Raoul Berger, *Government by Judiciary: The Transformation of the Fourteenth Amendment* (Cambridge, MA: Harvard University Press, 1977).

15.   Suzanne Fields, "Moral Deregulation," *The Washington Times*, May 27, 1993. Sen. Daniel Moynihan (D-N.Y.) describes a contemporary phenomenon called "defining deviancy down." He refers to our capacity for "moral deregulation," i.e., redefining deviant behavior so that it appears to be normal.

16.   See U.S. Constitution Art. I, Sec. 8 and 10 U.S.C. 5947.

17.   It is even so declared by homosexuals themselves, who revel in what they term "deviant" behavior. See Joan Smith, *San Francisco Examiner*, 25 April 1993, D-10:
        Queerness, says Browning with delight is about subversion. "It is a rather
        delectable word," he says. "More than the image of men doing forbidden
        things to one another in private, it represents, the peculiar and creative in all
        of us. . . ." Which is why the open acceptance of gays in the military would
        be subversive. "If you see your captain as a sexual object, as somebody's
        boyfriend, it subverts the whole notion of authority," he says.

18.   As described in "The Week," *National Review*, 16 April 1986, 16.

19.   See S. Alyson, *The Age Taboo* (Alyson, 1981). Alyson maintains that "man/boy love is a civil rights issue, and rejects the 'child molester' label." *Lambda Report*, No. 1, February 1993, 3.

20.   Walter Kendrick, Review of *Child Loving* by James R. Kincaid, *New York Times Book Review*, 24 January 1993. See also, Lynn Hecht Schafran, Letter to the Editor, "Pedophiles and the Law," *New York Times Book Review*, 23 February 1993.

21.   Schafran, "Pedophiles."

22.   Melissa Wells-Petry, *Exclusion, Homosexuals and the Right to Serve* (Washington, DC: Regnery Gateway, 1993), 43–49.

23.   Dean H. Hamer et al., "A Linkage Between DNA Markers on the X Chromosome and Male Sexual Orientation," *Science* 261 (1993):322.

24.   Robert L. Johnson and Diane K. Schrier, "Sexual Victimization of Boys: Experience at an Adolescent Medical Clinic," *Journal of Adolescent Health Care* 6 (1985):372–76.

25.   Michael Kramer, *Time*, 26 July 1993, 41.

26.   "As Deadline Nears, Gays Hold Out for Lifting Ban," *Washington Blade*, 9 July 1993.

27.   See, e.g., National Centers for Disease Control Report, 1988—61 percent of U.S. cases of AIDS resulted from homosexual activity. See also, "Teenagers and AIDS," *Newsweek*, 3 August 1992, 44: 87 percent of all AIDS cases in adults over age 24 attributable to needle-sharing and male/male sex; the same was true for 77 percent of AIDS patients aged 13–24.

28.   The army performed five combat transfusions during Desert Storm and five during Provide Comfort. Also, STDs other than AIDS can spread through an exchange of blood.

29.   The military screens for HIV at accession, within six months of deployments, and at least once every three years. It is worth noting that Daniel T. Bross, executive director of the AIDS Action Council called for the military to stop testing for HIV. He stated, "Someone's HIV status shouldn't be a determining factor for a job, and the military is a job" *Washington Times*, 1 December 1992.

30.   George Washington, cited in Henry Halley, *Halley's Bible Handbook* (Grand Rapids, MI: Zondervan, 1965), 18.

31.   Thompson Chain Reference Bible (Indianapolis: Kirkbride Bible Co., 1988), 1792.

Chapter 7

Anatomy of a Panic: State Voyeurism, Gender Politics, and the Cult of Americanism

BARRY D. ADAM

Despite the alarm raised in many quarters of American society over the idea of gays in the military, there is no intrinsic relationship, whether positive or negative, between homosexual relationships and military activity. Yet the American state and its most avid supporters have constructed a fantastic, paranoid vision of their supposed nexus and a complex, multimillion dollar surveillance apparatus to protect itself from its imaginary demons. A glance through the cross-cultural evidence on homosexuality and the military reveals that societies make diverse connections between the two phenomena, constructing the relationship as positive, irrelevant, or negative.

A dispassionate review of the military position justifying its persecution and purgation of the gay men and lesbians in its ranks shows that the military's claims are fanciful, bizarre, and contradictory. No sense can be made of the debate that has gripped American public discourse over the first half of 1993 by seeing the gays in the military issue as a clash of reason or evidence. The entire paroxysm of public debate around the issue can be made comprehensible only by probing into the psychoemotional underpinnings that charge its trajectory in order to reveal the tangle of gender politics and national identity that impelled it forward.

Homosexuality and the Military: The Evidence

What do homosexuality and the military have to do with each other? The answer is entirely dependent on specific cultural constructions of the meanings of both activities. Unlike the hegemonic American version, which has proven so durable that the Clinton administration has been able to make no more than an imperceptible reform to it, many societies around the world and throughout history have, in fact, drawn quite opposite conclusions about the connection between the two. The culturally entrenched answer to this question in American society is to posit the two as diametrically opposed. One is the subversion of the other.

The crux of the issue in the United States is the culturally embedded view that homosexuality represents a feminization of men and that this feminization entails a world of implications debilitating to military effectiveness, namely, all of the traditional traits assigned to the feminine—weakness, submission, passivity, softness, compassion, and peaceableness—all of which detract from military readiness. Seventy years ago, this same semiotic divide underpinned national debates over extending the vote to women. Opponents to women's enfranchisement were deeply convinced at the time that nations would soon be overrun by foreign invaders because the female electorate would choose surrender over violence.[1] Today the same meaning systems fuel debates over gays in the military.

The construction of a "homosexual threat to the military" is a story about the perceived potential emasculation of American masculinity. Certainly, lesbians bear the full brunt of the anti-homosexual policy, but the psycho-dynamic matrix of the issue revolves around a panic among men. The irony of this cultural axiom of American society is that it depends on a gender discourse with the most tenuous of foundations. An entirely opposite construction of the relationship between homosexuality and the military has occurred in many societies around the world. Homosexuality can just as easily be understood as having a masculinizing effect in males and therefore not only be compatible with, but an indispensable asset in military mobilization.[2] Most of these alternative conceptions of same-sex relations fall into some variant of the apprentice or acolyte model of intermale relationship.

In the ancient model, homosexuality is a medium for the transmission of folklore contained by the masculine gender and is a second stage of parenting, which succeeds the mother-child relationship.[3] In this social arrangement, boys are considered to be in need of masculinization, typically during their adolescence, as they leave behind the maternal influence of childhood. This masculinization occurs through the formal linkage of a boy with a man in a sexual relationship, the latter usually selected through kinship obligations or personal qualities valued by the boy's family. This kind of system can be easily adapted to military demands.

Examples can be drawn from Asia, Africa, Europe, Melanesia, and the Middle East. In Japan, the samurai tradition was characterized by intense erotic and emotional relationships between professional soldiers and their acolytes, who themselves eventually became samurai through a lengthy process of care and discipline.[4] The nineteenth-century central African Azande empire (crushed by British imperialism in the late nineteenth century) included a military class with a similar tradition. Evans-Pritchard wrote of the Azande:

> Many of the warriors married boys and a commander might have more than

one boy wife. When a warrior married a boy, he paid spears, though only a few, to the boy's parents as he would have done had he married their daughter.[5]

The ancient Greeks furnish the best known European example. Harmodius and Aristogeiton were credited in Greek mythology as the pair of lovers who slew a tyrant, thereby ushering in the democratic foundations of Western civilization. The sacred band of Thebes was said to be the most effective fighting force of its day, having been organized so that the younger men fought on the front line while their lovers backed them up. The story of Achilles and Patroclus is familiar to virtually every schoolchild.[6]

In parts of Melanesia, the male lineage was bound together as a cohesive fighting unit through the transmission of semen from older to younger males.[7] The people of the Siwa oasis in the Libyan desert maintained a military caste from ancient times into the twentieth century that functioned as a bachelor society bonded through sexual relationships.[8]

Even in homophobic societies, homosexual people are counted among some of their well-known military leaders. General Gordon, who fell at Khartoum, and Lawrence of Arabia are noteworthy British examples. Though not officially acknowledged, the homosexuality of *Sandinista comandantes* Jaime Wheelock Roman and Dora Marfa Tellez is widely rumored throughout Nicaraguan society. Both had distinguished careers as military leaders in the overthrow of the Somoza dictatorship, which had ruled Nicaragua for two generations. Both subsequently held high office in the revolutionary government which redistributed land to the dispossessed and organized the first democratic political system in the history of the nation.

Today, in comparing the advanced capitalist nations of North America, the European Community, Australia, and Japan,[9] only the United Kingdom and the United States remain mired in premodern policies excluding lesbians and gay men from military service. As Peter Tatchell points out in reviewing the European situation:

> Membership in the armed forces is open to homosexuals in eleven countries— Austria, Belgium, Denmark, Germany, Finland, France, Netherlands, Norway, Spain, Sweden and Switzerland—providing sexual relationships take place outside of barracks during off-duty hours. In the German armed forces, however, homosexuals are barred from officer rank.[10]

For these countries (with the partial exception of Germany), homosexuality has little or no bearing on military matters. In the Netherlands, in fact, lesbian and gay soldiers have an association that is recognized by the defense ministry. These countries continue to participate in the modernizing trend of extending equal rights to all of their citizens regardless of traditionally ascribed attributes or prejudices.

A perusal of the cross-cultural evidence, then, shows that there is no intrinsic or necessary relationship between homosexuality and the military.

Cultural representations of the relationship vary widely from the ancient and Melanesian models, which construct same-sex bonding as a military asset to modern conceptions, which find sexual orientation to be an irrelevant consideration in military recruitment. The United States, with the United Kingdom, remains exceptional in its continuing reproduction of homophobic ideology and its attachment to superstitious and paranoid postulations of a fictive connection.

The Spectacle of a Heterosexist Panic

One is left then casting about for an explanation of the ferocity and intransigence of the antigay ban in the United States. Complicating the picture is the fact that even the most extremist elements of the reactionary right have increasingly conceded the modernist critique. Even Senator Strom Thurmond (R-S.C.), a leading proponent of the ultraright, allowed for the "dedicated and heroic service by many gays in the ranks of our armed services" in testimony before the Armed Services Committee of the U.S. Congress.[11] Barry Goldwater wrote a widely published essay denouncing the injustice of the ban. The military itself commissioned two inquiries into the antigay ban, which concluded that its continuation was irrational and unwarranted. The 1988 report of the Defense Personnel Security Research and Education Center, "Nonconforming Sexual Orientations and Military Suitability," and the 1989 report, "Preservice Adjustment of Homosexual and Heterosexual Military Accessions," concluded that "homosexuals show preservice suitability-related adjustment that is as good or better than the average heterosexual."[12] Vice Adm. Joseph Donnell, commander of the Navy Surface Atlantic Fleet, admitted in a leaked memo that "lesbians may be among the Navy's 'top' performers."[13]

Reviews of social science research in the area come to similar conclusions. Gary Melton's 1989 summation of the research literature observed: "The army's self-declared rationale for excluding lesbians and gay men is contradicted by scientific research," and "[t]here is no rational basis for the army's counterproductive exclusion of gay people."[14]

A moment's reflection on the official rationale provided by the U.S. military for maintaining the ban demonstrates its absurd—even bizarre—logical contortions. Gregory Herek, who measures the official position against the social science research, shows that the claims forwarded by the official position are simply groundless.[15] Judith Stiehm, who examined their logical consistency, finds that they rapidly fall apart under scrutiny.[16] The claim that lesbian and gay soldiers pose a security risk lacks any evidence and even worse, contains a self-fulfilling element because the policy creates the very risk of exposure that is posited to be subject to blackmail.

The claim that lifting the ban lacks public acceptability and that no one would want to join the military if gay people were present must face the fact that the potential recruit who avoided the military because of the presence of gay people would then presumably seek employment in a larger society where gay people are present (and not systematically expelled from employment) and where, in at least seven states,[17] they are protected from workplace discrimination. The claim that lesbian and gay soldiers would destroy unit cohesion and themselves be subject to violence replays the primary argumentation used in 1948 against racial integration in the military.[18] As Stiehm points out, "trust and confidence develop not from homogeneity but shared experience."[19]

And yet, lesbians and gay men find themselves yet again in the gays in the military debate, the objects of a heterosexist orgy of sexual paranoia, vilification, and manipulation. Gay people confronted a circus-full of generals, senators, religious ideologues, and media commentators, all proud of their ignorance of homosexuality, busily engaged in legislating the meaning and worth of their lives. Like other inferiorized peoples, gay people discover themselves as symbols manipulated in the transmission of the dominant culture. Their "objective" identity lives beyond their control; the image of self, institutionalized by cultural agents, exists alien to their own experience and self-expression. The ongoing, emergent lives of a people are confronted by a "representation" that exists only as an object for the other. The social construction of the gays in the military issue reveals the powerlessness of reason and the weakness of such fundamental tenets of modern civilization as the idea that employment should be a matter of one's competence and not of an ascribed characteristic. The public discourse demonstrates once again, in the words of Eve Sedgewick, "how obtuseness itself arms the powerful against their enemies."[20]

Can one avoid the conclusion then that the gays in the military question is not about gays in the military but about the dynamics and practices of the heterosexist mind?

Gay and Lesbian Responses

While the dominant public discourse on the issue is about how the military constructed homosexuality in a manner that successfully fended off the modernizing probe of the Clinton administration, it is worth considering how lesbians and gay men constructed military issues in their press and in their movements. Military concerns have had their place in gay American history and have sparked debates within lesbian and gay communities concerning participation in this agency of the state.

War has had a much more multivalent effect on the development of homosexuality in the United States than the military itself imagines. Allen Berube notes that the vast mobilizations of entire generations of young men and women in the national efforts of World Wars I and II served as catalysts in realizing socially repressed desires.[21] At the same time as the military was developing its anti-gay repressive apparatus, military mobilization was moving millions of young people out of small towns and away from parental supervision, into large same-sex environments where personal relationships would be developed anew. Berube's meticulous historical account details how many gay Americans served in the military or even discovered their homosexual interests there. The military, as well, taught self-assertion to soldiers, demanding that they put their lives on the line, and then for many gay and lesbian veterans, threw them away, blocked their health and educational benefits, and issued them discharge papers that prevented them from securing employment even after the war.

When black soldiers, after defending their country against fascism, returned to the unemployment and racism of American society immediately after the two world wars, civil disturbances broke out in several major cities. Similarly, gay and lesbian soldiers were among those who took the first steps toward the organization of a modern gay and lesbian civil rights movement in the form of the postwar Veterans' Benevolent Association, which protested against the stigma of the "blue discharge." In Berube's words:

> The military, ironically, encouraged gay veterans to assume a stronger gay identity when it began to identify and manage so many people as homosexual persons rather than focus narrowly on the act of sodomy. . . . Having served their country well in a time of national emergency, gay veterans, especially those who had fought in combat, felt a heightened sense of legitimacy as citizens, entitlement as veterans, and betrayal when denied benefits. . . . A few began to speak of rights, injustice, discrimination, and persecution as a minority.[22]

In 1966, the small, low-profile homophile organizations that had survived through the 1950s and 1960s organized themselves into a North American Conference of Homophile Organizations, which adopted a resolution protesting the military ban.[23]

When a new wave of more militant organizing occurred in 1969 and the 1970s in the form of gay liberation and lesbian feminism, military issues took another term. In the midst of the deeply unpopular U.S. war in Vietnam, the movement took little interest in opposing a ban that, in the opinion of many, saved them from being conscripted to do the "dirty work" of forwarding the imperial ambitions of the U.S. elite. This was a time when many heterosexual men feigned homosexuality in an attempt to avoid engagement in a war that they believed to be morally bankrupt. Many gay activists remained suspicious of a state system that issued medals for killing men but expelled them for loving men.

In the post-Vietnam era, the problem of the military ban resurfaced. The gay and lesbian movement faced a dilemma not unlike the black and Latino movements of the day. While many abhorred involvement in the repeated military adventures of the U.S. state, which entailed the suppression of nonwhite peoples overseas, many others joined because of the attractive opportunities offered by the military for educational and social mobility—or because of their belief in the "patriotic" undertakings of the military.

In the more peaceable 1980s when many of the imperial exploits of the U.S. state were subcontracted to a variety of "contras" around the world, a series of lawsuits began to pick away at the military ban. With well over a thousand military people expelled every year for homosexuality over a fifty-year time span, a number of military men and women have been willing to take on the lengthy and expensive proceedings of challenging military practices of withholding diplomas from graduates of the naval academy, refusing re-enlistment to soldiers with distinguished service records, conducting witch-hunts of navy women fingered through rumors and personal vendettas, and denying pension and other benefits to those who had completed tours of duty.

Ultimately gay and lesbian organizations could scarcely ignore institutionalized state predation and terror directed against gay and lesbian people. Could anything be won from the state while it so actively engaged in the reproduction of homophobia within itself?

The Sex of the U.S. State

The "problem" of gays in the military, then, has very little to do with the lives and experiences of lesbians and gay men. It is, rather, a projection of a series of fears and anxieties characteristic of the ideologies of dominant classes in general, and more particularly, of gendered, nativist, and heterosexist discourses circulated and reproduced by certain constituencies in American society. State and military homophobia partakes of a general ideology of domination, which assigns similar traits to inferiorized peoples whether they are Jews, women, blacks, or the poor. The gaze of the powerful contains within it a fantasy image of the powerless. They are repeatedly found to be subhuman, impulsive, and instinctual, hypersexual, traitors and conspirators, and overvisible.

The "treason" charge is visible in the security risk claim forwarded by the official justification for the ban on gay people.[24] It surfaced again when the Navy convinced itself, in the absence of any supporting evidence, that a 1987 explosion that occurred in the gun turret of the battleship *USS Iowa* "must have been" the result of a "lover's quarrel" between two sailors.[25] More telling perhaps, is the barely concealed sexual paranoia of the "intimate quarters" claim of the official story.

Sexual Paranoia and State Voyeurism

The American public has been treated to a range of television clips and magazine stories picturing U.S. senators gazing upon the cramped living quarters of sailors and soldiers and worrying about their "sleeping and showering arrangements." In an article by Charles Moskos, reputedly one of the architects of the so-called "don't ask, don't tell" policy adopted by the state, the punchline narratologically positioned to deliver the knockout blow to convince everyone of the need to ban gay people from the military reads:

> Just as most men and women dislike being stripped of all privacy before the opposite sex, so most heterosexual men and women dislike being exposed to homosexuals of their own sex.[26]

In testimony before the congressional Armed Services Committee, Indiana Senator Daniel Coats'(R-Ind.) primary concern was what washrooms gay men would use if the ban were lifted.[27]

Gay men began to understand that the army, supposedly unafraid of a host of evil empires from Communism to Saddam Hussein, was terrified that gay men might catch a glimpse of their penes! Even though gay men have grown up with, showered with, and—yes—seen the penes of many men throughout their lives in schools, gyms, dormitories, and washrooms, it appears that in the military their gaze is so powerful as to virtually paralyze the phallocratic military machine. So serious is this threat that the military has constructed a massive voyeuristic system to spy upon the sexuality of gay men and lesbians by employing investigators and inquisitors to break into their sleeping quarters at 2:00 A.M. in the hopes of catching them *in flagrante delicto*, to read their mail and eavesdrop upon their conversations, and to squeeze out stories of sexual acts and contacts from its unsuspecting victims. Here we find an elaborate and expansive state machinery of surveillance organized by heterosexual men in order to gaze upon gay men, their bodies, and most prized of all, their erotic activity, all because gay men might happen to see their penes. The military has invented a real system of sexed desire in order to contain the imagined desires of gay men.[28]

None of this is unprecedented. It parallels racist phantasms about black sexuality. As the move to integrate public transit got under way with Martin Luther King, Jr., a leading Alabama politician charged that the main goal of the NAACP was "to open the bedroom doors of our white women to the Negro Man."[29] While the black civil rights movement worked to secure job rights and equitable treatment, the white opposition agitated itself with anxieties of black sexual predation and miscegenation. And while the gay and lesbian movement seeks fair employment practices in the military, the military is seized by anxieties of gay soldiers sleeping in the next bunk and lesbian sailors watching other women in the showers.

Lesbians and gay men have never been quite sure whether to laugh or cry in the face of heterosexist fantasies that such institutions as the military take so seriously as to inflict them upon gay people themselves. The paranoiac paradoxes of heterosexist phantasms create fertile ground for camp humor. This missive appeared in the gay press in the midst of the military debate:

> *Why Straight Men Should Not Be in the Military*
> 1.   Straight men are constantly flaunting their heterosexuality, and make gay men uncomfortable.
> 2.   Because of fear of being branded gay, straight men refrain from forming truly close relationships with other men. This interferes with the bonding and loyalty essential to military teamwork.
> 3.   Straight men are not used to seeing other men naked, so they are not psychologically equipped to shower with other men.
> 4.   Straight men are militant about converting others to their lifestyles, which includes unwanted pregnancies, disease, and cheap cologne.
> 5.   Straight men never get harassed, so they don't have well-developed defense techniques.[30]

Gender Politics

At the heart of the sense of terror among the military in the face of homosexuality is a semiotic chain, which binds aggression, masculinity, and self-esteem into a tightly wound mechanism designed to motivate and discipline the male soldier. This mechanism is a well-honed extreme of a larger social obligation, which threatens men with the loss of male prerogatives should they show signs of or sympathy with things "feminine." In basic training, homophobic and misogynist threats serve as a primary tool of combat preparation. Recruits are assailed with taunts of "little girl" or "faggot" for every sign of failure or weakness in order to forge an identification of violence with basic esteem.

R. Wayne Eisenhart argues that basic training works by fusing military authority and peer dynamics among recruits into a pressure cooker intended to shape every recruit in the image of aggressive masculinity.[31] Every recruit is threatened with psychological annihilation and physical jeopardy; his very being depends on his ability to show violence. The "alternative" is failure and expulsion as a "faggot" or a "girl." The fusion of military effectiveness with masculinity and concomitant demonization of femininity and homosexuality has become so fundamental a part of the military psyche that the prospect of gays in the military stimulates a psychological panic rooted in fears of loss of the self.

The integration of women into the military has suffered from the same dynamic, proceeding at a snail's pace and resisted by military authorities every step of the way. Once in, women are at an even greater risk of being expelled from the military on the grounds of homosexuality than are men.[32] Lesbianism carries its own set of associated meanings for the male regime ruling the military. Women who show independence, resistance to sexual harassment, or the "masculine" qualities so valued by the military are particularly vulnerable to the charge of lesbianism. Unlike the case of the gay male who is constructed as the nightmare simulacrum of the failed and emasculated soldier, women are caught in the acute contradiction that they are trained in the hypermasculinist ideology of the military as soldiers, at the same time as the same ideology demands their subordination to be seen as "proper" women at all. Not surprisingly the male military has no trouble catching all kinds of putative "lesbians" in its double binds.

The identification of the military task as fundamentally masculine, the manufacture of an anti-sexual male world based on the denigration of women, and the reliance on homophobia as a disciplinary tool all conspire to give the gays in the military issue an emotional charge that surpasses the *prima facie* merits of the issue.

The Cult of Americanism

The homophobic psychodynamic is further interlocked with national ideologies. Superpower states such as the United States are clearly gendered as male.[33] National identity and pride are caught up with masculinist ideologies of strength and belligerence. During periods when national populations experience a sense of threat, during wartime or self-doubt following military decline or defeat, conservative forces cast about for "fifth columns," traitors, or sites of moral weakness in an attempt to defend the overweening national ego of the superpower state. There are numerous historical examples where the British, German, and United States governments have launched campaigns of persecution against gay men and lesbians, along with series of other scapegoats, during times of national crisis or uncertainty.[34] As L. J. Moran contends, in reference to the British state:

> The male body becomes a device through which an idea of the nation is realised. . . . Thus manliness/nation is represented as order, strength, rationality, the upper part of the body, stiffness, harmony, proportion, stability, unchanging values, timelessness. . . . It is within the terms of the iconic repertoire set up in the idea of the Mannerstaat, that the homosexual is produced through a particular chain of associations: the emotional, effeminate, weak, subversive, conspiratorial, rebellious, revolutionary, corrosive, dark, dangerous, sensuous, irrational, unstable, and corrupt.[35]

Still, one must ask why the gays in the military question has become so major an issue in American society when it has occasioned only minor comment in other advanced industrial societies. Apart from its commonalities with other imperial nations past and present, American national identity has its exceptional characteristics as well. Despite the widespread acceptance of lesbian and gay recruits into the militaries of its allies (as discussed above), the public debate in the United States has shown no interest in the examples of these nations. Only the Israeli military attracts the attention of American commentators. Like the U.S. military, the Israeli military has been actively and repeatedly belligerent throughout the post-World War II period. The lengthy United Nations peacekeeping history of, for example, the Canadian military seem to hold little interest to the primary imperial army of the modern world system.

Unlike those of its allies, the military maintains a particularly central role in the American national imagination as the symbol of U.S. preeminence. Public discourse in the United States rarely questions the right or the consequences of the exertion of U.S. military power around the world.[36] The U.S. military has a special place as a medium through which the United States constructs itself in opposition to a long series of special "enemies." Public opinion polls show a surge of popular support for every act of military aggression such that presidents have learned to dole them out periodically in order to bolster their public profile, whether the target is Libya, Grenada, Panama, or continuing episodic attacks upon Iraq.

Finally, the issue indexes a much deeper divide in American society and must contend with powerful New Right constituencies who identify gay and lesbian rights with the effects of modernization. The United States has a particularly well-established coalition of right-wing constituencies that are able and willing to carry out symbolic crusades against a range of sociohistorical symbols associated with secularization, family change, and popular enfranchisement.[37]

Unlike many other countries, then, that now treat military recruitment as "another job," the U.S. military plays a more central role in the nation's self-image and self-esteem, thus raising the stakes for the issue of gays in the military.

The Closet Rule

The *denouement* of the public debate on gays in the military has been the imposition of a closet rule that supposedly takes away the active persecution and surveillance of homosexual service people but nevertheless removes none of the underlying policy that makes that persecution possible in the first place. The policy mandates the dismissal of anyone who "engages in

homosexual conduct," which includes merely saying, or having someone say
a person said, that she or he "is homosexual."[38] The "don't ask, don't tell"
rule reimposes a primary tool of homophobic assault. As Sedgwick remarks
in surveying numerous previous examples of the state practice of the closet
rule, "the space for simply existing as a gay person . . . is in fact bayonetted
through and through, from both sides, by the vectors of a disclosure at once
compulsory and forbidden." Lesbians and gay men become obliged to tra-
verse an unknowable minefield, "an excruciating system of double binds,
systematically oppressing gay people, identities, and acts by undermining
through contradictory constraints on discourse the grounds of their very
being."[39]

The U.S. state has adopted the homophobic doctrine propounded by the
Vatican in demanding that the sexual and emotional lives of homosexual
people be confined to the interior of their minds. The military/church re-
tains control of defining and interpreting the sign system by which "homosexuality" is to be read, while gay people get to be the mice in a cat-and-
mouse game of concealment and discovery.

Conclusion

The gays in the military issue has been an occasion for the gay and lesbian
movement to attempt to disrupt the semiotic chains that continue to bind
homosexually interested people. The approach of movement activists has
been to attempt to display the masculine soldiers, the patriotic women, and
the reasonable and competent people among its ranks. The 1993 March on
Washington featured a good deal of flag-waving, the application of basic
American values and constitutional rights to citizens who want to love and
live with the persons of their choice, and an attack on the popular prejudice
that labels gay men and lesbians as the Other, by advancing the truism that
gay people are among everyone's family, friends, and neighbors. It is a
strategy that is necessary and unavoidable in derailing the ideological ruts
and prejudicial precepts that have continued to give warrant to the homophobic regime of violence and exclusion that has assailed lesbians and gay
men throughout American history.

On the other hand, the entire gays in the military debate has been framed
in a characteristically American way as a question of the rights of individual
citizens to be accorded equal opportunity by the U.S. state. What has yet to
be considered is a question left over from the days of gay liberation that has
become muted in a more conservative era. That question is the relationship
of gay men and lesbians as a collectivity to the U.S. state and its foreign
policy.

Despite its size and relatively well-developed resources when compared with movements in other countries, the gay and lesbian movement in the United States has been peculiarly insular and myopic in relation to the plight of lesbian and gay men around the world. Despite the recognition of homosexual prisoners of conscience by Amnesty International and the work of the International Lesbian and Gay Association[40] in attempting to rally movement organizations against state and terrorist campaigns of assassination and imprisonment against homosexual people in many countries around the world, U.S. gay and lesbian groups have shown only limited interest in the relationship of U.S. foreign policy to the dilemmas of gay people abroad. The struggle to integrate the U.S. military may indeed one day win a success—but what will be the nature of the ultimate gain?

The struggle to integrate black and Latino people into the U.S. military has resulted in such high-ranking black military officials as Gen. Colin Powell acting as the efficient tool of the Reagan administration in carrying out its policy of torpedoing the Central America peace process in the 1980s. Fortunately, his mission to Costa Rica failed to destroy that peace process and the Costa Rican president went on to win the Nobel peace prize for his work. All the same, throughout the 1980s, the U.S. government carried out a campaign of low-intensity warfare, direct sabotage, and a propaganda barrage against the revolutionary Nicaraguan government eventually succeeding in installing a counterrevolutionary government more to its liking.[41]

While the revolutionary government had introduced anti-sexist education and a new opening for the rights of women and gay people, the succeeding reactionary government of Violeta Chamorro brought in a sweeping criminalization of homosexuality and restoration of Roman Catholic precepts on the status of women. The outstanding question raised by the gays in the military is: will the integration of lesbians and gay men into the U.S. military result in actions that are in the interests of homosexual people outside the United States?

Some four hundred gay men and lesbians "disappeared" during the "dirty war" perpetrated by the Argentine military dictatorship in the 1970s and 1980s with the active support and training of the Pentagon.[42] In both of these examples, and in hundreds of others, lesbians and gay men have made up only a small part of a much larger assault upon the basic living conditions and civil rights of the dispossessed in other countries, such that Edward Herman concludes:

> [U.S. foreign policy is] grounded in an ideology that rationalizes the collective interest of the military establishment, the local business and landed elite [in third world countries], and the multinational corporation—the joint venture partners who require terror to preserve and enlarge their privileges and the already gross levels of inequality prevalent in the Third World.[43]

The gay and lesbian movement, then, finds itself caught in a much wider geopolitical dynamic, which it can scarcely pretend to ignore: While solving one egregious case of heterosexist oppression, it may very well contribute to the reinforcement of a wider regime of repression against gay and nongay people around the world.

The gays in the military debate then has revealed a larger political dynamic involving state voyeurism, gender politics, and the cult of Americanism. Those who argue the merits of the issue on its face value have been swept aside by larger psychosocial and historical forces reliant on ancient prejudices, conflicting political agendas, and entrenched symbol systems. The further development of the issue will depend on the further playing out of this larger historical drama.

Notes

1.   Ramsay Cook and Wendy Mitchinson (eds.), *The Proper Sphere* (Toronto: Oxford University Press, 1976).

2.   This, of course, raises the question of why the military and masculinity are so closely connected in all of these societies. Female militarism has indeed been a rarity. Apart the occasional warlike female head of state or leader such as Joan of Arc, it is located most often in the mythology of the Amazons and of the ancient Celtic queen Boadicea.

3.   Barry D. Adam, "Age, Structure, and Sexuality," *Journal of Homosexuality* 11 (1985, 3/4):22.

4.   Saikaku Ihara, *Comrade Loves of the Samurai* (Rutland, VT: Charles E. Tuttle, 1972); *The Great Mirror of Male Love* (Palo Alto, CA: Stanford University Press, 1990).

5.   E. E. Evans-Pritchard, *The Azande* (Oxford: Clarendon, 1971), 199.

6.   J. Ungaretti, "Pederasty, Heroism, and the Family in Classical Greece," *Journal of Homosexuality* 3 (1978):291–300; John Boswell, "Battle-worn," *New Republic*, 10 May 1993, 15, 17–18.

7.   Gilbert Herdt (ed.), *Ritualized Homosexuality in Melanesia* (Berkeley: University of California Press, 1984).

8.   Barry D. Adam, "Siwa Oasis," in *Encyclopedia of Homosexuality*, vol. 2, ed. Wayne Dynes (New York: Garland, 1990), 1198.

9.   Stanley Harris, "Military Policies Regarding Homosexual Behavior," *Journal of Homosexuality* 21 (1991, 4):71.

10.   Peter Tatchell, *Europe in the Pink* (London: GMP, 1992), 81–82.

11.   Carroll Doherty, "Heated Issue Is Off to Cool Start as Hearings on Gay Ban Begin," *Congressional Quarterly Weekly Report* 51 (1993, 14):853.

12.   Thomas Stoddard, "Lesbian and Gay Rights Litigation before a Hostile Federal Judiciary," *Harvard Civil Rights—Civil Liberties Law Review* 27 (1992, 2):563.

13.   Judith Stiehm, "Managing the Military's Homosexual Exclusion Policy," *University of Miami Law Review* 46 (1992, 3):694.

14.   Gary Melton, "Psychology and Law on Gay Rights," *American Psychologist* 44 (1989):933–40.

15.   Gregory Herek, "Sexual Orientation and Military Service," *American Psychologist* (May 1993):538–49.

16.   Stiehm, "Managing the Military's Policy."

17.   Wisconsin, Massachusetts, Connecticut, New Jersey, Hawaii, and California.

18.   Gary Bass, "Their Words," *New Republic*, 22 February 1993, 15.

19.   Stiehm, "Managing the Military's Policy," 693.

20.   Eve Sedgwick, *Epistemology of the Closet* (Berkeley: University of California Press, 1990), 7.

21.   Allan Berube, *Coming Out Under Fire: The History of Gay Men and Women in World War Two* (New York: Free Press, 1990).

22.   Ibid., 249.

23.   Stuart Timmons, *The Trouble with Harry Hay* (Boston: Allyson, 1990), 221.

24.   On the manufacture of "gay treason" by the British state, see Simon Shepherd, "Gay Sax Spy Orgy," in *Coming On Strong* eds. Simon Shepherd and Mick Wallis (London: Unwin Hyman, 1989), 213–30.

25.   Randy Shilts, *Conduct Unbecoming: Lesbians and Gays in the U.S. Military—Vietnam to the Persian Gulf* (New York: St Martin's, 1993).

26.   Charles Moskos, "From Citizens' Army to Social Laboratory," *Wilson Quarterly* 17 (1993, 1):94.

27.   Doherty, "Heated Issue," 853.

28.   See Guy Hocquenghem, *Homosexual Desire* (London: Allison & Bushy, 1978) for a discussion of state territorializations of desire.

29.   Barry D. Adam, *The Survival of Domination* (New York: Elsevier/Greenwood, 1978), 45.

30.   Carol Magary, "Why Straight Men Should Not Be In the Military," *Cruise Magazine* (Detroit) 15 (1993, 25):19.

31.   R. Wayne Eisenhart, "You Can't Hack It Little Girl," *Journal of Social Issues* 31 (1975, 4):13–23.

32.   Judith Stiehm, *Arms and the Enlisted Woman* (Philadelphia: Temple University Press, 1989), 129.

33.   See Susan Jeffords, *The Remasculinization of America* (Bloomington: Indiana University Press, 1989). This book uses a critical strategy which is unfortunately common in psychoanalytic and feminist analyses where "authoritarian regimes or homophobic masculinist culture [is] damned on the grounds of being *even more homosexual* than gay male culture" (Sedgwick, *Epistemology of the Closet*, 154). This analytic tactic confuses homosexuality with the repression of homosexuality. See Adam, *Survival of Domination*.

34.   Barry D. Adam, *The Rise of a Gay and Lesbian Movement* (Boston: Twayne, 1987), 57–58.

35.   L. J. Moran, "The Uses of Homosexuality," *International Journal of the Sociology of Law* 19 (1991):160–61.

36.   Barry D. Adam, "The Imperial Gaze," *Research in Communication* (Forthcoming); Edward Herman and Noam Chomsky, *Manufacturing Consent* (New York: Pantheon, 1988).

37.   This thesis is developed in Adam, *Rise of a Movement*, ch. 6.

38. "Text of Pentagon's New Policy Guidelines on Homosexuals in the Military," *New York Times* 142 (20 July 1993).

39. Sedgwick, *Epistemology*, 70.

40. The International Lesbian and Gay Association information Secretariat is located at 81, rue Marche au Charbon, B-1000 Brussels 1, Belgium. There is a San Francisco-based ILGA affiliate in the International Gay and Lesbian Human Rights Commission, 520 Castro Street, San Francisco, 94114.

41. Peter Kornbluh, "The U.S. Role in the Counterrevolution," In *Revolution and Counterrevolution in Nicaragua*, ed. Thomas Walker (Boulder, Colo.: Westview, 1991), 323–49; Barry D. Adam, "Nicaragua, the Peace Process, and Television News," *Canadian Journal of Communication* 16 (1991, 1):19–39; Barry D. Adam, "Television News Constructs the 1990 Nicaragua Election," *Critical Sociology* 17 (1990, 1):99–109.

42. Carlos Jauregui, *La Homosexualidad en la Argentina* (Buenos Aires: Tarso, 1987), 171; Noam Chomsky and Edward Herman, *The Washington Connection and Third World Fascism* (Boston: South End, 1979), 27, 35, 45, 266–71.

43. Edward Herman, *The Real Terror Network* (Montreal: Black Rose, 1982), 84–85.

PART III

Homosexuality and the U.S. Military:
Critical Analyses

Chapter 8

Defensive Discourse: Blacks and Gays in the U.S. Military

GARRY L. ROLISON AND THOMAS K. NAKAYAMA

"Don't ask, don't tell, don't pursue" is, at the time of this writing, the proposed official military policy regarding gays. How this rather awkward phrasing became military official discourse with respect to homosexuality stands as a core focus of this paper. We argue that the proposed policy is a *defensive discourse* that attempts to protect a privileging of hegemonic masculinity in the military. As such, it is a discourse reminiscent of an earlier one that attempted to exclude African-Americans from the armed forces. Given this, we further offer analysis of similarity and difference of this discourse and how it has shaped the African-American and gay experiences of exclusion and incorporation in the military.[1]

The work of Foucault is a useful theoretical frame for our analysis, in particular, his discussion of the exterior limits to discourse. It recognizes that "in every society the production of discourse is at once controlled, selected, organised and redistributed by a certain number of procedures whose role is to ward off its powers and dangers, to gain mastery over its chance events, to evade its ponderous, formidable materiality."[2] It is to those "certain number of procedures" that we turn.

We also follow Foucault in privileging the importance of surveillance in the application of power to create societal objects, particularly the use of "gaze" and "nongaze" to structure individuals as social members. By this, we mean the ways in which surveillance through gaze (sight) is, in the words of Game, "exercised through the body of the individual: [such that] certain bodies, certain gestures, certain discourses, certain desires, come to be identified and constituted as individuals."[3] In essence, we wish to discover how surveillance or nonsurveillance through sight of the body or behavior of the body (i.e., language, movement, activity) comes to include or exclude those who are acceptable social members of the armed forces.

The primary texts used for analysis are contemporary newspaper and magazine accounts regarding gay attempts at inclusion in the U.S. military, Alan Berube's *Coming Out Under Fire: The History of Gay Men and Women in World War Two,* and Nalty and MacGregor's *Blacks in the Military: Essential Documents.*[4] We rely on these texts to look at the construction of the two debates of inclusion. Our analysis is intended more as a suggestive reading than a conclusive analysis of these discourses as both remain open and unfolding.

A Brief History of the African-American Military Experience

In 1792 the Militia Act excluded African-American participation in state militias by restricting recruitment to "each and every free able-bodied white male citizen of the respective states."[5] In so doing, as Berry and Blassingame point out, this act effectively equated citizenship with being male, white, and in the militia.[6]

In 1798 what had been made law for the state militia was further expanded and made more explicit in a letter from the secretary of war, Henry Knox, regarding recruitment into the Marine Corps. In part, the letter read that "[n]o Negro, mulatto or Indian [is] to be enlisted nor *any description of men* except natives of fair conduct or foreigners of unequivocal characters for sobriety and fidelity" [emphasis added].[7] Knox's letter is important not only because it excluded African-Americans, but also because it equated being African-American with character defects unacceptable to military service— unfair conduct, drunkenness, and infidelity. In short, African-American men were simply not among the "few good men" the Marine Corps wanted to recruit. The navy followed in the exclusion of blacks in 1818 and the Army in 1820.[8] This pattern of direct exclusion of African-American men held until the middle of the Civil War, when manpower needs forced Lincoln in 1863 to include them in segregated units.[9] Ironically, this pattern of segregation, which occurs coterminously with the "Emancipation Proclamation," ended some fourscore years later due to African-American protest.

The decade of the 1940s represented changed social conditions for African-Americans. In particular, following their migration to northern cities, which had begun with the labor shortages occasioned by the ending of European immigration and the disproportionate participation of white males in World War I, partially caused by the relative exclusion of black men from the armed forces, African-Americans became a more politicized population.[10] In particular, the black press became in the urban context a site for the articulation of African-American protest.

In 1940 the *Pittsburgh Courier,* arguably the preeminent African-American newspaper of the period, formed the Committee for Participation of Negroes in the National Defense to push for racial equality within the armed forces.[11] Significantly, in 1940, the *Courier* also endorsed Wendell

Wilkie for president of the United States.[12] Candidate Roosevelt responded by arranging a meeting between Secretary of War Robert Patterson, Secretary of the Navy Frank Knox, Walter White of the NAACP, T. Arnold Hill of the Urban League, and A. Philip Randolph, the head of the Pullman Porter's Union. The meeting accomplished little and as a result A. Philip Randolph threatened a "march on Washington" to protest for equal job opportunities and to end racial discrimination in the armed forces.[13] In response to Randolph's threat, Roosevelt issued a presidential order to include "fair" racial hiring practices in defense industries, including the armed forces, and the establishment of the Fair Employment Practices Commission to ensure the order's implementation.[14]

Opposition to attempts to promote racial "fairness" in the armed forces was entrenched, however; for example, point 7 of a memo sent to President Roosevelt by Assistant Secretary of War Robert Patterson on October 8, 1940, read:

> The policy of the War Department is not to intermingle colored and white enlisted personnel in the same regimental organizations. This policy has been proven satisfactory over a long period of years and to make changes would produce situations destructive to moral and detrimental to the preparations for national defense. . . . It is the opinion of the War Department that no experiments should be tried with the organizational setup of these units at this critical time.[15]

The NAACP's magazine, *The Crisis*, left little doubt of the African-American position when it termed the military policy of Jim Crow and "[o]fficial approval of the commander in chief of the army and navy of such discrimination and segregation . . . a stab in the back of democracy," and "question[ed] that [the] Jim Crow policy of [the] army 'has proven satisfactory,'" asserting "[s]uch segregation has been destructive of morale and has permitted prejudiced superiors to exercise their bigotry on defenseless Negro regiments."[16] In sum, the African American community and the military saw segregation in diametrically opposed ways.

In September 1941, Judge Hastie, a civilian advisor to the secretary of war on racial matters, suggested dismantling racial segregation in the armed forces. In response, the chief of staff for the secretary of war, Gen. George Marshall wrote in a memo:

> A solution of many of the issues presented by Judge Hastie in his memorandum to you on "The Integration of the Negro Soldier into the Army," September 22, would be tantamount to solving a social problem which has perplexed the American people throughout the history of this nation. The army cannot accomplish such a solution, and should not be charged with the undertaking. The settlement of vexing racial problems cannot be permitted to complicate the

tremendous task of the War Department and thereby jeopardize discipline and morale.[17]

In 1948, A. Philip Randolph, in testimony before the Senate Armed Services Committee, once again threatened black protest and civil disobedience if it was not dismantled. He stated:

> Negroes are in no mood to shoulder a gun for democracy abroad so long as they are denied democracy here at home. In particular they resent the idea of fighting or being drafted into another Jim Crow army. . . . I must emphasize that the current agitation for civil rights is no longer a mere expression of hope on the part of Negroes. On the one hand, it is a positive, resolute outreading [sic] for full manhood. On the other hand, it is an equally determined will to stop acquiescing in anything less. Negroes demand full, unqualified, first-class citizenship.[18]

In essence, Randolph's address clearly articulated the African-American community's keen awareness of the connection between equal citizenship, masculinity, and military service that the Militia Act of 1796 had earlier established. In July 1948, President Truman issued Executive Order 9981, which in effect ended racial segregation in the U.S. armed forces.

Creating Homosexuals in the 1940s

Randy Shilts, in a particularly insightful phrase, suggests that "the presence of gay men—especially so many who are competent for military service—calls into question everything that manhood is supposed to mean."[19] Below we develop a possible reading as to why this is the case. In doing so, we try to unravel why "the military is far less concerned with having no homosexuals in the service than with having people think there are no homosexuals in the service."[20] Shilts shows this tension to have existed since the Colonial Army, which accepted on the one hand an openly homosexual general, Baron Frederich von Steuben, who wrote the first "drill book" of the U.S. Army, and on the other dismissed the first soldier for sodomy, Lieutenant Gotthold Enslin.[21]

As Berube's work shows, the classification of gay military personnel as homosexual did not occur in the military until World War II. Prior to that time, the armed forces had simply defined as illegal, acts of sodomy. As Berube further develops, the large influx of men and women in the armed forces during World War II made it virtually impossible to punish by imprisonment all those who took part in what was broadly defined as sodomy. As a result, the armed forces looked for options. One option was psychiatry, which had in the 1930s advanced the argument that homosexuality was a mental illness.

In January 1944, the term *homosexual* had begun to supplant *sodomist* in official policy statements.[22] At the same time, the navy had issued a directive that for the first time spoke of "latent homosexuals," who supposedly were gay but had not engaged in acts of sodomy. That is, by 1944 the armed forces with the help of psychiatrists had constructed homosexuals outside the definition of illegal sexual behavior; and in its stead stood "certain tendencies" that marked a homosexual as mentally ill. The traits used to distinguish homosexual men were an effeminate manner, a strong maternal attachment, passivity, a sense of superiority, and fearfulness. These traits, Berube correctly points out, were antithetical to the "profile of the masculine, aggressive soldier" and were taken to be distinctively stereotypical and diagnostic of gay men.[23]

This construction of homosexuality by the armed forces represents a reasserted hegemony of masculinity that was formed in opposition to assumed homosexual traits. Indeed, R. W. Connell has suggested that homosexuality is often taken to be antithetical to masculinity.[24] As a result, homosexual men are "feminized" representations of real men and, hence, real masculinity. Moreover, the hegemonic definition of masculinity in Western societies over the past two hundred years embodies a strong measure of homophobia as a necessary constituent element.[25]

The upshot has been twofold and related with respect to gay men and hegemonic masculinity. First, gay men are constructed as "effeminate," and second, on the basis of that construction, homosexual men come both to anchor and be excluded from hegemonic masculinity. Viewed by these theoretical lenses, the exclusion of gay men from the military on the basis of presumed effeminate traits represents a fixing moment of hegemonic masculinity by separating homosexual behavior from assumed "effeminacy." In other words, the shift from punishing sodomy to diagnosing homosexuals is a shift toward establishing a hegemonic masculinity. That the discourse of masculinity rather than homosexuality lurks behind the exclusion of supposedly "homosexual men" from the armed forces is made manifest in the subdividing of the types of homosexuality that psychiatry and the armed forces develop.

The construction of the homosexual also allowed the armed forces some leeway with respect to sexual behavior among its personnel. In particular, the separation of homosexuality from acts of sodomy opened space for the "reclaiming" of men and women who "situationally" participated in acts of sodomy, without the necessity of imprisonment. With the scientific imprimatur of psychiatry, all individuals were viewed as having a "bisexual" nature, which at times and under certain conditions could express itself in acts of sodomy. Given this "scientific fact," acts of sodomy among same-sex partners could be "rationally" explained without invoking either criminality or mental illness. Men and women could be tempted by extraordinary conditions that were to a large extent heterosexually understandable. Of course, one temptation was those men who appeared homosexual whether they acted on that orientation or not. As such, these men were to be removed from sight and therefore not invested as objects of desire that could later serve to promote degenerate character among young men whose bodies the armed forces had responsibility over and the moral duty to protect.

Closely aligned with this "protective" stance is the further construction of "true homosexuals" as pathological in the dual sense that they are both "pathogens" to the body of the armed forces and psychologically deviant. As pathogens they threaten hegemonic masculinity by their presumed ability to seduce young men and as such must be ejected from the body of the armed forces. As deviants they are constructed as a clear example of what is not "masculine" and therefore not proper military material. As Connell developed it, the shift from Freud's notion of universal bisexuality to homosexual pathology is simultaneously a discourse that firmly privileges heterosexuality as the natural sexuality of men while defining homosexuality as being contrary not only to heterosexuality but to masculinity itself.[26]

Clinton's Compromise

Discussion about gays in the military comes at a particularly interesting historical moment. Now, more than ever before, white males are feeling threatened as their cultural space is being redefined in relation to Others—members of racial/ethnic minorities, women, and gays and lesbians. Recent discussion over the film *Falling Down* has focused on this renegotiation of the place and space of white heterosexual males in U.S. society. As *Newsweek* observed: "This is a weird moment to be a white man. True, one of them just became president—but one of them *always* becomes president."[27]

Despite the vulnerability that white heterosexual males are feeling at this time, they continue to remain in a position of incredible power in our society. Despite this privileged position, some have attempted to understand why they feel as threatened as they do. Contreras concludes:

> White males are everywhere. They control money and finance; they control the flow of information; they control corporate boards and union leadership. They predominate in police departments; they outnumber everyone in the officer ranks of the military. They are the majority of doctors and lawyers in the country. They dominate political offices at all levels of government. White males are simply not happy unless they have monopoly over everything they do.[28]

The fragility of white males in the social order is not particularly threatened, yet it is perceived to be under attack with the attendant defensive responses. As an article in the *Arizona Republic* directly stated: "Especially among middle-class men, the signs of gender panic are everywhere."[29] But this gender panic comes at the same moment as white panic. An article in the *Atlanta Constitution* pushed the focus on white people: "Aren't you just dying to know? You should demand that your local and national media get on the case. We need stakeouts of white America."[30] In one article, whiteness remains unstated, in the other, masculinity; yet both whiteness and masculinity are central to arguments of these articles.

The focus on masculinity as a cultural construction extends into the academic arena. A recent plethora of works on masculinity, especially white masculinity, underscores this point.[31] Academic as well as popular discourses on masculinity point directly to the social issue of renegotiating the space of white masculinity.

In his speech announcing the compromise on the military's policy, President Clinton recognized the relationships between the ban on gays and lesbians and the ban on African-Americans and women in the context of social change:

> Such controversies as this have divided us before. But our nation and our military have always risen to the challenge before. That was true of racial integration of the military and changes in the role of women in the military. Each of these was an issue because it was an issue for society, as well as for the military.[32]

Perhaps it is because the core issue is masculinity, more than race, that the parallels between the African-American experience and the gay experience get clouded. The editor of a national newsmagazine for black gays and lesbians recently lamented:

> The open hatred that used to be heaped on the African-American community has a new target: lesbians and gay men. But while most lesbian and gay activists see similarities between the two movements, most of straight black America does not.[33]

It is interesting to note that a dichotomy is made between those who see similarities and those who do not. Needless to say, the connections and divergences between these politics are much more complex.

The military, in part, claims to be a special arena that should be immune for such social concerns and politics. President Clinton addressed this issue, noting its unique situation, but also emphasizing that the military must change:

> Our military is a conservative institution, and I say that in the very best sense,

for its purpose is to conserve the fighting spirit of our troops; to conserve the
resources and the capacity of our troops; to conserve the military lessons
acquired during our nation's existence; to conserve our very security; and yes,
to conserve the liberties of the American people. Because it is a conservative
institution, it is right for the military to be wary of sudden changes. Because it
is an institution that embodies the best of America and must reflect the society
in which it operates, it is also right for the military to make changes when the
time for change is at hand.[34]

Clinton uses the special position of the military to turn the argument for
change.

The opposition facing lifting the ban, however, is focused on heterosexual
attitudes, much as the restrictions facing African-Americans hinged on white
attitudes. President Clinton summed up this situation by noting that the
issue is divisive, "with most military people opposed to lifting the ban because of the feared impact on unit cohesion, rooted in disapproval of homosexual lifestyles, and the fear of invasion of privacy of heterosexual soldiers
who must live and work in close quarters with homosexual military
people."[35] By discursively displacing the issue from lesbian and gay military
personnel to the attitudes of heterosexuals, the discourses about civil liberties, equality, and performance are sidelined from consideration. In short,
the central locus of discourse of white heterosexual masculinity regulates the
dialogue.

Discussion

In the 1940s, the military resisted racial desegregation with a discourse
similar to the one we hear in the 1990s regarding gays. First, exclusion of the
groups from military service has been justified by a discourse that suggests
only members of the privileged group, white males, have the moral "right
stuff" to serve in the military. Second, the military defended the exclusion of
blacks from white units on the premises that racial integration would inter-
rupt the morale, discipline, and efficiency of fighting units. Finally, the
military resisted using the armed forces as a site of social experimentation to
"solve social problems." Each of these defensive discourses against change
has been employed against gays in the 1990s.

The above we characterize as *defensive discourses* because they come
partly in reaction to the political mobilization of a disenfranchised group. In
the 1940s, the discourse developed in response to the political power of
African-Americans while in the 1990s the discourse comes in response to the
political power of gay Americans. That both discourses were centered in
the military is significant for at least two reasons. First, participation in the

military stakes claim to political and civil equality generally. Second, because the military is distinctly a governmental organ it is especially vulnerable in an expanding democratic state to political pressure. Indeed, this relationship between social concerns and changes in the military was pointed out by President Clinton in his appeal for his compromise.

The contours of discursive struggle around group inclusion are fundamentally formed and informed by the contentious relationship that the military occupies in an expanding democratic state. On the one hand, a military defensive discourse exists that asserts ascriptive differences between groups disallow membership in the military. On the other hand, a metadiscourse exists in civil society more generally to eradicate ascriptive differences as a barrier to equal political and civil participation. This discursive tension between the military and civil society is reminiscent of de Toqueville's more thorough and ambivalent aristocratic analysis of democracy.[36] For de Toqueville, democracy demands a political equality that has the potential to reduce the "quality" of government by creating disincentives for those most fit for governmental service. The military in a democratic society attempts to structure this aristocratically inspired dilemma in its defensive discourse against inclusion. The military reminds us that it is an aristocratic warrior society, a society that is inherently unequal and undemocratic, requiring only the "best" among us. It is, in short, no place to "conduct social experiments."

It is of more than passing interest that the proposed policy currently seeks to redefine gay identity in the guise of sexual behavior while not mentioning masculine identity or challenging military policy on sodomy. It is here where the discourses of race and gayness are most distinct. Nevertheless, the military's response has been to try and maintain a hegemonic masculinity hidden under the guise of efficiency and morale—the defensive discourse it developed earlier to segregate African-Americans and currently to restrict women.

African-Americans and Gays: A Useful Comparison?

From commentators as diverse as Gen. Colin Powell, former chairman of the Joint Chiefs of Staff, to John Sibley Butler, possibly the leading African-American military sociologist, the equating of African-American and gay experiences of exclusion by the armed forces has been forcefully critiqued. Butler succinctly states that it is "a major fallacy to compare homosexuals with a racial group with a history of exclusion from the military and other institutions in American society."[37] To a large measure, there is a resonance here that cannot be dismissed. Yet, the central issue may be less the history and nature of African-Americans and gay Americans with respect to military inclusion than it is the way in which these groups are discursively responded to by the military in its attempt to exclude their participation. This is particularly the case if a master discourse exists that is employed against both.

This is not to suggest that there are not differences in the historical and political experiences between the two groups, but is an attempt not to displace attention from the act of military exclusion and focus upon group attempts at inclusion in its stead. As Henry Louis Gates, Jr., reminds us, "although race is an ascriptive category whites have responded to blacks in the United States on the basis of presumed behavior, while homosexuality is a behavior that is responded to as if it were an ascriptive category."[38] This obverse homology is what gives much of the similarity to the two discourses of exclusion as we have discovered them.

The problematic of masculinity has informed the exclusion of both African-Americans and gay Americans from the military. For African-Americans, A. Philip Randolph's testimony serves best as a reminder that part of the struggle over African-American full inclusion in the armed forces was also a struggle for "full manhood." For homosexual men, the battle is also fought on the terrain of masculinity. However, this terrain more fundamentally challenges masculinity, as homosexuality was defined in wholly antithetical terms with respect to hegemonic masculinity.

Conclusion

In our analysis, we have identified three ways in which the discourse surrounding the military ban on gays and lesbians is defensive. First, it is defensive discourse in relation to the defense of the national body. As such, the military is protected, or wishes to be protected, from the influence of social groups and politics. It is not a part of the great social experiment in democracy.

Second, we find that this discourse is defensive in that it defends masculinity as a fragile, yet invaluable social construction. Hence, gays are seen as a threat to heterosexual male bonding, which is said to be critical to unit cohesion. The military argues that it needs to defend against this incursion. As such, the framework for the military appears to be one in which the older personnel are framed as "father-figures" who are protecting their "boys" from gays in order to make "men" out of them. Within this discursive logic, the term *gay men* becomes oxymoronic, as "men" cannot be gay.

Third, homosexuality continues to function as a discursive disease. Heterosexuality needs to be defended against this disease as heterosexuals can be "polluted," or become gay, through this contagion. Homosexuality is seen as a threat that must be defended against. Within this discourse, the stability of heterosexuality, and by extension white masculinity, is under siege. After all, heterosexuality is not fixed within this framework.

As of this writing, President Clinton's compromise position remains a locus of continued debate. For lesbian and gay activists, the compromise sparked protests from Los Angeles and San Francisco to Atlanta and beyond.[39] A recent Pentagon report stated that the ban on gays and lesbians in the military should be lifted.[40] This report may spark yet more defensive discourses aimed at protecting the military—an organization that should be protecting us.

Notes

1. Of course, a similar discourse has been and is employed regarding women and racial groups other than African-American in the armed forces. However, because of space constraints we will restrict discussion to gays and African-Americans.
2. Michel Foucault, "The Order of Discourse," in *Untying the Text*, ed. Robert Young (Boston: Routledge, 1981), 51.
3. Ann Game, *Undoing the Social* (Toronto: University of Toronto Press, 1991), 41, 42.
4. Allan Berube, *Coming Out Under Fire: The History of Gay Men and Women in the World War Two* (New York: Plume, 1990); Bernard C. Nalty and Morris J. MacGregor, *Blacks in the Military: Essential Documents* (Wilmington, DE: Scholarly Resources, 1981).
5. Berube, *Coming Out*, 13.
6. Mary F. Berry and John Blassingame, *Long Memory: The Black Experience in America* (New York: Oxford University Press, 1982), 298.
7. Knox quoted in Nalty and MacGregor, *Blacks in the Military*, 14.
8. Nalty and MacGregor, *Blacks in the Military*, 17. The exception to this evolving policy occurred during the War of 1812 in which Andrew Jackson had drawn among free men of color, mainly Creoles, within New Orleans. Again, this policy apparently stemmed from a "man"-power shortage.
9. Richard J. Stillman III, *Integration of the Negro in the U.S. Armed Forces* (New York: Praeger, 1968), 10.
10. August Meier and Elliott Rudwick, *From Plantation to Ghetto*, 3rd ed. (New York: Hill and Wang, 1976): 234–36.
11. Richard M. Dalfiume, *Desegregation of the U.S. Armed Forces* (Columbia: University of Missouri Press, 1969), 26.
12. Bernard C. Nalty, *Strength for the Fight* (New York: Free Press, 1986), 138.
13. Ibid., 140–41.
14. Ibid., 141–42.
15. Quoted in Nalty and MacGregor, *Blacks in the Military*, 108.
16. Quoted in Ibid., 109.
17. Quoted in Ibid., 114–15.
18. Quoted in Ibid., 237.

19. Randy Shilts, *Conduct Unbecoming: Lesbians and Gays in the U.S. Military, Vietnam to the Persian Gulf* (New York: St. Martin's Press, 1993), 5.

20. Ibid., 6.

21. Ibid., 7–12.

22. Berube, *Coming Out*, 142.

23. Ibid., 159.

24. R. W. Connell, "A Very Straight Gay: Masculinity, Homosexual Experience, and the Dynamics of Gender," *American Sociological Review* 57 (December 1992): 735–51.

25. Ibid., 736.

26. Ibid., 737.

27. David Gates, "White Male Paranoia," *Newsweek*, 29 March 1993, 48.

28. Raoul Lowery Contreras, "White Males Are Bad Sports About Having to Share Power," *Tempe Daily News Tribune*, 4 April 1993.

29. Nicolaus Mills, "Men Wage Battle of the Sexes—For Identity, " *Arizona Republic*, 20 May 1992.

30. Derrick Z. Jackson, "Admit the Failures of White America," *Atlanta Constitution*, 23 November 1991.

31. See, for example, J. A. Boone and M. Cadden, eds., *Engendering Men: The Question of Male Feminist Criticism* (New York: Routledge, 1990); R. Chapman and J. Rutherford, eds., *Male Order: Unwrapping Masculinity* (London: Lawrence & Wishart, 1988); Steve Craig, ed. , *Men, Masculinity, and the Media* (Newbury Park, Calif.: Sage, 1992); Richard Dellamora, *Masculine Desire: The Sexual Politics of Victorian Aestheticism* (Chapel Hill: University of North Carolina Press, 1990); Barbara Ehrenreich, *The Hearts of Men* (Garden City, N.Y.: Anchor, 1983); Alice Jardine and Paul Smith, eds., *Men in Feminism* (New York: Methuen, 1987); Susan Jeffords, *The Remasculinization of America* (Bloomington: Indiana University Press, 1989); Sam Keen, *Fire in the Belly: On Being a Man* (New York: Bantam, 1991); Denise Kervin, "Advertising Masculinity; The Representation of Males in Esquire Advertisements," *Journal of Communication Inquiry* 14 (1990): 51–70; Constance Penley and Susan Willis, *Male Trouble* (Minneapolis: University of Minnesota Press, 1993); E. A. Rotunda, *American Manhood: Transformations in Masculinity from the Revolution to the Modern Era* (New York: Basic Books, 1993); Jonathan Rutherford, *Men's Silences: Predicaments in Masculinity* (New York: Routledge, 1992); Cathy Schwichtenberg, "Of Phallic Proportions: The Construction of Arnold Schwarzenegger's Prosthetic Masculinity," paper presented at the annual meeting of the Speech Communication Association, Atlanta, 1991; Victor J. Seidler, *Recreating Sexual Politics: Men, Feminism & Politics* (New York: Routledge, 1991).

32. William Jefferson Clinton, "The Right Thing to Do," *Frontiers*, 13 August 1993, 15–16, 18.

33. Don Thomas, "Liberty and Justice for All," *The Advocate*, 5 October 1993, 5.

34. Clinton, "The Right Thing," 18.

35. Ibid., 15.

36. Alexis de Toqueville, *Democracy in America* (New York: Vintage, 1945).

37. John Sibley Butler, "Homosexuals and the Military Establishment," *Society* 13 (November/December 1993): 15.

38.   Henry Louis Gates, Jr., "Blacklash?" *New Yorker*, 17 May 1993.

39.   "Bill Clinton is a President without Honor," *Southern Voice*, 6/23, 29 July 29–4 August 1993, 8; Joe Carrithers, "After the Anger," *Frontiers*, 13 August 1993, 25–26, 28–29; Karen Ocamb, "'Betrayed by Bubba," *Frontiers*, 13 August 1993, 22–23, 66.

40.   John Gallagher, "Terrible Timing," *The Advocate*, 5 October 1993, 28–29.

Chapter 9

Best-Kept Secrets: A Comparison of Gays and Women in the United States Armed Forces (The Hidden Life of Uncle Sam)

M. C. DEVILBISS

Behind every secret lies a purpose. For example, certain military secrets are vital to the conduct of effective military operations. Grand strategies and battlefield tactics, weapon systems and troop movements—all are kept from knowledge or view, hidden from everyone except those with a need to know. Sometimes, even who is in the military is a secret—a secret particularly important to the success of covert military operations.

Those who make (and keep) military secrets will tell you that secrecy is important for a variety of reasons: to achieve victory in combat, to ensure national security, or to obtain certain larger political objectives. And they are right. But at the very heart of any military secret lies an even deeper purpose than victory or national honor. That purpose is survival, both individual and collective.

Some of the best-kept secrets in the United States' two hundred plus years are the participation and contributions to the military mission by many hidden groups. Such groups have included those who are not U.S. citizens, those who are not white, those who are not men, and those who are not heterosexual. This paper is about the military experience of two of these historically invisible groups—gays and lesbians, and women. It is about their participation in "the hidden life of Uncle Sam" and about the organizational parallels between them. It is also about survival, both individual and collective.

Two Important Starting Points

The hidden life of Uncle Sam regarding the participation of women and of gays and lesbians in the U.S. armed forces begins with two "family secrets"

135

or unacknowledged realities of military experience. Our inquiry into these issues thus begins with articulating these hidden truths. They are:

Family Secret #1: Persistent Presence.   Both women and gay men and lesbians have been present from the beginning of the U.S. military and have continued to serve in the U.S. armed forces throughout our nation's history. This "persistent presence"[1] is a well-documented one, though only recently as historical fact rather than historical fiction.[2] There is also evidence that the persistent historical presence of women and gay men and lesbians in military organizations is not limited to U.S. forces alone, but is a transcultural reality as well.[3]

Family Secret #2: Lack of Conceptual Clarity.   The categories "women" and "gays" in the military are not mutually exclusive. Put another way, it is crucial not to think of the category "gays in the military" as composed entirely and exclusively of military men, an often unstated assumption. The category "lesbian" is a classification that bridges both of the categories. Hence, the phrase *women and gay men and lesbians* in the military is more accurate and precise. Further, a category that overlaps two characteristics often helps us see more clearly the strengths and limitations of comparisons between the two "main" categories.

Key Comparisons

It is important to emphasize several initial points about the use of analogies as a methodological tool. First, we know that virtually all analogies have limitations and one should be careful about extending them too far. We also know however that analogies can be useful heuristic devices.[4] That is the spirit in which they are presented and analyzed here. Second, the comparisons between women and gay men and lesbians in the military that follow should not be thought of as all-inclusive. They are an attempt to identify important comparisons between these groups and to highlight them for further study.

Third, the analogies presented here may be seen as five major factors of potential utility in comparing the military experience of women and gay men and lesbians in the armed forces. They can also roughly be thought of as five historical stages in the U.S. armed forces' attempts to deal with the "women issue" and the "gay issue." Finally they represent certain themes (we may term them *rallying cries*) in the military's reaction to the women issue and the gay issue; they are the additional secrets necessary to cover up the original secrets of the hidden life of Uncle Sam.

Theme 1: They're Not Here

There have been many attempts to deny the persistent presence of women and gay men and lesbians in the U.S. armed forces. This denial has most often manifested itself in the form of official restrictions ranging from "no access" (keep all women and all gays out of the U.S. military) to "limited access" (allow these groups in the military but impose limitations on service).

For women, their status as a group within the military has alternated between no access and limited access.[5] Under limited access, women's participation has ranged from service in gender-segregated units to service in gender-integrated units without access to combat slots. For gay service members, a policy of no access in practice has been one of limited access, emphasizing individual merit and retention criteria rather than entrance requirements (which could be gotten around). Thus, excellent job performance and/or critically needed skills—and especially keeping quiet about one's sexual orientation—might allow individual gay service members to stay in the military once they had slipped in. Here our bridging category, "lesbian," is useful since it informs us of the doubly limited access for women: Upon entrance, one filter of potentially limited access because of gender, and upon retention, a second filter of potentially limited access because of sexual orientation.

The limited access solution has operated similarly for women and gay men and lesbians in the military's attempts to impose job restrictions on both of these groups. Typically, these restrictions have applied to what the military terms its combat roles. In practice, this has meant laws and policies have excluded servicewomen and gay service members from the military's central (warrior) roles. Lesbians would presumably be prevented from serving in combat roles for reasons of both gender and sexual preference, but gender would probably be the primary reason for exclusion.

Another important commonality of the they're-not-here experience for servicewomen and gay service members has been their dual-level hiddenness, that is, organizational and personal invisibility. On the organizational level, the military has maintained a veil of secrecy about servicewomen and gay service members, keeping their presence in the organization from general public knowledge. On the individual level, service members have had to hide their own self identities in order to remain in the military. In the case of women, this need to hide or to disguise one's gender, particularly to serve in combat roles, was an eighteenth- and nineteenth-century phenomenon (although some women did openly serve in the military and in combat roles during this time).[6] For gay men and lesbians, hiding one's sexual orientation in order to serve was an eighteenth-, nineteenth-, and twentieth-century necessity.[7]

Theme 2: If They're Here, I Don't See Them

Organizationally hiding women and gay men and lesbians in the military (keeping them from general public knowledge and view) is related to organizationally disowning them by refusing to acknowledge their history or their contributions to the military. The more than two hundred year history of both women and of gay persons in the U.S. armed forces has been both unreported and underreported. Only in the late twentieth century have books and articles describing the contributions of these groups been available to the interested general reader.

A denial of the historical and ongoing organizational contributions of women and gay men and lesbians in the military has resulted in a further denial of organizational dependence. Such denial makes it easier for individual service members and for the military as an organization to promote hostility toward people in the denied groups, and to sanction organizational prejudice and discrimination (and even violence) against them. The reality of this organizational abuse secret, only now coming publicly to light, is an important understanding and a key point of comparison between women and gay men and lesbians in the military.[8]

The U.S. armed forces are not the only organizations, however, that have denied or ignored women and gay men and lesbians in the military. Civilian groups that would seemingly have an interest in them, especially in the area of civil rights, often have turned away from women and gay men and lesbians in the military. It is only since the 1980s, for instance, that civilian activist groups such as the American Civil Liberties Union (ACLU), the Gay Liberation Front (GLF), and the National Organization for Women (NOW) have publicly taken on the cause of women and of gays in the armed forces. Both the GLF and NOW came to public prominence in the 1960s and were connected historically with the anti-war movement. These organizations thus were not readily sympathetic to women and gays in the military. Whatever its root cause(s), however, the historical effect was the same: Both women and gay men and lesbians in the military were denied or ignored by civilian groups who, at the same time, were among those groups who were advocating for women and for gay men and lesbians who were not in the military.[9]

A related historical analogy for women and gay men and lesbians in the military is the silence, not only about their history, but also about their present concerns. Books written by women and gay men and lesbians about their experiences in the armed forces are still rare enough that they may all be contained on a single bookshelf. The record of their personal and collective experience was once simply unspeakable, and it is only in the last decade of the twentieth century that this is beginning to change.[10]

In fact, the claim of rights in general for women (and for both men and women) was once considered unspeakable, unacceptable, and radical. In the United States, while acceptance and equal rights are still not a reality, these ideas are now much more mainstream. In some respects, change has come very rapidly for women and for gays and lesbians in the military in the 1990s. An important factor in that change has been the lifting of the organizational veil of secrecy, denial, and silence.

Theme 3: I Think They're Here, and They're a Marked People

Women and gay men and lesbians in the military have been the object of labeling. Virtually all these labels have been negative ones. For instance, women (as a class) and gay persons (men and women) as a class are traditionally seen in the military as "them" or as "the other".[11] This perception has been extended to include notions that "they" (women and gay men and lesbians) are not really armed forces personnel; thus "they" are not full or real members of the military organization. "They" are different from the "real" members of the military organization, i.e., those who are not women and who are not gay.[12]

To support the notion of otherness, both women and gay men and lesbians in the armed forces have been the object of demeaning stereotypes that emphasize their differences and alleged inferiority. Gay men are seen as effeminate and as incapable of "being real men;" women are seen as either "whores or dykes."[13] In both cases, the individual is defined first by his or her sexuality, and then in particular by his or her sexuality in relationship to male heterosexuality.

Two other negative stereotypes have paralleled the military experience of women and gay men and lesbians: They are morally tainted and are security risks. These perceptions have contributed to the judgment that both groups (women and gay men and lesbians) are organizationally unfit, unstable, and unsuitable for military service. The ideas underlying these negative stereotypes (and the subsequent exclusions based on them) are themselves based upon unarticulated ethical or moral precepts, which in turn are based upon certain interpretations and understandings of particular religious doctrines, especially those of Western Christianity.[14]

Labeled by the military in which they served, women and gay men and lesbians have been a marked people in other ways. Once it could no longer be credibly claimed, for example, that there were no women or gay people within its ranks, the U.S. military has typically reacted by "studying the issue." In particular, it has turned to the experience of other countries (especially to Israel and to NATO member nations) and asked the question, Hey, what do you people do with "them" in your militaries?[15] The fact that there are different responses to this question worldwide has made the study of such issues a help to scholars (since there is now more factual information available), but somewhat less of a help to policymakers (since there exists no worldwide consensus on which to base recommendations or make decisions).

The overall effect of zeroing in on women and gay men and lesbians in the military for research or other purposes has been to stigmatize and ghettoize them. It has been argued, for example, that both women and gays should be physically isolated or set apart; in particular, that they should be given separate living quarters and separate toilet and shower facilities, and that this should be done for their own protection. The question then becomes: Protection from what and from whom? And, since both women and gays in the military have been the target of physical assault and even murder by their fellow service members, it is an especially important question to ask. We will explore this point below.

Theme 4: I Believe They're Here, and Anything Goes

A fourth theme contains the realities of both interpersonal prejudice and of structural discrimination. Structural discrimination against women and gays and lesbians in the military can be seen in the currently evolving combat exclusion policies pertaining to all women and in the currently evolving policy of mandatory separation for gay men and lesbians. No matter what the reason for such institutionalized discrimination, it exists in the military and it is targeted toward all individual members of certain groups regardless of individual talent or merit.

Related to institutional discrimination is the reality of interpersonal abuse and mistreatment of those in the stigmatized groups, and—until only very recently—the organizational sanction, by tacit approval, of such behavior.[16] Such mistreatment has taken the form of physical and psychological abuse of individual women and gay men and lesbians at the hands of their fellow service members.[17] For many years, abuse and mistreatment was kept quiet by the military, or simply accepted as part of the culture of the armed forces. This reality could no longer be denied or ignored in the U.S. armed forces in the 1990s. In the wake of the Gulf War and of the Tailhook sexual abuse scandal in the navy, and in the opening up of the gay issue at the highest political levels, the hidden life of Uncle Sam suddenly had been exposed and in a way never before articulated in U.S. military history. The family secrets could no longer be denied or somehow explained away. They were now a part of public knowledge, public discourse, and public concern.

Theme 5: I Know They're Here; Let's Deal Responsibly with Their Presence

The climate created by these events of the early 1990s produced an unprecedented opportunity for women and gay men and lesbians in the military. It created for both groups an opportunity for the military as an organization to deal realistically and responsibly with their persistent presence.

Increasingly, "intolerance will no longer be tolerated" has become the rule in attitudes and actions toward women and (less so) toward gay men and lesbians in the military. Two examples of this are the implementation of policies against sexual harassment and of not asking service personnel about their sexual orientation. Linking sexist behavior to negative job performance evaluations is one organizational response aimed at eliminating such behavior, improving the overall working atmosphere, and enhancing the mission performance of the group. Such an approach takes its precedent from the military's earlier (and continuing) work to battle racism within its ranks.

However, true organizational change with regard to women and gay men and lesbians in the military cannot fully occur without an institutional paradigm shift—a change in the military's basic perceptions of and attitudes toward women and gay men and lesbians. For the five analogies that we have cited, what are the reasons for these commonalities? And why do they persist? To answer these questions, we must now move beyond description to analysis.

Analytical Perspectives

In this section, we present two hypotheses for the commonalities of experience we have identified between women and gay men and lesbians in the military. The hypotheses suggest two major explanatory factors for these commonalities: (1) organizational power, and (2) organizational values.

Hypothesis 1: Organizational Power and Limited Access

The dominant group within the U.S. military (the one that holds the most power within the organization) is composed of heterosexual white males, who fashion organizational solutions that either prevent minority groups from holding organizational power or limit their access to such power. Such organizational solutions are enacted by the dominant group to ensure that they retain power within the organization.

Helpful to us here is a framework developed by Cynthia Enloe to describe the selection and utilization of another minority group: "ethnic soldiers."[18] Enloe looks at the state's agents of legitimate force (the military and the police) and asks how state planners shape the ethnic composition of these forces. Her approach is historical (emphasizing the seventeenth through the twentieth centuries), cross-cultural (examining the state security maps of

Western as well as non-Western societies), and primarily focused upon the experience of male ethnic soldiers. She presents an "ideal ethnic security map" of five concentric circles with the state apparatus at the center or bull's-eye. Going out from the center are four ethnic groups: Group A, most reliable and most politically resourceful; Group B, very valuable to the state though reliability not total; Group C, useful to the state but of questionable reliability; and Group D, least necessary to state maintenance and least politically reliable.[19]

Enloe states: "The group closest to the state core—Group A—ideally would have maximum access to the state apparatus. Its members would be the primary target for military recruitment."[20] In our analogy, Group A thus would correspond to the placement within the military of the dominant group—heterosexual white males. But what of the minority groups, especially women and gay men and lesbians in the military? Where are they in this framework?

The situation of women in the U.S. armed forces has historically been a case of movement from periphery to center.[21] The incorporation of women in the U.S. military in the late twentieth century is nearing a level comparable to Group B (valuable but not totally reliable). Historically, this is a step up: The status of women in military organizations prior to the midtwentieth century mirrored Group D (least necessary and reliable) and then Group C (useful but of questionable reliability). Where are gay men and lesbians in the military on the state's security map? As in the case of women, there has been a movement from periphery toward the center. The status of gay men and lesbians in the late twentieth century moved from Group D to a point near Group C. Their historical progress, however, lags behind that made by other hidden groups in the military, especially women and racial minorities.

It is important to explain the reasons behind the relegation of women and gay men and lesbians to this organizational periphery. Looking at the concept of organizational power, we see the need to examine the notions of otherness, of class exclusion, and of organizational centrality more closely. Why, for example, are women in the military not at the level of Group A at the present time? Although the military now regards individual women as "most reliable and resourceful," it still regards women as a class as "the other." Thus their participation in the military as a class is restricted—the participation of all women is restricted because they are women. There are rules on the types of military jobs from which women are excluded, especially from combat or warrior roles. Such a class exclusion restricts the access of any and all women to the central or core roles of the military, and thus to those roles that are the most organizationally powerful ones.

Why are gay men and lesbians in the military relegated to peripheral roles? Again, the concept of "as a class" applies here. Although individual gay men and lesbians may be considered highly reliable and useful to the military (Group A), in the final analysis they too may be classified by their group status and prevented from occupying key roles in the U.S. armed forces. The key words are *discovered* or *self-identified* gay men and lesbians. At the present time, individual gay men and lesbians in the military can only hold such key positions if they hide their sexual orientation. Once their sexual orientation becomes known, their ability to perform their military duties is immediately suspect.

The organizational solutions fashioned by the dominant group (for example, proposals to keep women and gays out of the core combat roles) may be attempts by the dominant group (heterosexual [white] males) to limit the access to organizational power of the minority groups (nonheterosexuals and nonmen). Such structural-level explanations bridge social-psychological explanations as well. For example, to the extent that the dominant group is threatened by, fearful of, or angry about sharing organizational power with nonheterosexuals and nonmen, physical and verbal aggression increases by individual dominant group members toward individual minority group members. This displaced-aggression explanation may also help to explain possible interactive or additive effects of race, gender, and sexual orientation. Thus, lesbians in the military face the double discrimination of being both gay and women, while lesbian women of color face compounded discrimination from lingering aspects of racism, sexism, and homophobia.[22]

Hypothesis 2: Organizational Values and Limited Access

In the military, combat or warrior roles are (a) the most central or core roles, (b) the most organizationally powerful roles, and (c) the definitional roles, i.e., they form the essence of what it means—both individually and collectively—to be in the military. The traditional military has difficulty including women and gays and lesbians in the military within these central, powerful, and definitional roles. Therefore, we must identify and examine some of the key notions in the military's core belief system. In particular, we must explore the ideas of organizational self-concept and organizational survival.

One of the values at the heart of any organizational belief system is how the organization perceives itself. This organizational self-concept includes perceptions of the organization's mission or purpose, notions of the appropriate ways to perform that mission, and ultimately the perception of what the organization itself looks like, both individually and collectively. Combat roles describe the military's mission, how the military is to perform that mission, and what the organization "looks like."

It thus comes as no surprise that at the core of the military's belief system is the archetype of the warrior. This concept has evolved over the U.S. military's more than two hundred year history. For example, the concept of warrior has expanded to include those in the enlisted ranks as well as officers, a change from the earlier notions of the dashing, property-owning, horseman gentleman-warrior. Since the mid–twentieth century, the concept of warrior in the U.S. military has also evolved to include white ethnic and nonwhite racial groups.

As the concept continues to evolve, the U.S. armed forces face more questions about what this archetype includes. These are difficult and painful questions for the military. What will happen, for instance, to the traditional ideas and beliefs within the military culture if the U.S. military's most central and defining roles are occupied not only by nonwhites but also by nonheterosexuals and/or nonmales? It is here that we find a most compelling explanation for why women and gay men and lesbians are treated as they currently are in today's armed forces and why they are excluded from central organizational roles. The entire mythos of the organization—its notion of what it looks like—is being challenged.

For the military to reexamine, reevaluate, and possibly (once again) alter its core concept is not an easy task. It is probably the largest organizational issue that the presence of women and of gay men and lesbians in the military evokes. The military had to deal with the issue on a subconscious level first but must do so now on a conscious one. Such an organizational confrontation is necessary, however, because in the 1990s the hidden life of Uncle Sam—the reality that nonheterosexuals and nonmen are an important part of that life—can no longer be ignored.

This focus helps us explain the reality of organizational discrimination and mistreatment of women and gay men and lesbians in the military. Why, for example, would loyalty to and support for one's fellow service members (loyalty and support also being central military virtues) not apply in such cases? Why would some members of the military (the dominant group) abuse, assault, and even murder other members of that same military (the minority group)? We have already suggested one possible reason: Both women and gay persons represent a potential power threat to the military's dominant group (heterosexual white males). We now suggest a related reason: Women and gay persons represent a threat to the military's central organizational archetype.

Now we are able to see more precisely the nature of this threat: Servicewomen and gay service personnel pose a threat to the U.S. military's current understanding of its individual and collective manhood.[23] This is the case because neither women nor gay people in the military are perceived as "real men." We may conclude (as, for example, demonstrated by the Tailhook scandal) that, however it is masked, the U.S. military culture historically has been steeped in aggressive extremes of male behavior. The U.S. military therefore has argued that anything other than male heterosexuality is incompatible with military service (and especially incompatible with bravery and valor in the armed forces).[24] This position fosters hostility toward groups other than male heterosexuals.

It is not necessarily the organizational concept of male heterosexuality that is the problem here. Rather, the problem is the organizational focus on the aggressive extremes of male behavior, i.e. *male hyperheterosexuality*. Possibly, aggressors (for the most part, hyperheterosexual men) fear that they will be unable to impose their will (i.e., will be unable to satisfy their need for conquest) over either male homosexuals or women (heterosexual and homosexual). There may also be related fears (on the part of the aggressors) of homosexual rape or of female sexual superiority. It should be emphasized that all of the above suggestions represent additional hypotheses to be tested; they are possibilities that may help us better understand and explain the shared organizational experience of individual mistreatment of women and of gay people in the military by their comrades.

Organizations, like individuals, strive to survive.[25] Women and gay men and lesbians in the military have been survivors for more than two hundred years. They are still here. And so is the U.S. military. But now they must survive together rather than being at odds with one another. Now that the family secrets are out, Uncle Sam's family relationships must change.

This is a defining moment in military history. The 1990s present the opportunity for addressing the presence of women and gay men and lesbians in the U.S. military. There are, of course, several ways to deal with these issues. There could be policy change in the direction of further inclusiveness and centrality—both women and gays and lesbians in the military could become most reliable and resourceful Group A members—or of further restriction—they could return to "least necessary" Group D status. The current uneasy truce over women and gay men and lesbians in the military is probably not a viable, long-range organizational solution. Future policy change probably will be in the direction of greater inclusiveness, but will be a cautious movement and one that will not be accomplished without a great deal of organizational kicking and screaming.

Why is this the case? A shift toward inclusiveness for women and gay men and lesbians in the military hinges upon the simultaneous occurrence of several important trends: the emergence of a changing world order, a resultant evolution in the military's mission and training, and an organizational archetype in transition. We will comment upon the organizational archetype in transition because it is so germane to the issues we have discussed already.

We said at the outset that behind every secret lies a purpose. The United States armed forces are used to keeping many secrets, and to keeping them for good or higher purposes (for national security, to win wars, etc.). What of the military's silence surrounding women and gays in the armed forces? What was the reason behind this secret keeping, and what has been the effect of keeping this information hidden?

Keeping the participation of women and gay men and lesbians quiet has, from the point of view of organizational power, been functional: It has served to preserve the myth. It has enabled the institution to survive in its historical form as a white, male, heterosexual (and, we would add here, hyper-heterosexual) citizen armed force. This is the reason for the secret keeping. But such is not the reality of the military in contemporary times, if, in fact, such a reality was ever historically true.

However, the consequences of keeping these particular organizational secrets hidden also has been costly and dysfunctional for the military. It has forced the military to squander human resources and talent; further, the banding together of dominant group members against women and gay men and lesbians has contributed to negative cohesion that compromises rather than enhances mission performance, group spirit, and organizational integrity. The root cause of this secret keeping revolves around a no longer appropriate archetype for the armed forces. The traditional warrior archetype with its male hyperheterosexuality is neither a positive nor a desirable model to emulate and pass along: It just doesn't work anymore. It casts a shadow over the military that must be identified and revised before positive changes may occur both on the individual and organizational levels.

Conclusion: Metanoia and Change

If there is to be a real change in the U.S. armed forces regarding its servicewomen and gay service members (and not just a cosmetic change), then there must not only be policy change but a change of heart as well. *Metanoia* is a theological term which refers to a conversion or change of heart. Its definition includes the sense, first, of real repentance, then of a true desire to live differently, and finally a visible and notable change in behavior. A real paradigm shift and institutional change regarding women and gay men and lesbians in the military (and, we would add here, regarding racial minorities in the military, for real acceptance is not yet complete here either) will occur only if there is this institutional change of heart. Only then can a much-needed new warrior archetype emerge. Only then can a new military model evolve. Only then can positive change and real healing (both individual and collective) begin.

Notes

1.   Randy Shilts, *Conduct Unbecoming: Lesbians and Gays in the U.S. Military, Vietnam to the Persian Gulf* (New York: St. Martin's, 1993), 3.

2.   See, for example, Linda Grant De Pauw, *Battle Cries and Lullabies: A Brief History of Women in War* (New York: William Morrow, forthcoming); Jeanne Holm, *Women in the Military: An Unfinished Revolution*, 2nd. ed. (Novato, CA: Presidio, 1993); Shilts, *Conduct Unbecoming*; Allan Berube, *Coming Out Under Fire: The History of Gay Men and Women in World War Two* (New York: Free Press, 1990).

3.   Shilts, *Conduct Unbecoming*, 7-11; De Pauw, *Battle Cries and Lullabies*; and Tom Philpott, "Homosexual Policy in the Armed Services: An International Overview," paper presented at the Inter-University Seminar on the Armed Forces and Society (IUS) International Biennial Conference, Baltimore, October, 1993.

4.   M. C. Devilbiss, "Cynthia Enloe's *Ethnic Soldiers: State Security in Divided Societies*," in *Women's Studies International Forum*, Special Issue; "Women and Men's Wars," Vol. 8, (1982):380.

5.   Holm, *Women in the Military*; M. C. Devilbiss, *Women and Military Service: A History, Analysis, and Overview of Key Issues* (Montgomery, AL: Air University Press, 1990), 45–49, 69–70.

6.   Holm, *Women in the Military*; De Pauw, *Battle Cries and Lullabies*.

7.   Shilts, *Conduct Unbecoming*, 13–18.

8.   See Shilts, *Conduct Unbecoming*; Department of Defense Inspector General (DOD IG), *Tailhook 91—Part 2: Events of the 35th Annual Tailhook Symposium* (Washington, DC: Superintendent of Documents, 1993); M. C. Devilbiss, "The Tailhook Debacle: Sex Discrimination and Military Values," paper presented at the Inter-University Seminar on the Armed Forces and Society (IUS) International Biennial Conference, Baltimore, October, 1993.

9.   See Shilts, *Conduct Unbecoming*, 93–97.

10.   See, for example, Carol Barkalow with Andrea Robb, *In the Men's House: An Inside Account of Life in the Army by One of West Point's First Female Graduates* (New York: Poseidon, 1990); Rhonda Cornum, as told to Peter Copeland, *She Went to War: The Rhonda Cornum Story* (Novato, CA: Presidio, 1992); Berube, *Coming Out Under Fire*; Shilts, *Conduct Unbecoming*; and Winni S. Webber, *Lesbians in the Military Speak Out* (Northboro, MA: Madwoman, 1993).

11.   See De Pauw, *Battle Cries and Lullabies*.

12.   William P. Mahedy, *Out of the Night: The Spiritual Journey of Vietnam Vets* (New York: Ballantine, 1986), 117–25; Devilbiss, *Women and Military Service*, 78–79.

13.   Shilts, *Conduct Unbecoming*, 210, 213, 139–47; Devilbiss, *Women and Military Service*, 59–60.

14.   M. C. Devilbiss, *Women in the Military and Women in the Church: Historical Parallels, Organizational Impacts, and Institutional Implications*. Unpublished master's thesis, Lutheran Theological Seminary, Gettysburg, Pennsylvania, 1991.

15.   See, for example, Nancy Loring Goldman (ed.), *Female Soldiers: Combatants or Noncombatants? Historical and Contemporary Perspectives* (Westport, CT: Greenwood, 1982); Sandra Carson Stanley and Mady Wechsler Segal, "Military Women in NATO: An Update," *Armed Forces and Society* (1988): 559–85; Philpott, "Homosexual Policy."

16.   DOD IG, *Tailhook 91*; Devilbiss, "The Tailhook Debacle."

17.   See especially DOD IG, *Tailhook 91*; Shilts, *Conduct Unbecoming*; Berube, *Coming Out Under Fire*.

18.   Cynthia H. Enloe, *Ethnic Soldiers: State Security in Divided Societies* (Athens: University of Georgia Press, 1980).

19.   Ibid., 19.

20.   Ibid., 23.

21.   See Devilbiss, *Women in the Military and Women in the Church.*

22.   Shilts, *Conduct Unbecoming,* 4; Webber, *Lesbians Speak Out.*

23.   Shilts, *Conduct Unbecoming,* 5–6.

24.   Mahedy, *Out of the Night,* 117–25; Devilbiss, "The Tailhook Debacle."

25.   See Anne Schaef, *The Addictive Organization* (New York: Harper and Row, 1990).

Chapter 10

The Military Ban on Homosexuals and the Cyclops Effect

JUDITH HICKS STIEHM

This essay represents an effort to contribute a new way of thinking about the military's ban on homosexuals by separating the discussion into two parts: (1) the effect on cohesion of including known homosexuals in a male group, and (2) the effect on cohesion of including them in a female group. The assertion here is that the debate has been by men and premised on male behavior, but treated as though men's behavior were general behavior. The question is, What if: What if the analysis were done by women, based on observations of women, and what if rules designed to facilitate women's cohesion were then applied to men?

This essay will not be so bold as to provide the answer to the above "what if," but hopefully it will persuade the reader that it is worth trying to answer. Social scientists have been painfully aware that the implementation of their well-thought-out-advice too often results in new (and unanticipated) problems. Sometimes this happens because the new policy has been based on a one-eyed vision. That is, the new policy is focused on what is known about one set of people, but then affects a larger set of people differently and sometimes adversely. That unfortunate, sometimes even monstrous, set of events is well-labeled the *Cyclops effect.*

This essay sees the military's ban on homosexuals as an example of the Cyclops phenomenon. The military's exclusion of homosexuals is an example of men supporting a policy grounded in arguments based on men's behavior and experience that binds both servicewomen and -men but that affects them differently. Hence, a policy for men and women designed primarily to control men's violent and/or shunning behavior ends by disproportionately punishing women—women whose behavior was not identified as a problem (apart from violating the regulation). Taking into account Rosabeth Kantor's discussion of the consequences of proportionality in a group, this paper will describe a group that is 85 percent or more male as a "male group." A group that is 60 to 85 percent male will be described as male-dominated. Gender will go unnoted in groups that are 40 to 60 percent male.[1]

The Military As Shaper of Views on Homosexuality

Since the end of World War I, sodomy has been a criminal offense under the Articles of War. By the beginning of World War II, though, a new understanding of homosexual behavior began to affect military policy related to homosexuals. This was that homosexuality was a mental disorder, a medical condition, and that it was something susceptible to diagnosis and possibly treatment. Further, it was decided that individuals with the condition, homosexuals, should simply not be inducted. They should instead be screened out by physicians rather than be enlisted or commissioned and then punished and/or discharged if found out.

This policy change had profound consequences. First, instead of focusing on particular unacceptable behavior it looked globally at the individual. Instead of saying, "Don't do X," it empowered medical authority to say, "People like you won't do."

Second, it gave extraordinary salience to a particular aspect of the individual. Every single male recruit was specifically queried and categorized as being or not being "a homosexual."[2] This was done even though physicians had a difficult time identifying homosexuals (failure to gag when the tongue was depressed was once considered evidence) or, for that matter, defining or categorizing homosexuality.[3]

Third, even if the individual identified as a homosexual was not "blamed," he was stigmatized—stigmatized so severely that he was legally forbidden to serve his country in uniform, even during a time of great national need.

In addition, because personnel needs were great, the military could not afford to let a declaration of homosexuality become an easy way of avoiding service. Therefore, while drafting millions, it actually prevented only a very limited number of people from serving and also discharged only a limited number on grounds of homosexuality.[4] But scorn, stigma, humiliation, and dishonorable or general discharges are powerful weapons, and the military used those weapons—perhaps more to keep homosexuals invisible than actually to exclude them.

The military, then, has played a significant role in the education about homosexuality of men (especially men over forty for they were once subject to the draft). It taught them that homosexuality was a condition some people had, and that homosexuals were not fit to serve their country. Again, the military negatively socialized the very men now making military policy about homosexuals, and it socialized them to disdain homosexuals, and to refuse to associate with them.

Individual views on homosexuality were also influenced by families, by friends, and by churches, of course. But few other institutions spoke so clearly, with such authority, to so many, and with such exclusionary intent as did the military. Indeed, the military must be understood as a (if not the) primary teacher for men. The military has never been a neutral institution on this subject or one that merely reflected public views. It has reinforced and taught prejudice.

During the 1970s and 1980s civilians became accustomed to public, assertive, organized, and political behavior by homosexuals. Also, during this time the American Psychiatric Association and American Psychological Association decided that homosexuality was not a mental illness. Many states repealed their sodomy laws, and political and judicial initiatives were begun to remove various restrictions upon persons identified as homosexuals.[5] Legal tests typically drew upon civil rights law and sought to characterize homosexuals as a class deserving of equal protection. The military was even challenged in court. In response, the military tried to construct a comprehensive policy that would bar behavior, bar kinds of people, and even bar people with desires or propensities. In January 1981, military policy became more rigid and exclusive even as American society was becoming more tolerant.

Being (or not being) like the societies they serve is a general problem for nonconscript militaries, and one that needs further consideration both by scholars and elected officials. For two decades the United States has had a large and professional standing (peacetime) army, something we have not had before in our history. Moreover, questions about the unrepresentativeness of the all-volunteer military may become more critical. A professional military necessarily develops vested interests, and as it becomes more and more separate from civilians, it becomes more and more likely that civilian authorities (both executive and legislative) will find their legitimacy diminished as fewer and fewer of them have had military experience.

Militaries expect their troops (especially their men) to be sexually active. However, management is easier for the military if sexual activity is not with others also wearing a uniform, that is, if sexual partners are not both in the military. In recent decades the increasing numbers of military women have created problems related to harassment, fraternization, rape, assignment, and deployment. Many commanders would probably have been happy to keep the number of women at one percent and mostly nurses (or possibly nurses and secretaries) in order to avoid such problems. One can well understand, then, that military commanders (and lawyers) did not welcome the possibility of having to deal with the issue of intimate relationships between members of the same sex too. Indeed, arguments that existing policies related to harassment and fraternization would suffice for same-sex sex were hardly persuasive to those who thought the policies had not worked well for opposite-sex sex.

The best thinking about the military's ban on homosexuals has evolved. However, it is not at all clear that, as it evolved, thinking has become clearer, more reliable, or more valid. While the policy of the 1980s listed a variety of reasons for excluding homosexuals, in 1992-1993 the overriding concern became unit cohesion. The argument was that sodomy is a crime and that homosexuality or bisexuality, or even a propensity toward either, or declarations of either, all so significantly reduce cohesion that the result of lifting the ban would be a second-class military.[6] The policy assumed that the mere presence of homosexuals made folks uncomfortable and impaired unit efficiency. Hence, the dominant argument against service for homosexuals was not that they lacked competence or were security risks, but that the negative reception accorded them by others made their service impossible.

The Military and Gay Men

Libraries and bookstores now provide abundant resources on gay and lesbian life. One can learn about gender roles and how they relate to homosexuality, the history of homosexuality, and variations in status in other cultures. One can review theories of causation—biological, psychoanalytical, cultural/environmental—and consider the views of religious authorities. One can read gay and lesbian fiction and study gay and lesbian culture and political action. Military policy, however, has not been based on research, logic, evidence, or controlled observations. It has been based on the experience of senior commanders who, of course, have not knowingly had much experience with homosexuals.[7]

Reduced cohesion is the umbrella conclusion, but this conclusion covers several elements—elements that seem to apply to men but not necessarily to women. One element involves the desire to minimize violent attacks on gays, sometimes called *gay bashing*. One study reported that one in five gay males had been "punched, hit, kicked, or beaten" because of their sexual orientation.[8] Such violence is usually the work of a group of young men and is basically recreational. The military is primarily composed of young men and they often find themselves creating their own recreation. Therefore, what happens in civilian life also occurs in the military. Indeed, two dramatic incidents occurred during the debate on lifting the homosexual ban. One was the murder of a young sailor in Yokosuka, Japan, by a shipmate; the other involved testimony by a marine colonel before the Senate Armed Services Committee.

The grisly beating to death of Seaman Allen Schlindler after he had made his homosexuality known and was preparing for discharge has been chronicled by the media—but might not have been, if the ban had not been a concurrent news item and if his mother had not worked with the media to bring her son's murder to public attention. One sailor who incriminated another in that murder got off lightly; the second received a life sentence.

Marine Col. Fred Peck testified before the Senate Armed Services Committee in May 1993. He had probably expected to argue that the presence of homosexuals would have a deleterious effect on discipline, good order, and morale—this was the position being advanced by the corps. However, shortly before he was to appear before the committee, his college-aged son revealed to him that he was a homosexual. Peck gamely gave his testimony, including the information he had recently learned from/about his son. After expressing his love for his son, he made clear his belief, nevertheless, that his son should not serve in the military. Peck said "I would be very fearful that his life would be in jeopardy from his own troops."[9] Again, the military was arguing that there would be a high risk of personal, physical violence directed toward gays.

Discussion of bashing is usually oblique and subdued enough that one has no sense as to whether or not military service is more hazardous than civilian life for gays. One does know that it is sometimes condoned in civilian life.[10] One does not know if it is condoned in military life, but the military has powerful disciplinary tools and does not have to tolerate a great deal of behavior that is permitted in civilian society. Since most people do not bash gays, it seems fair to ask why the military cannot eliminate those few who do. We entrust soldiers with lethal weapons. Self-control would seem a basic requirement. If anyone, soldiers should know that violence is not for fun.

A second element involves same-sex rape. This, too, is a known civilian phenomenon. In particular it is a part of prison life.[11] Large numbers of men are confined there with little access to women and the stronger use the weaker. Sodomy occurs frequently in prison but often neither participant considers himself a homosexual. It is just sex. Further, in some U.S. subcultures (ones represented in the military) a man who participates in same-sex sex does not consider himself a homosexual if he is the "active" participant.[12] This, too, is considered recreational; additionally it is characterized as dominance asserting—something that occurs regularly in all-male groups. As children, each of us has probably at least heard stories of an older bully who threatened or perhaps even forced a younger child or a misfit to touch or suck his penis. An absolute ban on homosexual behavior makes it possible for the military to punish both recreators and dominance asserters without having to deal with motivation. The behavior of persons who might be called hypermacho is controlled in the military by labeling it homosexual and proscribing it.

A third element that has more recently become a part of the discussion involves the privacy rights of heterosexual military men—in particular their right not to be seen nude by someone who might be sexually interested in them. These men have taken "gang" showers in school and at health clubs, have swum nude at YMCAs and, perhaps, "streaked" across a campus. Our culture expects men to bare themselves before other men without inquiring about sexual orientation, and it expects homosexuals to conceal any attraction they may feel. Military men are attended by women nurses and doctors; mission rather than sex defines the context. Similarly, in field operations both women and men long ago learned to "let 'em look."[13] Privacy is not always a fact of life.

The military argues, though, that it is a special case; that military men are entitled to privacy and that it is more efficient to exclude homosexuals than to provide privacy for heterosexuals. One might guess that those who plead their need for privacy do not hesitate at all to "snark" or to mentally undress women who have not the faintest interest in them. It seems that military men heterosexuals are projecting their own sexually aggressive behavior toward women onto men homosexuals.[14]

Homosexuals in our culture mostly conceal their sexual orientation, but that has not prevented a stereotype from developing. For men, it is the sensitive, slight-of-build man sometimes described as effeminate. These individuals may or may not be homosexual. One source suggests that perhaps 15 percent of both homosexual and heterosexual men are effeminate.[15] Those who look effeminate may well find life difficult because other men are so busy establishing dominance over them. If they willingly or easily submit, it is possible that they will be deemed not reliable as fighting men—because of their submissiveness, their unwillingness to retaliate or, literally, to fight. This concern, though, should not apply to the 85 percent of homosexuals who do not fit the effeminate stereotype—and should apply to the 15 percent of heterosexuals who are perceived as effeminate. Feminine men and homosexual men are not the same thing, although both may have difficulties in the military.

If cohesion is diminished by the bashing of gays, by recreational sex between men, by assertions of dominance, by worries about being looked at, by worries about frail comrades, should not these issues be addressed explicitly? And if they are so addressed, do they not seem to be primarily male problems, especially young male problems, rather than general problems?

The Military and Lesbian Women

For men the problems related to homosexuality mostly involve action. The operative definition of homosexuality among men focuses on the penis and where it is inserted, although the definition of a homosexual act according to Department of Defense Directive No. 1332.14 is now simply "bodily contact

. . . for the purpose of satisfying sexual desires." However, the military wants to promote appropriate love—bonding—between male buddies. Its policies, therefore, seek to encourage but also to control that love by forbidding absolutely sexual acts between persons of the same sex. The military has not actually proscribed feelings, but it has forbidden their expression. Thus, for even saying that one has homosexual desires or "otherwise demonstrating" that one has a "propensity" to engage in a homosexual act one can be discharged.

The military's rules, developed for men, are also applied to women. This, even though women's culture is very different from men's, and lesbian culture is very different from gay culture. For example, there is certainly more intimacy, more touching, more verbal expression of affection among women, homosexual and heterosexual. Women's behavior done by men could well be considered a demonstration of propensity. Also, women are not as discomfited by homosexuals as men are, and neither women nor men are as disturbed by lesbians as they are by gays.[16] Moreover, thinking about lesbianism continues to change. The most serious scholars of the subject most certainly do not hold identical views.[17]

The end of the twentieth century is highly sexed. Sexuality is extolled, promoted, exhibited. It intrudes in virtually every element of U.S. culture. But sexuality has not always been so important, and sexual acts may not be as important to women as to men. Further women have long had deep and emotional friendships with other women, described in the nineteenth century as "romantic friendships."[18] In other times women's relationships may or may not have had a genital component. In our sexually charged era, two women living together and committed to each other are often assumed to be sexual partners too. However, even if sexuality is suspected, merely living together would probably not result in employment or social sanctions for them. (The military, though, was recently considering whether or not it would permit two individuals of the same sex to rent a one bedroom apartment off-base!)[19]

Perhaps because the penis is considered so essential to sex, and because sexual acts are done in private, it has not been same-sex sexual acts that have led to trouble and/or criminal charges for women historically. It has been nonsexual, gender inappropriate behavior—e.g., dressing and acting like a man—that has brought them censure. Short haircuts, direct language, lack of makeup, interest in machinery, socializing with other women, wearing men's clothing—these are the elements of lesbianism for much of the public. The woman homosexual, then, is characterized by heterosexuals as much by acting like a man as she is as a person who takes part in sex with a woman—after all, it's not clear she can even perform "the" act.[20]

Regardless of intellectual, political, and legal formulations, large numbers of Americans do think of homosexuals, especially women homosexuals, in a

fairly simple way: as people who present themselves with significant characteristics usually associated with the opposite sex. This would include being
sexually attracted to a person of their own sex—which is, after all, whom a
person of the opposite sex (whom they are imitating) would be attracted to.

Earlier in the century the concept of an "invert" was well known. However, less attention was paid to the willing, same-sex, lover-companion of the
invert. Apparently because those lover-companions were playing the gender
role appropriate to their sex, they were not seen as objects of mystery and
stigma even though their affections did belong to a person of the same sex.
The point is this: Inversion has long been seen as an inadequate conceptual-
ization for homosexuality. Nevertheless, it remains important to people's
everyday interpretation of and reaction to other people's behavior. This
formulation (of the homosexual as an invert) places great emphasis on appearance and on appropriate sex roles. It resembles the position the military
now takes when it demands that people "don't tell," i.e., that they conceal
their sexual orientation. This emphasis on the visible, however, also means
that virtually every military woman is at risk for being suspected as a homosexual. This is because she will be perceived by some as an invert for merely
enlisting in the military, unless she is a nurse. (Nurses are now, but once
were not considered both essential and womanly).[21]

Men who are effeminate and make no effort to conceal it are treated as odd
ducks. After all, why would any member of the more privileged sex choose
to act like the more restricted? They may be suspected of homosexuality but
there is also a pretty clear act that defines male homosexuality. Women,
though, often have good reasons for wanting to avoid being treated as wom-
en, particularly as feminine women. To be treated as a feminine woman is to
be treated as dependent, as incompetent, as "no threat," even as prey. Thus,
for women to appear and to act like men has benefits: release from confinement, legitimacy accorded to aspirations for power, and for income, too. A
downside is that acting like men casts doubt on one's sexuality, and doubts
can be damaging when homosexuality is punishable.

Women can feel powerfully identified as women but still reject femininity.
They can reject femininity without disliking men and also without any desire
to be men. Still, nontraditional work and social life make women suspect.
Information about a woman's actual emotional commitments or information
about her actual sexual behavior may not be available, but may also not be
thought necessary for making a judgment about her sexual orientation. Indeed, misjudgments seem especially likely in an institution (the military)
that attracts the most conventional men and the least conventional women—
and expects them to bond or expects those men to make authoritative judgment's about the nature of the women's sexuality.

The military did not play as powerful a role in creating the concept of
lesbian or in shaping lesbian cultures as it did in defining gay men and in

developing a gay culture. Women have never been drafted, and therefore few have had to make an official declaration about themselves. Also, their numbers in the military have been small; only in recent years have women become more than 10 percent of what remains, essentially, a male military. Lesbianism has, though, played a significant role in the women's movement for the last several decades. Indeed, feminists are routinely lesbian baited, which helps to explain the frequently heard phrase, "I'm not a feminist but . . ." With this assertion the speaker denies being a lesbian but asserts the right to speak on and in support of feminist principles.

Feminists have differed on abortion rights, but generally those who stayed in the movement came down in favor of choice. The inclusion and support of lesbians caused tension in the 1970s, but soon a conscious decision was made (in particular by the National Organization of Women [NOW]) that the movement would not be split by the issue, nor would it respond to lesbian baiting. This may mean that heterosexual women, especially feminists, (1) know they know lesbians, (2) are accustomed to working with lesbians, and (3) are more tolerant of homosexuality than are heterosexual men. In fact, if the military wished to study a cohesive organization in which heterosexuals and known homosexuals work very well together it might examine any of several feminist organizations.

Part of the women's movement has placed great emphasis on taking control of naming, i.e., on seizing the power to label. Lesbian feminists and feminists who are not lesbians sometimes present a united front by declining to proclaim their sexual identity at all. Or they may make a political decision and all proclaim themselves lesbians. For some women, being a lesbian simply means loving and identifying with other women; genitality need not be central or necessary; for others genitality is an important part of love. The point is that lesbians have become self-defining and that their heterosexual sisters seem to be more accepting of them and accustomed to being their sisters than is the case for heterosexual men and gay men.[22]

Again, gay culture and lesbian culture often were and are separate and distinct. During the AIDS crisis, though, lesbians have come to the support of gay men. The military ban also provided an important occasion for joint action. Nevertheless, the cultures do differ. In addition, there are many different kinds of gays and lesbians and they participate in distinct subcultures.[23] The subcultures vary in visibility, in the desire to be visible, and in heterosexual response to them. Only the military finds the response so negative as to require the exclusion of homosexuals. (One group that also requires high cohesion, for example, is a surgical team, but its members would not be screened for sexual orientation.)

Again, most of the important reasons given for keeping male homosexuals out of the military do not apply to women. There is not a concern that violence will be done to them (at least not more than is done to women in general) and, if there is a fear that they would not be capable of using violence, it has not been expressed. There is, though, one worry that surfaces in relation to women that is not central to the discussion of men: the seduction of younger women by older ones.

Women seem to come to awareness of their bisexual or lesbian identity later than men—ages twenty to twenty-five.[24] This means that many of them join the military without concluding that they are lesbians, and it is during their term of service—when they are away from home and more free to experiment—that they come to an understanding of their sexuality. For those who knew those women "when," it may look like they were seduced, perhaps even taken advantage of, during their time in service. However, for women the military is not like the prison experience (a sex-segregated isolated environment). They have ample opportunity to meet men. And any military woman gets lot of experience with predators—most of whom are heterosexual men and some of whom are far from subtle.

It is worth noting that some lesbian women say it is harder to be a female in the military—even though it is legal—than it is to be a lesbian (which is illegal but more concealable).[25] Lesbian seductions may occur, and might even occur more often if lesbians were permitted to be open about their sexuality, but surely this concern is a molehill and male marauders the mountain!

The Ban's Different Consequences for Women and Men

The bottom line is that women are dismissed from the services for homosexuality at a rate far higher than that of men. Between 1980 and 1990, women constituted 23 percent of discharges for homosexuality although they were only 10 percent of military personnel.[26]

Since the military deplores visibility and declarations, stereotypical behavior, associations, and perceptions may be more relevant than actual behavior and feelings. This means that the strong, independent, short-haired, no-makeup-wearing woman who wears men's clothes, radiates confidence, and is seen as a topnotch troop is also likely to be seen as a possible lesbian. In contrast, because the stereotype of a gay man is one of being frail, fashion conscious, and nonviolent, his image is very much at odds with that of a good soldier. Therefore, the ban affects women and men differently. For women, looking and acting professional makes one suspect as a lesbian; for men, looking and acting professional means one is not likely to be suspected.

It is not just that military women choose an appearance that is masculine. Military men select the uniforms for women that make them look like men— stripes down the pants, bulky sweaters, baggy camis, wide belts with heavy buckles. The need to have a unit look uniform has meant that women's uniforms have been designed to look like men's, but men's have never been adopted to take into account what would become a woman. By regulation, makeup is limited, hair must be above the bottom of the collar, and the wearing of jewelry is restricted.

The willingness to take on physically demanding tasks, to be emotionally controlled, to give and take raw commentary, to use a command voice—these are all valued by the military. They are also widely perceived as masculine. Therefore, acquiring or having these capacities makes a woman suspect. Again, it means that any woman top performer needs to prove that she is not a lesbian. Again, this is because homosexuality is popularly associated with looking and behaving like a member of the opposite sex.

The legal/administrative definition of homosexuality is quite different. It is restricted to one sphere of activity—the sexual—and to one element of sexuality—the sex of one's partner or desired partner. Information that would qualify as evidence is not readily available about who does what with whom. As a result, it is observable but nonsexual acts and signs that are thought to indicate propensity and that are most likely to create trouble for lesbians (and those perceived as lesbians).

Women's increased numbers and efforts to move them into a wide range of assignments have greatly increased the number of military women in "nontraditional" jobs. These jobs, which often require the daily wearing of camis or other work uniforms, the carrying of weapons, the use of heavy equipment, and the repair of machinery, add to the perception of military women as "inverts"—and it may be that women in nontraditional jobs bear an extra burden of harassment.[27] That harassment is likely to be of two kinds—first, pressure to prove that they are not lesbians, and second, simple pressure to run them out for having invaded men's turf.

A second way that the ban on homosexuals affects women and men differently stems from the fact that women are so low a proportion (now 11 percent) of the military. This means that they are always visible. Everything they do and everything they say is observed, commented on, and becomes material for stories. Women have little chance to go unobserved.[28]

Women's relatively low numbers mean that most men (who always experience some pressure to "score") will not have access to them. A ten to one ratio may be terrific for a heterosexual woman, but for a homosexual woman it means she will have to turn down invitation after invitation after invitation and always wonder as she does so whether a disgruntled suitor will assert she is a lesbian and jeopardize her career.

Women's low numbers also mean that they will rarely have any "naturally occurring" all-women's event, meeting, or party. Any all-women's function will be visible and talked about. It will be seen as divisive, as a publicity stunt, or possibly as lesbian. There will not be advisory boards, work details, or promotion boards that just happen to be all women. In contrast, men have many opportunities to be with the guys. Many of them only have to deal with women when they choose to do so. Military women, though, are always surrounded. Thus, the very numbers work differently for women than men.

One time women can be on their own is when they participate in women's athletic events, e.g., softball. However, playing on teams and the sisterhood that is displayed there (including hugs and kisses too) make them suspect. Men once left the management of women troops to women. Now men command women as well as men. This involves a responsibility for promoting bonding—between women and between men and women. Bonding women and promoting cohesion that includes women has not been high on the military's agenda. (Indeed, there appears to have been more discussion about how a women's presence prevents bonding!) Again, athletics are a given for men but when women participate in athletics they sometimes feel they are taking a risk. The risk involves being considered a lesbian, either because team sports are male and women who do them they must be lesbians, or because the camaraderie of team members includes expressions of affection that are suspect. Military women do constrain themselves in their relationships with other women to avoid suspicion of being lesbians.[29]

Expressions of affection, friendship, and camaraderie among women are not the same as among men. Sharing secrets, for example, may be an extremely important part of female friendship. Thus, sharing the secret of one's homosexuality could be a profound form of bonding. That bonding could be between lesbians or between a lesbian and a heterosexual woman. It is apparent that policy-makers, though, do not see "telling" as enhancing bonding—but they could be wrong.

Conclusion: The Cyclops Strikes Again

The ban on homosexuals was made to make managing a large number of young men easier in a world where litigation often makes it complicated. The 1980s version of the ban was intended to remove all discretion and, therefore, common sense and leadership. It functions as a taboo. It eliminates gay bashing by eliminating gays. It removes sexual dominance by making "consent" an unacceptable explanation. It forbids any same-sex sex and makes no distinction between the giver and the receiver even though that is, in fact, a common distinction. The taboo, then, may really not be so much about sex as about preventing violence—by men to men. These underpinnings of the ban, however, are not relevant to women.

The problem is the rule is general. The ban does apply to women even though violence by women has not been a problem for the military. This is because sex is not done in public. Therefore, appearance and other public behavior are taken to indicate what kind of sex one is practicing, and the popular assumption is that people who look like and act like the opposite sex practice homosexual sex. This means that women who act like men become suspect. And, simply by joining the military they become suspect—often wrongly. If not wrongly, women are put in a position of finding it much harder to maintain their privacy because "cues" constantly draw attention to them. What is worse, those cues are often the same ones that indicate that they are doing a good job professionally.

Ironically, then, women, who do not have the problems the ban was created to solve, are the persons disproportionately affected by it. There is almost never legal proof that one has engaged in same-sex sex. Decisions are taken based on other evidence, in particular assertion, association (although you are supposed to bond with fellow troops), and appearance and behavior typical of the other sex (although you are supposed to be military/manly). What began as an effort to prevent certain acts by men (sodomy) became an effort also to eliminate persons who presented "inappropriate" appearance and behavior, and finally to exclude persons with "inappropriate" feelings. Each time, the ban made the military more exclusive and more punitive to women.

The Cyclops struck again!

Notes

1.   See Rosabeth Kantor, *Men and Women of the Corporation* (New York: Basic Books, 1977), chapter 8.

2.   The World War II medical exam for women did not ask recruits about their sexuality. Homosexual behavior by women was not explicitly proscribed until 1944. See Alan Berube, *Coming Out Under Fire* (New York: Free Press, 1990), 32.

3.   Ibid., chapter 6. See also *Theorizing Lesbian Experience,* special issue of *Signs*, Vol. 18, No. 4, (Summer 1993).

4.   Rand Corporation, "Sexual Orientation and U.S. Military Personnel Policy: Options and Assessment" (Santa Monica, CA: Rand Corp., 1993), 6.

5.   Ibid., 463–64. By 1992 a (slight) majority of states no longer had anti-sodomy laws and eight states prohibited discrimination on grounds of sexual preference. The military can no longer argue that removing the ban would be a social experiment.

6.   Lt. Gen. Calvin Waller, U.S. Army (ret.), deputy commander of Desert Storm, gave this testimony before the Senate Armed Services Committee, April 29, 1993.

7.   GAO, "Defense Force Management: DOD's Policy on Homosexuals" (Washington, DC, 1992), 59. (DOD response to the report).

8.   Warren J. Blumenfeld and Diane Raymond, *Looking at Gay and Lesbian Life* (Boston: Beacon, 1988). 250.

9.   *Miami Herald*, 12 May 1993.

10.   Several examples are provided by Blumenfeld and Raymond, *Looking at Life*, 245ff.

11.   Daniel Lockwood, *Prison Sexual Violence* (New York: Elsevier, 1980).

12.   Thomas Almaguer, "Chicano Men: A Cartography of Homosexual Identity and Behavior," *Differences* 3 (Summer 1991): 77.

13.   Capt. Rhonda Cornum, former POW, at Quail's Roost Conference, University of North Carolina, April 2–4, 1993.

14.   Laura Miller's interviews with servicemen suggest this is the case. Among those supporting the ban, Miller found, there was a fear that gay men would act toward heterosexual men as straight men do toward women, i.e., "aggressively pursue their interests and possibly use force." See Miller's chapter, this volume.

15.   Blumenfeld and Raymond, *Looking at Life*, 368.

16.   See Miller, this volume.

17.   See *Theorizing Lesbian Experience*. While it is agreed that homosexuality is neither criminal nor clinical, real debate continues about the degree to which it is one's identity and whether it is essential or constructed. See also Lillian Faderman, *Odd Girls and Twilight Lovers* (New York: Viking Penguin, 1991).

18.   Lillian Faderman, *Surpassing the Love of Men* (New York: William Morrow, 1981).

19.   *Los Angeles Times*, 16 July 1993.

20.   Joan of Arc was burned at the stake for heresy but provoked many of her troubles by wearing men's clothing. For a contemporary example of a (Portuguese) woman passing as a retired general, and being punished for fraud see the *Miami Herald*, 30 April 1993. See also Martin Duberman, Martha Vicinus, and George Chauncey, Jr., *Hidden from History* (New York: Meridian, 1989). See especially the articles by Judith Brown, Martha Vicinus, Carroll Smith-Rosenberg, Esther Newton, Leila J. Rupp, and Madeline Davis and Elizabeth Lapovsky Kennedy. See too Faderman, *Surpassing the Love of Men*, chapter 4.

21.   Melissa Herbert, "Amazons and Butterflies: Gendered Attributes and the Construction of Sexuality as Mediators in the Participation of Women in the Military," University of Arizona, an unpublished paper. Herbert discusses the conflict for military women between their professional and gender roles.

22.   Women were more approving of Clinton's desire to lift the ban on homosexuals than men (and nonwhites than whites) according to a Times Mirror Center for the People & The Press press release, August 5, 1993.

23.   For example, lesbians are more likely to live together and expect fidelity. Their relationships are also more likely to be between women of a similar social class and of a similar age. There is more equality in their relationships. There is little anonymous sex. Blumenfeld and Raymond, *Looking at Life*, Chapter 8.

24.   Ibid., 91.

25.   Examples are provided in Winnie Webber, *Lesbians in the Military Speak Out* (Northboro, MA: Madwoman Press, 1993). 3, 60, 119.

26.   GAO, "Defense Force Management," 20.

27.   Michelle Benecke and Kirsten Dodge argue that this is the case in, "Military Women in Nontraditional Fields: Casualties of the Armed Forces' War on Homosexuals," *Harvard Women's Law Journal* 13: 215–50.

28.   Kantor, *Men and Women of the Corporation*.

29.   Herbert, "Amazons and Butterflies," 19. Thus, an argument could be made that the fear of investigation and investigations themselves have a more adverse affect on women's bonding than does the presence of homosexuals.

PART IV

Evidence from the Militaries of Other Nations

Chapter 11

Opening the Canadian Forces to Gays and Lesbians: An Inevitable Decision but Improbable Reconfiguration

ROSEMARY E. PARK

On October 27, 1992, the federal court of Canada declared that the policy prohibiting the enrollment or retention of known homosexuals in the Canadian Forces (CF) was in violation of the Canadian Charter of Rights and Freedoms. The federal court's decision was prompted by an out-of-court agreement reached prior to a court hearing involving a former military officer released from the CF because she was lesbian.

As a result of the out-of-court agreement, the Canadian federal government accepted that the CF could not justify continued discrimination on the basis of sexual orientation. The trial ended without evidence presented by either side. Four other federal court cases involving similar complaints then required settlement; and, the CF undertook to expunge all related orders, policies, and practices deemed discriminatory.

Gays and lesbians who are citizens of Canada may now enroll in the Canadian military. Gay and lesbian service members may openly declare their sexual orientation without official censure. Same sex partners in uniform may now dance together at official military social functions with official approval. If gay or lesbian members feel harassed or have been sexually assaulted, their commanding officers must investigate the complaint and take appropriate action in accordance with formal regulations dealing with personal harassment or sexual misconduct, as applicable.

The court ruling simplified the issue of homosexuals in the CF by identifying those aspects of the issue that were discriminatory. It was also unequivocal in its direction to the CF to abandon the policy. This essay examines the rationale used to explain earlier policies preventing homosexuals from serving in the Canadian military, the inability of the military to defend in law its flawed policy, the process of making the policy change, the new CF policy on sexual orientation and initial reaction, the type of "acceptance" officially endorsed, and the problems the CF will likely experience with this approach.

In sum, while the CF is complying with the legal intent, the organizational and social realities suggest that the acceptance of known homosexuals will be minimal.

A History of Exclusionary or Restrictive Policies

The Canadian military has had a long history of opposing the enrollment or retention of homosexuals in all of its regular or reserve forces plus Cadet Instructor List. The three separate services—Canadian Army, Royal Canadian Navy, and Royal Canadian Air Force—prior to 1967, had regulations dealing with the detection, investigation, and disposal of cases involving suspected or known homosexuals, or commission of homosexual acts. Known or suspected homosexual applicants were not permitted to enroll. It was the duty of all service members to report suspected or known homosexual members, and the duty of every commanding officer to investigate each reported case. Investigations were to be conducted with care, medical examinations were to occur, and higher headquarters were to review each case to avoid errors in identification and embarrassment to the CF and persons involved. Confirmed cases resulted in the release of the member(s).

In 1964, the Canadian government brought in legislation (Bill C-90) to integrate the separate command structures of Canada's armed services. In 1967, the CF Reorganization Act was passed combining the three services into a unified body—the Canadian Forces. All regulations were necessarily rewritten and a single, new CF Administrative Order, CFAO 19-20, Sexual Deviation—Investigation, Medical Examination, and Disposal, replaced the three former services' orders in May 1967.[1] Homosexuality, and other "sexual deviations" continued to be part of the new order. Few changes were made to the new order in its procedures to report, investigate, and dispose of members.

Over the 1968–1969 period, the Canadian Parliament also passed amendments into legislation reforming the Canadian criminal justice system. Of relevance, the Criminal Law Amendment Act decriminalized certain types of homosexual behavior and permitted same-sex sexual relations to occur in private between consenting adults. As a result, the military could not rely upon federal criminal law to support its blanket prohibition of all forms of homosexual behavior or tendency contained in CFAO 19-20. Rather, the policy was consistent with federal criminal law only when a specific offense was committed still listed under the federal Criminal Code of Canada, e.g., gross indecency, assault, or exhibitionism.

A small but significant change was made to CFAO 19-20 in 1976 when the order was amended and retitled. The revised CFAO made a distinction between homosexuality and "sexual abnormality." Homosexuality was defined as having "a sexual propensity for persons' of one's own sex." Sexual abnormality was defined as "any form of sexual behavior not conforming with accepted moral standards or constituting an offence under the Criminal Code of Canada," e.g., bestiality, voyeurism, or gross indecency. As a result, homosexuality was no longer officially a moral issue. However, virtually all procedures remained requiring the reporting, investigation, and release of members confirmed homosexual or having committed a homosexual act.[2]

CFAO 19-20 was not reprinted following the 1976 amendment until the entire order was revoked in 1992. During that time, however, there was considerable legal, political, and "special interest group" pressure exerted to make the CF disband its exclusionary policy. The Canadian military responded to such pressure by introducing successive revisions to the policy that progressively weakened the policy intent. Two significant pieces of federal legislation—the Canadian Human Rights Act passed in 1978, and the Canadian Charter of Rights and Freedoms that came into effect in 1985—gave legitimacy to the pressure.

The Canadian Human Rights Act (CHRA) prohibits discrimination on ten grounds: age, sex, race, color, national or ethnic origin, religion, physical or mental disability, marital status, family status, and pardoned conviction. To accommodate occasions when discrimination must occur, e.g., public safety, the CHRA requires employers, as an example, to demonstrate bona fide occupational requirements justifying an exclusionary or restrictive policy. The CF was not exempt from any part of the legislation.

The CHRA did not include sexual orientation as a prohibited ground of discrimination and pressure began almost as soon as the act was passed to include such protection. The CHRA also created a requirement for the CF to defend its personnel policies with legal argument and supporting evidence. In the case of possible discrimination against women caused by the limiting of their employment to noncombat roles and nonisolation environments, the CF created a series of trial employments from 1979 to 1985 of servicewomen in near-combat, all-male occupations and environments (the SWINTER Trials).[3]

The second piece of individual rights legislation that specifically forced the revocation of CFAO 19-20 was the Canadian Charter of Rights and Freedoms, the supreme law of Canada. Nine prohibited grounds of discrimination are listed in Section 15: race, national or ethnic origin, color, religion, sex, age or mental or physical disability. Akin to the CHRA, sexual orientation is not mentioned. However, Section 15 can prohibit other forms of discrimination beyond the nine listed, if ruled analogous by a court.

The 1980s in Canada "belonged" to the Charter. From 1982 to 1985, the federal government and Parliament reviewed over eleven hundred federal laws that were of general application "to test them against likely interpretations of the Charter, in particular, Section 15."[4] In response, the most significant pledge made by the government in terms of sexual orientation was its promise in 1986 to "take whatever measures are necessary to ensure that sexual orientation is a prohibited ground of discrimination in relation to all areas of federal jurisdiction" (i.e., the CHRA), given that "one's sexual orientation is irrelevant to whether one can perform a job."[5]

Throughout this process, the CF was named as possibly in legal violation of Section 15 of the Charter by having an exclusionary policy on homosexuality. The CF failed to impress especially a parliamentary committee in 1985 with the rationale it provided to justify the policy. The committee suggested the Canadian military acted on and perpetuated prejudicial thinking based on stereotypic views of homosexuality, gave undue weight to the presumed sensitivities of those objecting to homosexuals in the military, and offered a circular argument when suggesting that homosexuals were at greater risk of blackmail. Yet, in 1986, a specially created military Charter Task Force continued to recommend the CF not change its position for reasons of cohesion and morale, discipline, leadership, recruiting, medical fitness, and the rights to privacy of other members.[6]

The policy was revised even as the task force was gathering its material. In successive statements made in 1986 to parliamentary committees, the minister of national defense, associate minister of national defence, and chief of the defence staff (CDS) variously stated that inappropriate behavior, not propensity, was the basis for releasing members labeled homosexual, and agreed to "frozen action on the release of homosexuals."[7] The policy thereafter directed that a member "not be released simply on the basis of being homosexual rather [because of] behavior resulting from homosexuality if not in the interests of the CF."[8]

A specific amendment to CFAO 19-20 was also made in February 1986 that removed the obligation of service members to report to their commanding officer an awareness or suspicion that another military member was homosexual. Finally, in 1988, an "interim reply" was announced that permitted practicing homosexuals to be retained in the CF but under the severe career restrictions of no promotion, no career courses, no occupational transfers, no advancement in qualification level status, and ineligibility for reengagement, subsequent periods of engagement, or extension of service contracts.[9] The next-to-last policy change occurred in 1990, when the CDS directed that the CF Special Investigation Unit cease investigating suspected homosexuals as required under CFAO 19-20.

The 1990 revision was prompted by external pressure, this time by a junior military officer, who had been placed under the interim policy because of her admitted lesbianism, and who had subsequently taken her voluntary release from the CF. In 1989, Michelle Douglas complained to the federal Security and Intelligence Review Committee (SIRC), appealing the loss of her security clearance, following an improperly conducted investigation of her suspected lesbianism while in the CF. The SIRC strongly supported the complaint made by Douglas concluding that she should be reinstated in the CF and given back her full security clearance. The directive had the power of law unless the CF chose to appeal.

In 1990, Michelle Douglas also filed a wrongful discrimination suit against the CF. Her complaint became the lead case filed in federal court against the interim policy, and was finally scheduled to be heard on October 27, 1992. The stage was set for the CF to defend in court its "interim policy," which permitted known homosexuals to serve but with transient and marginalized status. From an exclusionary policy based on societal perceptions of morality and deviancy, through one justified by military reasoning, to a restrictive interim policy, the CF had adjusted its policy on homosexuality when obviously required, yet maintained over time a policy consistently discriminatory in its intent.

The Inability of the CF to Construct a Legal Defense

Lawyers for Michelle Douglas sought to challenge the constitutional validity of the Canadian military's interim policy. As noted above, Section 15 of the Charter does not specifically include sexual orientation as a prohibited ground of discrimination. However, the claim of discrimination made by the plaintiff's lawyers was consistent with other court interpretations, following the 1985 Charter enactment, which judged sexual orientation to be an analogous ground under Section 15.

Because of these previous judgments, the Department of Justice, representing the military in court, would have had difficulty arguing that sexual orientation was not an analogous ground of discrimination. Rather, justice lawyers had to seek exemption for the CF from the Charter Section 15 guarantees. Section 1 of the Charter does provide for possible limits on and exclusions of Canadians' individual rights protected under Section 15 in order to protect the rights of others or in light of other constitutional values. However, such "reasonable limits" must be *"prescribed by law* as can be *demonstrably justified* in a *free and democratic society"* [emphasis added].[10] The first difficulty for the CF in its argument for a Charter exemption was the Section 1 stipulation that the interim policy be prescribed into law. The methods used to repeatedly revise CFAO 19-20 and further lack of precision in the wording of the order itself strongly suggested that the interim policy did not legally satisfy the Section 1 requirement.

The case of Michelle Douglas also did not augur well for the military seeking an exemption from the Canadian Charter. An exceptional junior officer, she had finished first on her basic officer and basic security officer training courses. She was given an outstanding annual performance evaluation by her superior officer, even when under the interim policy. In addition, information contained in the 1990 SIRC report and reported later in Canadian newspapers suggested that "deplorable" behavior had been shown by certain CF members during the investigation of Douglas's possible relationship with another servicewoman.[11] These "bad facts" suggested that the interim policy had caused the most unfortunate consequences, unreasonable to expect in Canadian society.

Finally, the Canadian military had to provide convincing evidence of its need for the policy. From 1989, when the first of five court challenges was filed, and onward until 1992, the CF and Department of Justice worked to collect evidence and identify expert witnesses. Nine arguments relating to national security, other nations' policies, recruiting and the CF image, medical concerns, discipline, compromised leadership, service members' attitudes, restrictions on the employment of servicewomen, and social science findings regarding the nature of prejudice and organizational change, were dismissed for a myriad of reasons. In the end, the CF was left with two arguments from larger social science research.

Arguments Used in the Preparation of a CF Defense

The invasion of privacy was considered a key underlying factor in service members' perceived unwillingness to accept homosexuals into the CF. Without a sense of control over interpersonal access, members might be under such stress as to impair their task performance, group cohesiveness, and personal and mental health. An expert on "privacy in the person-environment transaction" under varying conditions of "privacy stress" was consulted. He was willing to state that the enrollment of homosexuals could represent a significant source of discomfort for members in conditions of limited privacy exacerbated by environmental stressors such as isolation, danger, and confinement. However, he also identified several methods to provide an "optimal level" of privacy for members. They included a formal recognition by the CF that privacy is an important factor, a physical redesign of the environment, and "psychosocial adjustments" to group selection, training, and leadership.[12]

A key aspect of the privacy stress expected to occur as a result of heterosexual and homosexual members working and living together was the "modesty discomfort" experienced by individuals in situations where bodily modesty was not possible. Dr. Lois Shawver, an expert on the subject of bodily modesty, provided a thorough literature search. Her findings suggested that, when considered as a habit or fashion, bodily modesty could be readily modified. Greater tolerance of known homosexuals was forecast in situations including undressing, sleeping, and showering.[13] While the research did not necessarily describe the military's often intense working and living conditions, the optimism shown by most researchers that individuals could modify their privacy concerns did not help the CF defense. At the same time, there was a clear recognition by scholars that individuals require some degree of privacy, and that privacy includes a desire to be free from unwarranted observation.

The potential problems relating to privacy concerns, discipline, health fears, etc. were thought to influence negatively a unit's cohesion. In 1990, one researcher, Dr. Daryl Henderson, was asked to provide a complete explanation of the impact of cohesion on the combat performance of military units.[14] He also provided a later research evaluation of the 1986 CTF survey and its accompanying report. With appropriate qualifications, he specifically examined the possible effects on military unit cohesion and effectiveness should homosexuals be introduced into small-unit primary groups. Dr. Henderson concluded that the recruitment of homosexuals into the CF "would probably result in a clear and significant decrease in combat effectiveness."[15]

Henderson's review obviously could not cite examples of decreased cohesion having occurred as a result of known homosexuals within military units. His forecast of problems for the CF might have been criticized by expert witnesses called to testify against the CF case because of the "static" features of the analysis, e.g., servicewomen were not present in the unit scenarios depicted; opinions and values of heterosexual members who opposed homosexual members were considered fixed, etc. Nevertheless, the identification of specific problem areas, and conceptual explanation of the unique features characterizing military operations and organization would have assisted the CF explain its concerns to the court.

Analysis of the New CF Policy on Sexual Conduct

Trying to Make the Policy Change

On October 10, 1991, Canadian newspapers carried articles reporting that the CF had made the decision to accept homosexuals.[16] Copies of an internal military message announcing the change, a media news release, and possible questions and answers regarding the policy for use when speaking to the media were later reprinted as proof of the planned change.[17]

The day after the articles appeared, the prime minister of Canada would not acknowledge the existence of the draft news release, and insisted he could not comment on a government policy change while the issue was before the courts.[18] Other members of Parliament (MPs) were more outspoken in disclosing that the Conservative government had backed away from the policy change at the last moment, following the adamant refusal by certain Conservative MPs to support the decision. This vacillation was not resolved until a year later, when the out-of-court agreement was announced on October 27, 1992. At that time, one Conservative MP conceded the change an inevitable consequence of the legal challenges to the CFAO 19-20 policy. Asked to explain the prior 1991 decision not to change the policy, he replied: "Some [government] caucus members were upset, . . . [and] some Armed Forces members were upset."[19]

This hesitation on the part of the Canadian government, played out in the national media, once again highlighted the enormous ambivalence that characterized extending to homosexuals those rights of citizenship and societal entitlements available to others. The call to action by the government finally occurred, according to one MP, only when the ruling party "faced the prospect of a humiliating loss in [its] court case."[20] In essence, the judicial system was used to decide what parliamentarians could not.

The Current Policy

Following the federal court decision on October 27, 1992, the CDS immediately issued two simultaneous announcements. Significantly, a description of the new policy was contained in a media release intended for the Canadian public: "Canadians, regardless of their sexual orientation, will now be able to serve their country in the Canadian Forces without restriction."[21] Additional detail about the new policy was also provided designated military spokespersons handling media queries.[22]

The new policy represented a clear and forceful change from past policies. Applicants to the CF or service members who declare their homosexuality or who engage in homosexual behavior are not to be treated differently from others. No inquiry or record of their homosexual orientation is to be made, unless deemed necessary by a specialist, in dealing with an associated counseling, legal, or medical problem. There are to be no changes in the provision of accommodation, ablution, and messing arrangements. (However, as Canadian law does not recognize the family status of homosexual couples, homosexual members will not be entitled to occupy military married quarter accommodations or to designate a homosexual partner for pension purposes.) HIV testing is to continue on an as-required, specifically identified basis, and conducted with the consent of the individual member. Homosexual military members are permitted to proceed on foreign military courses/ training and on foreign duty, including to countries whose militaries do not permit homosexuals to serve or where homosexuality is considered a crime.

The conduct of homosexuals when in uniform is expected to conform to the same standards of dress and decorum as that expected of heterosexual members. A new order has been issued dealing with inappropriate or criminal sexual conduct committed by either heterosexual or homosexual members, and suitable amendments have been made to existing orders dealing with personal harassment and personal relationships between two service members. Heterosexual members refusing to share accommodation with known homosexual members will not be permitted to exempt themselves from the operational requirements necessitating such quartering. Members refusing to work with homosexual members, or making disparaging comments about them or homosexuality in general, will be considered demonstrating a personal failure to adapt to a military requirement.[23]

The second announcement leaving the CDS's office on October 27 was a message sent to all CF units. The CDS did not describe the new policy but focused on the cancellation of the existing order. He acknowledged the difficulty some members might have accepting the revocation and cited changing "national attitudes," "Canadian legislation," and "evolving government policy" as reasons for the change. Nonetheless, members were expected to adhere to any direction given by commanders. A policy on sexual misconduct was introduced to allay concerns: "Inappropriate sexual conduct by members of the Forces, whether heterosexual or homosexual is unacceptable and will be dealt with effectively."[24]

Two months later, senior commanders were given additional direction to assist in the implementation of the policy change.[25] First, the letter put into context, i.e., placed limits on, the organizational change required by the policy change. The aim and rationale for the change were limited to a recognition that the CF had to honor the rights and freedoms of its members protected by the Canadian Charter of Rights and Freedoms. Professional duty, by extension, required members "to observe and follow the new policy."

Second, because the policy change was externally imposed without any identified military requirement, the emphasis was placed on the CF leadership to endorse the policy change and to motivate members to behave properly, again relying on members' "sense of duty that transcends individual differences." This reliance on the formal leadership to promote the policy's acceptance and appeal to a higher purpose provided the best chance of success. It permitted concentrating on an individual to behave properly versus requiring a member to change basic values, beliefs, or attitudes.

Indeed, there was no expectation or demand made of members to alter their own personal views regarding homosexuality. Rather, the method for promoting policy change was to answer specific questions related to members' behaviors with clear, uncompromising answers, e.g., no member could refuse assignment to a barrack room, tent, mess deck, etc. with a known homosexual. On a final note, the CF sought to limit the policy's impact by predicting that little would change for most members, and that adequate protection against sexual misconduct would be provided heterosexual and homosexual members alike. This reassurance was given in part because few were expected to come forward and declare their homosexual orientation.

Since October 1992, some military members have chosen to state publicly their homosexual orientation. However, some members speaking to the media on the condition of anonymity have suggested that nothing has changed in the unwillingness of CF members to accept homosexuals.[26] On the other hand, no one has taken their release directly as a result of a disagreement with the policy, and no incidents of violent retribution have been reported. Some senior noncommissioned officers have stated on television that job performance is more important than sexual orientation in determining a member's likely acceptance within a unit.

In essence, an externally imposed, legal requirement to permit the enrollment and retention of homosexuals in the Canadian military was accepted by the CF's CDS and further organizational, legal, or parliamentary attempts to resist a policy change abandoned. Since October 27, 1992, formal policy aspects have been addressed, leadership involvement has been highlighted, members' obligations have been identified, and acceptable personal behaviors have been prescribed. It can be said that the CF has endeavored to act immediately and responsibly in response to the legal direction given.

Analysis of the Policy Change

A Qualified Type of Acceptance. The CF, unwittingly or not, has ascribed to a particular model for introducing the presence of known homosexuals and managing the display of homosexual affectionate and sexual behavior. Homosexuals will be assimilated using an approach best described as "benign neutrality."[27] Specifically, the CF has not endorsed homosexuality but rather has said it should not matter. Three key elements comprise the approach.

First, the Canadian military has sought to reduce the uniqueness of the incoming homosexual group, i.e., homosexuals are no different. To the extent possible, homosexual members are officially invisible, i.e., unknown. The organization has no interest in or intention of inquiring about or recording a member's homosexual orientation or behavior other than when problems occur specific to the person's sexual preference, e.g., sexual harassment, sexual assault, or counseling/medical/legal requirements. This is quite different from an organizational endorsement of, let alone enthusiasm for, homosexuality as an alternative or accepted sexual orientation. Consistent with this approach of indifference, there is also no plan to educate members about the subject. Further, there is no plan or agency to monitor the policy and its effect on the homosexual member. Indeed, there is little expectation that homosexual members will demand attention. The sexual subtext underlying the military culture, and working and living conditions, will remain heterosexual.[28]

This effort to reduce the uniqueness of the incoming homosexual group is totally respecting of homosexual members' individual rights of privacy and military entitlements. However, a distinction can be made between the CF approach, which seeks to downplay the key characteristic defining the known homosexual, and an approach that respects the defining characteristic. Evidence from efforts to introduce CF servicewomen into formerly all-male units showed the difficulties of trying to dismiss gender or treat women as if they were "men in drag."[29] Rather, women's chances of successful integration into a unit occurred when their military status as women was recognized and valued.

Because the approach seeks to mask the presence of homosexuals and homosexual behavior in the CF, it will be the person himself or herself who will self-identify. However, unlike employment equity (a.k.a. affirmative action) initiatives, there will be no active organizational support for the member who does self-identify, e.g., special measures, targets, goals, or timetables that recognize the difficulties faced by and seek to improve the status of a disadvantaged group.

The second element characterizing the CF approach has been the limited response of the Canadian military in its management of the issue. That is, the CF has made only the most legal and formal of responses. The CF has cited the Charter as requiring the legal change. The CDS's legal authority to order a policy change has been used. The legally constituted CFAO 19-20 regulation has been canceled, and two other regulations dealing with personal harassment and personal relationships have been amended. The CDS has formally directed the leadership corps to ensure the policy's successful implementation, and has formally stated his expectation that members will comply. Those in clear defiance will be officially punished, e.g., face disciplinary charges or receive lower performance ratings. These actions are commendable, yet represent a partial response. Other components of the formal organization's structure and process have not changed. Furthermore, the informal organization and related norms remain officially uninvolved.

The third element of the CF approach is the official limiting of reactions by members having difficulty with known gays and lesbians or open displays of homosexual behavior. Members will be permitted to believe whatever they want and will not be expected to change personal values, etc. However, their outward behaviors must be in keeping with the organization's acceptance of the homosexual member's right to serve. This "partitioned" interpretation does not suggest a model of human consistency and does not necessarily assist members understand their resistance to the formal order.

As one liberal-minded, well-educated man, dependent upon communicating effectively in his job, was heard to say: "I don't know what it is, but it makes me feel creepy."[30] In sum, the CF has suggested the independence of cognitive and affective processes from behavioral outcomes, in order to limit the responses possible to the new policy. This interpretation of mental functioning allows the CF to act immediately if problems occur. However, it does not provide for difficulties occurring among those not accepting the new policy.

Assimilation versus Integration.   The current CF policy regarding homosexuals and homosexual behavior was described earlier as one of benign neutrality. The combination of the three elements of the policy suggests a balancing act of (1) the homosexual member's entitlement to serve, (2) an acknowledgement of the organization's two formal responsibilities to permit homosexuals to serve and to suppress dissent, and (3) recognition in part of the resistant heterosexual member's private entitlement to disagree. By using the strategy that homosexuals are not different, that a limited response on the part of the CF is appropriate, and that members' behaviors can be isolated and targeted to control dissent, the CF will conduct "business as usual."

The model strongly suggests that incoming homosexuals will be assimilated into the larger heterosexual group as long as the homosexual member accepts the dominant heterosexual worldview and does not cause others to think differently. It requires the homosexual member to support the values of the dominant group after having taken advantage of the legal right to serve in the CF, i.e., nothing has changed. On the other hand, if incoming homosexuals decide to highlight differences or reject the dominant heterosexual culture, the CF will not provide strong organizational support. Such occurrences could well lead to a segregation of homosexual members by emphasizing their distinctiveness, discouraging their participation in heterosexually oriented activities, or pointing out other differences. The time spent erecting barriers and fighting such differences can make group cohesion very difficult.

Previous research examining attempts at successful integration of cultural groups in Canada,[31] and perhaps of greater relevance, of servicemen and servicewomen in the CF,[32] suggests that a successful social integration occurs when both the dominant group already in place and the incoming group are mutually valued for their respective characteristics and contributions. This would be the ideal scenario for the successful introduction and full membership of homosexuals in the CF, as well as acceptance of affectionate and/or sexual same-sex behavior between consenting adults.

The difficulty for the CF in pursuing such an objective lies in the type of prejudice that characterizes the rejection of homosexuality.[33] Groups who experience discrimination in North American society have been variously described as dependent, disabled, despised, or possessing some combination of the three. Using this simple characterization, homosexuals and homosexual behavior fall under the label of "despised." As such, the issue prompts a type of prejudice unlike that displayed toward other minority groups attempting to integrate in the CF and military culture. Because of such negative labeling, it is difficult to describe a situation where homosexual members, as an incoming group attempting to gain acceptance in the CF, will be able to "trade up" on the chief feature that defines their difference from the dominant heterosexual group, i.e., their homosexual orientation and associated behavior.

Instead, alternative types of interaction are more likely, i.e., assimilation or segregation. This difficulty may also explain why the CF has chosen a strategy that only partially acknowledges the homosexual member's presence, partially uses measures available to promote the homosexual member's full status, and partially accepts heterosexual members' resistance. Under the circumstances, a full integration may not be possible. While the legal decision to open the Canadian Forces to gays and lesbians was inevitable, the model now followed by the CF suggests an improbable reconfiguration, likely to result in a minimal acceptance of known homosexuals in the CF.

Summary

Since October 1992, the CF has had an unrestricted employment policy permitting Canadian citizens who are gay or lesbian to enroll and serve in all military occupations and environments open to their heterosexual counterparts. Revisions to the Canadian military's personnel policy on homosexuality have ended for the moment, although additional entitlements may be granted, such as military housing or legal family status of homosexual couples, as a result of ongoing legal cases. While political and legal action required the Canadian military to successively amend its policy on homosexuality, a reconfiguration of the Canadian military that fully accepts and endorses homosexuals and homosexuality on an equal plane with the more dominant heterosexual orientation is highly improbable. An indecisive assimilation of homosexual members with the existing, larger CF membership is the more likely result.

The U.S. military's current attempts to revise its policy on homosexuality (including the government's difficulty finding a compromise) show a marked similarity with the Canadian military's experiences. The intensity of the debate will likely be greater as military service figures more centrally in American culture and identity than in Canada.[34] The end result may, nevertheless, be the same.

Notes

1.   See Canadian Forces Administration Order 19-20, "Sexual Deviation Investigation, Medical Examination, and Disposal" (Ottawa: Queen's Printer, 1967).

2.   See Canadian Forces Administration Order 19-20, "Homosexuality—Sexual Abnormality Investigation, Medical Examination, and Disposal" (Ottawa: Queen's Printer, 1976).

3.   Rosemary E. Park, "Overview of the Social/Behavioral Science Evaluation of the 1979–1985 Canadian Forces Trial Employment of Servicewomen in Non-Traditional Environments and Roles," *Canadian Forces Personnel Applied Research Unit Research Report 86-2* (Willowdale, Ontario, 1986).

4.   Canada, Department of Justice, *Equality Issues in Federal Law: A Discussion Paper* (Ottawa: Communications and Public Affairs Department of Justice, 1985), 1.

5.   Canada, Department of Justice, *Toward Equality: The Response to the Report of the Parliamentary Committee on Equality Rights* (Ottawa: Communications and Public Affairs, Department of Justice, 1986), 13.

6.   Department of National Defence, *Charter Task Force Final Report* (Ottawa, 1986), 21.

7.   Canada, Parliament, House of Commons, *Minutes of Proceedings and Evidence of the Standing Committee on National Defence,* (Ottawa: Queen's Printer, April 15, 1986), 35.

8.   Ibid., December 11, 1986, 33.

9.   See National Defence Headquarters letter "CFAO 19-20 Interim Reply on Homosexuality" 1620-12-20 (Ottawa: DGPCOR, January 20, 1988).

10.   Canada, Department of Secretary of State, *The Charter of Rights and Freedoms A Guide for Canadians,* (Ottawa: Communications Directorate, 1986), 5.

11.   "Military to Lift Its Ban on Gays and Lesbians," *Toronto Star,* 10 October 1991.

12.   Peter Suedfeld, *Privacy in the Person-Environment Transaction: Implications of the Psychological Literature,* Report prepared for the Department of National Defence (Ottawa, February 1991).

13.   Lois Shawver, *The Development of Bodily Modesty.* Report prepared for the Department of National Defence (Ottawa, July 1991).

14.   Darryl Henderson, *The Impact of Cohesion on the Combat Performance of Military Units.* Report prepared for the Department of National Defence (Ottawa, August 1990).

15.   Darryl Henderson, *Analysis of the Canadian Forces Survey on Homosexual Issues by Major R. A. Zuliani, September 1986.* Report prepared for the Department of National Defence (Ottawa, March 1992).

16.   "Ottawa Expected to Forbid Anti-Homosexual Policies in Military," *Vancouver Sun,* 10 October 1991.

17.   "Homosexuals in the Military," *Whig Standard Magazine,* 19 October 1991.

18.   "Ban on Gays Still in Place," *Toronto Star,* 11 October 1991.

19.   "Forces Agree to End Anti-Gay Policies," *Globe and Mail,* 28 October 1992.

20.   Ibid.

21. See Department of National Defence News Release, "Change to Sexual Orientation Policy," (Ottawa, October 27, 1992), 30.

22. See Department of National Defence Public Affairs Document, "Canadian Forces Policy on Sexual Orientation Questions and Answers" (Ottawa, October 27, 1992), 1-5.

23. Ibid.

24. See National Defence Headquarters message, "Homosexual Conduct," (CANFORGEN 54/92 271550Z OCT 92 (Ottawa, 1992), 1–4.

25. See National Defence Headquarters Associate Deputy Minister (Personnel) letter, "Revocation of CF Sexual Orientation Policy: Post Announcement Action," 1745-42-7 (ADM Per) (Ottawa, December 10, 1992).

26. Luke Fisher, "Armed and Gay," *Maclean's Magazine*, 24 May 1992, 15–16.

27. Rosemary E. Park, "Organizational Factors Enhancing and Impeding the Integration of Servicewomen in the CF." Paper presented at the International Applied Military Psychology Symposium, Copenhagen, Denmark, June 1983.

28. B. Az, "A Materialistic View of Men's and Women's Attitudes toward War," *Women's Studies International Forum* (1982) 5:355–64.

29. Rosemary E. Park, "Final Report of Social Behavioral Science Evaluation of the SWINTER Land Trial," *Canadian Forces Personnel Applied Research Unit Research Report 85-1* (Willowdale, Ontario, 1985).

30. Personal communication.

31. J. W. Berry, "Psychological Aspects of Cultural Pluralism: Unity and Identity Reconsidered," *Topics in Cultural Learning*, (1974) 2:17–22.

32. Park, "Overview of Social/Behavioral Science Evaluation."

33. Geoffrey Haddock, Mark P. Zanna, and Victoria M. Esses, "Assessing the Structure of Prejudicial Attitudes: The Case of Attitudes towards Homosexuals," *Journal of Personality and Social Psychology* (1993):1105–18.

34. Randy Shilts, *Conduct Unbecoming: Gays and Lesbians in the U.S. Military—Vietnam to the Persian Gulf* (New York: St. Martin's, 1993).

Chapter 12

Gays in the Military: Policy and Practice in the Israeli Defence Forces

REUVEN GAL

A recent official review, conducted by the U.S. General Accounting Office (GAO) of policies and practices of various foreign countries regarding homosexuals in the military service found Israel to be one of 11 countries (out of twenty-five included in the review) who had official policies that permit homosexuals to serve in the military.[1] As in other countries in this category, the policy of the Israeli Defence Forces (IDF) concerning military service of homosexuals developed over time, reflecting general changes in civilian law and social attitudes toward homosexuals. Furthermore, though the official policy enables homosexuals to serve openly without discrimination in the IDF, in practice, gay soldiers in Israel may still face sporadic obstacles during their military years of service.

Thus, the following review will begin with a background and history of Israeli society pertinent to our subject, followed by a description of relevant characteristics of the IDF in general. The main part of this paper will describe the policies and practices regarding military service of homosexuals in Israel throughout the years. Finally, we will draw some comparisons between the Israeli and the American cases.

Background and History of Israeli Society

The State of Israel was established in 1948, based on Zionist-Jewish-democratic principles. Its current population is approximately 5.2 million, with the Jewish inhabitants at about 82 percent. The society itself is quite diverse and multiethnic, with immigrants coming from all over the world.

Though quite westernized in its norms and culture, and in spite of a growing tendency toward a capitalistic-individualistic orientation, Israeli society is still very much influenced by the socialistic-collective ideology that characterized its founders, the early Ashkenazi (European origin) Zionists.

This ideology, which was a secular-sectarian reaction movement against the traditional religious Judaism of the Diaspora, stressed sexual as well as other equality among all members of the community.[2] On the other hand, the huge waves of immigrants coming to Israel after 1948, especially those from Arab countries (Sephardic Jews), reinforced more traditional and religious trends within the evolving Israeli society.

A further elaboration on the composition of contemporary Israeli characteristics is relevant here. Ethnocentrism is usually quite high among Israelis, especially among the Israeli Jews.[3] A part of that ethnocentrism is the lack of tolerance expressed towards the "other," the "different."[4] Another aspect is the central role of family in the Israeli self-identity: In a recent survey conducted on a representative Israeli sample, a large proportion (48.6%) of the sample rated Family as the leading component of their self-identity.[5] In regard to religion, while only three percent of the surveyed Israelis ranked Religious Observance as their primary identity component, the Jewish religion is nevertheless a predominant factor in Israeli society: between 58[6] and 65 percent[7] of the Israeli-Jewish population consider themselves as orthodox or traditional (as opposed to secular) Jews.

Thus, in addition to their differing cultural, economic, and educational backgrounds, Israelis vary widely in their attitudes toward religion and sexuality. Nevertheless, most remain bonded by their common religion (Judaism), their pride in the state, and the perception that the state and its armed forces provide the only means of ensuring their safety in a region historically accustomed to war and hostility from Arab neighbors and terrorist activities within its own borders.

Although Israel does not have a constitution or provisions similar to those of the United States' Bill of Rights, the Declaration of the Establishment of the State of Israel provides guarantees for freedom from discrimination on the basis of sex, race, or religion. Israel's laws regarding citizen rights, including homosexual rights, are still evolving and are gradually becoming more specific. In the absence of a human rights law, Israel has had to rely on the courts to safeguard civil rights and liberties.

Public awareness about homosexuality has been quite restricted until recently, and most Israelis have traditionally held negative views toward homosexuals—either because Judaism condemns homosexuality or, more simply, Israeli society (as compared to several Western European countries) is relatively conservative.

In the only known study conducted in Israel on this subject, the researcher administered an attitude questionnaire—based on MacDonald's (1974) Attitudes Toward Homosexuality Scale—to a mixed sample of Israeli and American students (the latter were on a one-year foreign-student program in Israel).[8] On a scale ranging between 28 and 252 (the higher the score, the more negative the attitude toward homosexuals), the Israelis scored, on the average, higher (mean = 108.5) than their American counter-parts (mean = 89.5). Women in both samples scored relatively lower than the men.

Indeed, throughout the years, most Israeli homosexuals remained hidden, and the gay communities or gay movements that did exist were merely surreptitious. The first structured Israeli gay organization was founded as early as 1975, but under the name of the Society for the Protection of Personal Rights (SPPR). Recently however, Israel has gradually become more accepting of homosexuality and more homosexuals are readily reveal-ing their sexual orientation. Still, most do not come out until later in life due to fears of negative parental and societal reactions.

Also, recognition of the rights of homosexuals is on the increase as demon-strated by the decriminalization of sodomy in 1988. In December 1991, Israel's parliament (Knesset) amended its labor law to prohibit discrimination against homosexuals in the workplace. According to the amendment, em-ployers cannot discriminate against employees and job seekers because of their "sexual inclination." The amendment covers all conditions of employ-ment, including hiring, working conditions, promotion, training, and dismissal.

In February 1993, the Knesset's subcommittee dealing with homosexual rights hosted a conference to draw attention to the need for legal equality of homosexuals. As of this writing, this subcommittee is working to obtain full rights for homosexuals and is developing legislation to establish partnership rights for homosexual couples. Presently, homosexual marriages are not rec-ognized in Israel and homosexual partners do not have conjugal rights.

Characteristics of the Israeli Military

Israel has a full-draft system of regular conscript service with an extended period of reserve duty, for males, which is also compulsory. Structurally, the IDF is divided into three main components:

1. *Sherut Hova*: compulsory conscript service which is based on universal conscription of men and women, who become eligible for service at the age of eighteen.
2. *Sherut Keva*: the permanent service corps, consisting of a relatively small nucleus of career officers and noncommissioned officers who have chosen the military as a long-term vocation. After completion of their three (or two) years of compulsory service, these men and women volunteer for prolonged career service.
3. *Sherut Milluim*: the reserve service, which is the main core of the IDF's

fighting capability. This encompasses all demobilized conscripts who have successfully completed their compulsory-service period. These reservists are called up annually for thirty to sixty days of active duty, men until age fifty-five and women until age twenty-six (unless exempted by marriage or children).

The Israeli Defence Forces has an estimated 141,000 men and women on active duty (comprised of both Sherut Hova and Sherut Keva) and 504,000 in the reserves. Most of the IDF's personnel are Jewish Israelis, with only a small number of Druze male soldiers who also serve as draftees. Arab Israelis and Bedouins are not required to serve, but may volunteer to do so. Based on their religious (and somewhat anti-statehood) beliefs, ultra-Orthodox Jews are also exempted from mandatory military service.

With this wide range of universal service—conscripts, reservists, and careerists; men and women; Jews and non-Jews—military service has become a core aspect of Israeli life. There is hardly a family in Israel that does not have a family member serving in the military at any given time. Furthermore, military service is often considered to be a precondition to a successful career because military service influences the networks and associations used later in life. Since nearly everyone is required to serve in the armed forces, establishing a military record is an important prerequisite for the young man or woman entering mainstream Israeli life, and deferments are not viewed favorably. In fact, youngsters with medical or psychological problems often try to hide their difficulties in order to serve. Motivation to serve in the IDF is further enhanced by Israel's political and security conditions, by its history of repeated wars, and by the highly prestigious status the IDF normally boasts. These, then, become the ingredients of the extremely powerful normative system that makes serving in the IDF so highly appreciated, so socially desirable, and—for most Israelis—so taken for granted.[9]

A final note should be made concerning the nature of military service in Israel: Because of the size of the country (approximately the area of New Jersey) and since IDF bases do not have civilian housing facilities (such as the U.S. parallel HBQs), Israeli soldiers normally spend, especially in peacetime, minimal time away from their homes. Many return home almost every day. Even those in remote bases usually have weekend passes to be with their families and thus are not critically isolated from their private lives.

Policies

Under Israeli military policy, homosexuals are not exempted or banned from military service in the Israeli Armed Forces. As described earlier, almost all Israeli men and about 60 percent of Israeli women enter the mandatory service at the age of eighteen. Homosexuals are no exception. Conscripts are not particularly questioned about their sexual orientation and individuals who are openly gay are not exempted or discharged from the service because of it. Further, no special effort is made by the military authorities to identify homosexuals, and the military places no restrictions upon the promotion potential of these individuals. Military regulations on sexual behavior state that sexual activity is not to take place in the barracks (males and females may live in the same barracks); the regulations make no distinction between heterosexuals and homosexuals. Any problems related to homosexuals are required to be handled through normal channels, such as the unit psychologist, or as strictly disciplinary matters.

However, until very recently, military regulations published in 1983 by the IDF Manpower Division did apply restrictions on the placement of homosexual soldiers, thereby barring them from serving in "sensitive" units, and the continuation of their service (whether as conscripts or careerists) was to be determined by the military mental-health authorities and the chief security-classification officer. According to the 1983 regulations, under no circumstances could a soldier who was openly homosexual serve in a position requiring a top-secret security clearance in the intelligence community. Likewise, homosexual soldiers could be excluded from some combat units that are highly consolidated and perform under high stress. They could also be prohibited from serving on those bases where soldiers or sailors must live and work under close conditions or must endure prolonged periods of seclusion.

Indeed, under the former regulations, some homosexual conscripts were exempted from the draft service if their psychological assessment revealed personality disturbances relating (or not) to their homosexuality. More specifically, those who identified themselves as homosexuals were required, under the 1983 regulation, to undergo additional psychological testing. These tests were intended to determine whether (1) the individual's inclination could prove to be a security hazard or (2) the individual had the mental fortitude and maturity to withstand the pressures of serving in the defense forces.

On June 10, 1993, Israel adopted a new military policy concerning homosexuals. The change came after several years of behind-the-scenes attempts by various civil rights movements to invoke new policy, and following a dramatic disclosure made by a reputable Israeli academic—Professor Uzi Even—who for years had held a top-secret research position in the military. The new policy states that no restrictions shall be placed upon the recruitment, assignment, or promotion of homosexual soldiers and civilians, both males and females, due to their sexual inclination. This policy was implemented immediately, albeit amid several voiced protests, particularly from the Orthodox Jewish community.

Interestingly, it was noted by many (journalists, civil-rights activists, students of military sociology, etc.) that the radical change occurred in Israel in the midst of the public and political debate developing in the United States regarding President Clinton's campaign to change policy on homosexuals in the U.S. military. Apparently the transitions evolving in America, as well as the growing awareness of civil rights in Israel, have directly contributed to the change in the IDF policy regarding homosexual soldiers.

Practices

Even though Israel's military policy toward homosexuals has just very recently been modified, its practices can be, nevertheless, reviewed in retrospect. The reality of gay soldiers in Israel diverged from the official policy in both directions: On the one hand, the 1983 regulation prohibiting the assignment of homosexuals to "sensitive" positions was never fully implemented. Commanding officers, even in highly classified intelligence units, who had homosexual soldiers who performed satisfactorily under their command, refrained from enforcing this regulation.

Similarly, much latitude was normally given in IDF units when a seasoned soldier, already serving in a certain unit, was suddenly discovered to be a homosexual. If that soldier was regarded as a good soldier, most likely he would not be reported by his commanders. A highly cohesive unit would retain its esteemed soldiers even if their sexual proclivities were disclosed. Indeed, a recent GAO review reports the findings of committee members who investigated the situation in Israel and spoke with a number of reservists and retired IDF personnel who stated that, while on active duty, they had openly served as homosexuals.[10] They said they had still received promotions and had not been restricted in their assignments. Apparently, these individuals were evaluated by their occupational proficiency and not by their sexual orientation.

On the other hand, though homosexuality is not banned and no longer suffers any legal restrictions within the Israeli military, it is still viewed as abnormal, deviant, and dangerous by many in Israeli society. Subsequently, many IDF servicemen and -women, especially in the permanent (career) corps, refrain from revealing their homosexuality, even if they are highly regarded by their supervisors. One such story, which appeared as a cover story in a recent *Army Times* report, tells of a thirty-year-old reserve lieutenant in the Israeli navy who skillfully commands a fast-attack patrol boat, but who nervously conceals his homosexuality from both his subordinates and his superiors.[11]

More publicized is the case of Professor Even, a reserve captain in Israeli intelligence, who testified at the February 1993 conference hosted by the

Knesset subcommittee dealing with homosexual issues. He related that he had been summarily dismissed from his reserve unit in which he had served devotedly for many years when his homosexual orientation became known to his commanders. However, this case seems to be the exception, not the rule, in the Israeli military. As confirmed recently by representatives of the leading homosexual and civil rights organizations in Israel, homosexuality has almost no bearing on an individual's military career. Homosexual soldiers are usually judged on their performance, like any other soldier. Other than the case involving the former captain stated above, no other case is known in which a homosexual's career has been directly harmed because of his/her sexual orientation. [12]

The military authorities consider the inclusion of homosexuals in service to be very effective. IDF officials responsible for the mental health of the troops have recently reported that homosexual soldiers adjust to military life as well as heterosexuals. And security officials have stated that homosexuals, especially those who have come out openly, may hold security clearances without posing an unnecessary security risk. [13] It should be noted that the IDF applies a very rigorous screening procedure to its conscripts. [14] In addition to aptitude and intelligence tests, this procedure includes a special assessment of the soldier's prospective adjustment to the military (notably field units) environment. Part of the successful adjustment of the homosexual soldiers during their years of service can be accredited to this early screening.

As of now, no specific studies have been conducted as to if and how the inclusion of homosexuals in the IDF has affected unit readiness, effectiveness, cohesion, or morale. However, a recent GAO document reports that the inclusion of homosexuals has not had an adverse impact on these areas. Generally speaking, it seems that homosexual soldiers serving in the IDF perform as well as their heterosexual counterparts. [15] The IDF does not provide any educational or training courses dealing with homosexuals. Military officials from the Education Corps see no need for training because there are actually few problems related to the presence of homosexuals in the military environment.

Conclusions

A recent review published in the *American Psychologist* by Greg Herek reflects on the animated national discussion that erupted in the United States following President Clinton's pledge to reverse the ban on lesbians and gay men in the U.S military. [16] The President's plan created considerable controversy, including intense opposition voiced by the Joint Chiefs of Staff.

This opposition arose partially from the historical policy of the U.S. military to reject gay draftees.[17]

Conversely, the Israeli military has allowed homosexuals to serve for forty-five years, ever since the state and its armed forces were created. Hence, most Israelis do not have strong feelings about a homosexual presence in the military and, in reality, homosexuals and their rights in general are just not issues at the forefront of public debate in Israel. Likewise, several other points presented by Herek as obstacles for homosexual equality in the U.S. armed forces are either irrelevant or are not prevalent in the Israeli case.[18] Thus, for example, the assumed difficulties derived from sharing living quarters is minimized in the Israeli case because of the relatively short periods that Israeli soldiers stay away from their homes or are isolated from their private lives.

Even more dramatic is the difference resulting from the conscription system. Unlike the U.S. all-volunteer force, the IDF is a full-draft system, applying to all the diverse segments of Israeli society. Furthermore, military service is highly regarded and deferments are not viewed favorably. The inclusion of homosexuals thus cannot affect recruitment rates or levels of motivation.

Finally, based on the Israeli experience, gay males and lesbian females have, in general, served and performed as well as heterosexual soldiers. According to military reports, their presence, whether openly or clandestinely, has not impaired the morale, cohesion, readiness, or security of any unit. Perhaps the best indication of this overall perspective is the relative smoothness with which the most recent (June 1993) repeal of the remaining restrictions on homosexuals was received within the IDF and in Israeli society on the whole. While perhaps more biased in other areas, the Israeli people evidently seem to be fair and square where the military is involved.

Notes

1.   General Accounting Office (GAO), *Homosexuals in the Military—Policies and Practices of Foreign Countries*, Document No. GAO/NSAID-93-215 (Washington, DC, 1993).

2.   A. Elon, *The Israelis: Founders and Sons* (New York: Pelican, 1983).

3.   D. Horowitz and M. Lissak, *Trouble in Utopia: The Overburdened Politics of Israel* (Tel Aviv: Am-Oved, 1990), (in Hebrew).

4.   M. Zemach, *Do Israeli-Jews Practice the Phrase "Thou Shalt Love Thy Neighbor as Thyself"* (Jerusalem: Van Leer Institute, 1980), (in Hebrew).

5.   B. Kimmerling, "Yes, Back to the Family," *Politics* 48 (March, 1993): 40–45, (in Hebrew).

6.   O. Mayseless, R. Gal, and E. Fishkoff, *Perceptions and Attitudes of*

High-School Students regarding Issues of Security and Military Service (Zikhron Ya'akov: Israeli Institute for Military Studies, 1989, (in Hebrew).

7. Kimmerling, "Back to the Family."

8. G. Friedman-Grayevski, *Attitudes toward Homosexuals and Sex-Role Perceptions among Israeli and American Students.* Unpublished master's thesis, Hebrew University, Jerusalem, 1983, (in Hebrew).

9. R. Gal, *A Portrait of the Israeli Soldier* (Westport, CT: Greenwood Press, 1986).

10. GAO, *Homosexuals in the Military.*

11. T. Philpott, "No Easy Answers," *Army Times,* 11 January 1993, 10–14.

12. GAO, *Homosexuals in the Military.*

13. Ibid.

14. Gal, *Portrait of the Soldier.*

15. GAO, *Homosexuals in the Military.*

16. G. Herek, "Sexual Orientation and Military Service: A Social Science Perspective," *American Psychologist* 48 (1993): 538–49.

17. A. Berube, *Coming Out Under Fire: The History of Gay Men and Women in World War Two* (New York: Free Press, 1990).

18. Herek, "Orientation and Service."

Chapter 13

Sexual Orientation and Military Service: The British Case

GWYN HARRIES-JENKINS and CHRISTOPHER DANDEKER

The issue of homosexuality in the British military has attracted considerable attention and has produced a small but significant body of literature.[1] Much of what has been written, however, starts from a value-based position in which rational discussion is often subordinated to the presentation of polemics and political arguments. This paper sets out to look critically at the current position of gays and lesbians in the British armed forces by considering the three basic questions of policies, practices, and problems.

Policies, in this context, refer to the declared aims and objectives of the military organization that govern the employment of personnel within national armed forces. Such aims and objectives are not static and they change over time. The term also relates to the rules and regulations that, in the guise of military law, govern the behavior of individual service personnel.

Practices equally refer to the employment of personnel. Specifically, the term acknowledges that the culture of military organizations, in reflecting an amalgam of symbols, rituals, heroes, and values, provides a set of operational criteria. These may imply accord with declared policies; they may enlarge upon them through the provision of examples and rules of good practice. They will in some situations provide an alternative to formal rules and regulations.

Problems are the "garbage can" of decision-making. Notwithstanding legislative provision and an acknowledgment of the impact of culture on management practice, the military, in common with other large, complex organizations, is consistently faced with the existence of major operational problems. Minor issues can be readily solved; major questions require more consideration and deliberation.

The Development of Policy

In the United Kingdom, the traditional policy of the government with regard to the recruitment and retention of homosexuals in the armed forces was based on the premise that military law should replicate common and statute law. Effectively, this meant that homosexual acts were a criminal offense. In the military, their commission and detection led to the court-martial of the offender; in civil society the full panoply of the law was equally exercised.

This policy was changed in civil society following the recommendations of the Wolfenden Report (1957). Under the subsequent Sexual Offences Act (1967), it was laid down that homosexual acts undertaken in private between two consenting males over the age of 21 would not be a criminal offense. Such acts where one party was under the age of twenty-one continued to be a criminal offense, as did the commission of homosexual acts in a public place. Since lesbian acts had never been a criminal offense, their commission was not affected by the reforms of the 1967 act.

Section 1(5) of the act, however, enacted special provisions for the armed forces of the United Kingdom. For males in the military, traditional policy continued to apply. The rationale for this had been given in the Wolfenden Report:

Offences in Disciplinary Services and Establishments 144. We recognise that within services and establishments whose members are subject to a disciplinary regime it may be necessary, for the sake of good management and the preservation of discipline and for the protection of those of subordinate rank or position, to regard homosexual behaviour, even by consenting adults in private, as an offence. For instance, if our recommendations are accepted, a serving soldier over twenty-one who commits a homosexual act with a consenting adult partner in private will cease to be guilty of a civil offence or of an offence against Section 70(1) of the Army Act, 1955 (which provides that any person subject to military law who commits a civil offence shall be guilty of an offence under that section, and hence liable to be dealt with by court-martial). The service authorities may nevertheless consider it necessary to retain Section 66 of the Act (which provides for the punishment of, *inter alia,* disgraceful conduct of an indecent or unnatural kind) on the grounds that it is essential, in the services, to treat as offences certain types of conduct which may not amount to offences under the civil code. Similar problems may arise in relation to other services and establishments.[2]

Accordingly, as a result of an exemption from the 1967 act, service personnel could still be charged under military law for the commission of homosexual acts in circumstances where an offense would not be committed in civilian life. The offense would usually be identified as "disgraceful conduct of an indecent kind," "conduct prejudicial to good order or discipline," and possibly, but very rarely, "scandalous conduct by officers" (*Manual of Military Law*). Coincidentally, the military could use the mechanism of an administrative discharge ("services no longer required" or a "return to shore") as an alternative to the legal process of the court-martial. Indeed, thirty-nine service personnel were dismissed from the armed forces between 1988 and 1992 following conviction for an offense involving homosexual activity (navy, 9; army, 22; air force, 8) while 296 were discharged as a result of administrative action. Of those discharged on administrative grounds from the army during this period, over half were women who under British civil legislation had committed no criminal act.

During the course of considerable discussions in the House of Commons on the 1991 Armed Forces Bill, it was pointed out that society outside the armed forces was now much more tolerant of differences in sexual orientation than it had been. This was contrasted by the British pressure group, Stonewall, with what happened in the military. In an undated press release (probably early 1993), they argued that exemption from the 1967 act had allowed the armed forces to:

> punish consenting sex between men, even during off-duty hours and in private. In theory this could also apply to heterosexual sex; in practice only gay sex was punished this harshly. On average, 10 men a year were sent to prison, often for 18 months. Lesbians were often threatened in prison. In addition, lesbians and gay men faced automatic discharge if they were discovered to be gay.

Official policy, however, was vigorously defended by Archie Hamilton, the then responsible minister, during the course of the 1991 debate on the Forces (Discipline) Bill. He argued:

> [B]oth homosexual activity and orientation are incompatible with service in the armed forces. The main reason centres on the need to maintain discipline and morale. The services are hierarchical, close knit overwhelmingly single sex and young communities. Units can work to full effectiveness only on the basis of mutual trust and the expectation of equal treatment among each rank. The formation within these units of sexually motivated relationships are potentially very disruptive of discipline and morale, particularly when they cross rank boundaries.[3]

As a result of the debate, however, the government was forced to concede that the exemption for the military from the provisions of the Sexual Offences Act of 1967—the section 1(5) clause—was no longer tenable. Accordingly, civil and military law were to come into line so that homosexual acts were decriminalized. The Select Committee on the Armed Forces Bill of 1991 recommended:

> [H]omosexual activity of a kind that is legal in civilian law should not constitute an offence under Service law. We look to the Government to propose an appropriate amendment to the law before the end of the next Session of Parliament.[4]

The government, in the form of Archie Hamilton, responded cautiously to this recommendation but gave no firm undertaking as to the timing of any legislative changes.[5] In July 1991, the Earl of Arran announced an internal review to be carried out within the Ministry of Defence in which the experience of other countries would be examined in the development of policy on this issue. In June 1992, in connection with the annual renewal of the Armed Forces Discipline Acts, it was announced that the Select Committee recommendation was to be accepted and implemented immediately in administrative practice and the requisite legislative changes would be introduced as soon as the parliamentary timetable allowed, i.e., the Sexual Offences Act of 1967 would require amendment. This concession did not change the basic policy of the government towards homosexuality in the armed forces. The British position is that overt homosexuality continues to be incompatible with service in the armed forces.

Although criminal charges will not be and cannot be laid against servicemen and -women for the commission of acts that are not offenses under civil law, official policy is unyielding. Homosexuality is incompatible with military service.

Policy Issues and Assumptions

In any discussions of this policy, however, it is necessary to be clear about the terms that are being used. Three terms can be distinguished: *homosexuality*, *homosexual acts*, and *homosexual offenses*. The dictionary and legal definition of the first term states simply that "homosexuality is having a sexual propensity for persons of one's own sex." This definition, as is pointed out in the 1957 *Report of the Committee on Homosexual Offences and Prostitution* (the Wolfenden Report), involves the adoption of some criteria for its recognition. As in other psychological fields, the conclusion that such a propensity exists has to be derived from both subjective and objective data. The former will reflect what is felt by the person concerned; the latter, what is done. The use of such data as the determinant of the presence or absence of the sexual propensity has to be treated with caution, for its use is subject to the strict rules of evidence. That is particularly so where subjective data are the basis of evaluation.

For example, individual service personnel may not be aware of either the existence or strength of a feeling or propensity. The Wolfenden Report notes that "rationalizations and self-perception can be carried to great lengths and in some cases lying is also to be expected."

The British military leans heavily toward the use of subjective data in taking disciplinary action in that it is the feelings of the individual concerned that are critical. Hence the reference by Hamilton in the June 1991 debate to "both homosexual activity and orientation":

It is MoD [Ministry of Defence] policy neither to recruit nor to retain any person who admits to being homosexual. Being lesbian or gay is grounds for instant dismissal ("administrative discharge"). You do not have to be caught having sex to be dismissed—the very fact of being gay is enough.[6]

The policy of the military in this context, as the pressure groups such as Stonewall continue to stress, imposes restrictions that would not be tolerated in civilian employment. The policy is often seen to be contrary to the policy of the European Community. In its resolution of March 13, 1984, the European Parliament stated:

[I]n the campaign against discrimination of all kinds, it is impossible to ignore or passively to accept *de facto* or *de jure* discrimination against homosexuals.

In the United Kingdom military, however, an admission by individuals of their homosexuality, makes them liable to dismissal from the armed forces.

Whereas homosexuality, by definition, is a state or condition the existence of which has to be determined from primarily subjective data, homosexual acts are evidenced by objective data. A latent homosexuality may be influenced by behavior that is not overtly sexual. It may thus be inferred from an individual's outlook or expression of opinion or preference for a certain mode of conduct. Homosexual acts, in contrast, are overtly sexual. They are, for example, defined in current U.S. Army Regulations as:

bodily contact, actively undertaken or passively permitted, between members of the same sex for the purpose of satisfying sexual desires.[7]

It is, however, a question of legislation as to when such acts become homosexual offenses. The concept of homosexual offenses extends by definition the identification of homosexuality as a state or condition, and the identification of homosexual acts as a form of sexual behavior. Homosexual offenses are those overt acts that, because they are contrary to law, render the perpetuating individual or individuals liable to prosecution. On conviction, the offender is punished, the severity of that punishment varying in accordance with the dictates of national practice.

What constitutes a homosexual offense varies by country and has changed over time. There are no absolute homosexual offenses. Notwithstanding the prescriptions of a Judeo-Christian tradition, it is in actuality contemporary legislators who define the legality or otherwise of a specific homosexual act. Legislation in the United Kingdom, however, follows three precepts: (1) There is need for laws to safeguard those in need of protection by reason of their youth or mental incapacity; (2) a major function of law is the preservation of order and decency in public places; and (3) there is a requirement to regulate conduct seen to be contrary to the public good.

To these determinants of civil legislation, military legislation in the United Kingdom adds the need to regulate conduct prejudicial to good order and discipline.

Some of the offenses here will be common to all service personnel irrespective of their sexual preference. Offenses such as coercion or harassment irrespective of whether the associated sexual relationship is homosexual or heterosexual are punished as "conduct prejudicial to good order and discipline." The latter term can have a wider interpretation to include conduct such as a sexual relationship between service personnel of different ranks, although such a relationship would not be an offense in a civilian organization. The United Kingdom also stipulates that major breaches of these rules of conduct will constitute offenses punishable by court-martial as an alternative to administrative discharge.

The rationale that underlies U.K. policy on homosexuality in the military can be discussed more fully under the headings of practices and problems to which we now turn.

Practices

In order to understand the position of homosexuals within the British military, one must address not only the formal policy context of legal and administrative regulations but also the organizational culture of the armed forces, because this influences the ways in which regulations are interpreted and enforced. This culture comprises the self-image of the British military. Traditionally, military socialization in the United Kingdom has been linked to the development and maintenance of an occupational culture, the symbols, rituals, and values of which have constituted an idealized self-image.

In British society, the latter has stressed the importance of such qualities as toughness, aggressiveness, endurance, and controlled deviancy. These, irrespective of the logic of the arguments that have been put forward, have been perceived as masculine traits; inadequate or poor performance, on the other hand, has been equated with a femininity that is the antithesis of effective soldiering. To maintain and develop the military self-image, British armed forces have established complex personnel policies and practices. Almost without exception, these have emphasized the notion of conformity, and from the moment of recruitment through induction and advanced training, military personnel have been conditioned to believe that these male traits and this concept of masculinity are desirable qualities. Hockey comments:

> This self-image is one which combines traditional masculine values with a competence in the techniques of survival and liquidation. Recruits perceive

themselves very much in the same fashion as the Corporal who saw that soldiers should be young and fit, rough and nasty, not powder puffs.[8]

One long-standing effect of this interpretation of the desired qualities of the traditional military image has been the opposition within the British military to any demonstration of homosexual tendencies. Those service personnel who have shown a sexual propensity for persons of their own gender have been thought to exhibit a pattern of behavior that contradicts the conventional identification of the idealized self-image. They have been seen to be deviants and the military has persistently taken draconian steps to ensure that such individuals do not form part of the military organization. This is not to deny that homosexuals were always found within military organizations. Nevertheless, deviant behavior was always punished on discovery and the British military continues to exercise a policy of exclusion, which contrasts markedly with the attitude toward the recruitment and retention of homosexuals adopted by other European armed forces.

Indeed, it has been claimed that current personnel policies breach legal and human rights. To take one example, it has been reported recently that in the Royal Navy, if officers suspect the sexual conduct of their personnel they can resort to invasive medical procedures in pursuit of their enquiries. It has been claimed that the legal basis of these procedures would be questionable if the United Kingdom possessed a Bill of Human Rights, and they in any case confirm that official policy is based on stereotypes and prejudice rather than well-informed analysis. Thus Stonewall has reported:

> Experienced medics are told men suspected of being the passive partner in a gay sex act can be spotted by their feminine gestures, clothes and make up. Senior officers are warned to be "on the alert" for servicemen who spend their time in clubs during shore leave as this is a tell tale sign. And they are warned sailors could get involved in gay sex if they seek out the "haunts of civilian homosexuals" and accept drinks and hospitality from them. The MoD tells the medics a thorough medical examination can be conducted immediately after gay sex has taken place because "homosexual acts are not in themselves life threatening" but they are warned that "homosexuals are often the source of sexually transmitted diseases" and that more than usual care is needed by the examiner.[9]

In addition, it is claimed that a good deal of scarce resources are being spent on investigating the sexual orientation of personnel even when actual or supposed homosexual relations are taking place between consenting adults off duty and off base.

In current circumstances, it is obviously difficult to establish the number of personnel in the U.K. services who experience the effects of the current policy toward homosexuals, but it is interesting to note that gay rights organizations have reported that many homosexual service personnel are, not surprisingly, reluctant to reveal their identity for fear of the consequences on their own careers and those of other personnel.

However, given that current policy is geared to the assumption that homosexuality is incompatible with service life, homosexual personnel are denied the social benefits or rights that are available for heterosexuals, such as pensions and housing benefits. Similarly, bearing in mind the number of personnel administratively discharged from the service on grounds of homosexuality (225 over three years from all three services from 1989 to 1991), it has also been argued that insufficient resources have been devoted to the resettlement of these individuals into civilian society.

Such personnel policies are thus deeply rooted in aspects of the organizational culture of the military. Whatever rules are adopted in regard to the homosexuality issue in the armed forces, any departure from current practice must manage the process of change by addressing problems of organizational and cultural resistance within the services.

Problems

Having discussed the development of policy toward homosexuality in the armed forces and the rationale underlying it, we now turn to the problems and controversies associated with the presence of homosexuals in the British military. These can be analyzed under two headings: social problems and medical problems.

Social Problems

The initial problem is derived from the status of the military as a disciplined organization. It is thought necessary that there should be cohesiveness and a proper sense of purpose among a group of service personnel if their morale is to be maintained in adverse conditions. Intimate personal relationships, whether heterosexual or homosexual, may affect that sense of cohesion and coincidentally affect the morale of the group. At the same time, behavior that affects traditional superior-subordinate relationships is considered to weaken the continuance of a preferred style of leadership, which skillfully blends the exercise of impartial authority with the maintenance of a sense of group camaraderie. The enduring and primary relationship between leader and led, implicit in the term, is thought to be at risk from the presence of homosexuals within a military unit.

The critical issue is the maintenance of small-group (unit) integrity and stability. The creation of a strongly cohesive unit is a major objective of many military training programs. Cohesive units tend to discourage members from belonging to autonomous groups with possibly deviant norms or from exhibiting a pattern of behavior that is considered to threaten the sense of cohesion. An important factor is the extent to which homosexuality whether overt or covert is deemed by group members to be "deviancy" or "threatening" behavior.

Hockey brings out very clearly the manner in which training practices within the British military bolster this sense of "belonging" to the small group.[10] As has been noted, many of these practices reinforce the perceived link between masculinity and military effectiveness; this link becomes the very basis of cohesiveness. Whether this should or should not be so is irrelevant; what is important is the reaction of individuals within the group, a group that on the streets of Northern Ireland may be as small as the "brick" of two men supporting each other on street patrol in a hostile environment. For these men, the critical variable is the ability to rely without question on the commitment of the other person, a commitment that is believed to be most evident in "a mate who is like I am."

A second no less important social problem is the violence and assaults that homosexuals may suffer. In the United Kingdom, as in most European countries, numerous incidents of anti-lesbian and anti-gay violence—"queer bashing"—are reported. Similar assaults occur in military organizations and, as in the parent society, they may lead to the death of the victim. While military law can deal with the problem of assault irrespective of the sexual orientations of those involved, such violence has a negative effect on the discipline and cohesion of the military unit. In recognition of this, some European armed forces, notably the Scandinavian and Dutch, have instituted major training programs designed to change the attitudes of those who are instrumental in promoting such violence. However, there seems to be little recognition within British armed forces of the problem of homophobic violence. The conclusion seemingly reached is that the way to avoid any potential problem is to remove the perceived cause of the problem. The exclusion of the homosexual reduces the possibility of tensions or acts of violence that adversely affect discipline, order, morale, trust, and confidence among service members or impair the system of rank and command.

A lesser form of homophobic violence is the sexual harassment to which individuals in the British military may be subject. A harassment Code of Practice was adopted in November 1991 in the European Community along with a European Commission Recommendation advocating supporting action by E.C. member states. The code aims to give "practical guidance" to employers, trade unions and employees on the "protection of the dignity of women and men at work." It seeks to "ensure that sexual harassment does not occur and, if it does occur, to ensure that adequate procedures are readily available to deal with the problem and prevent its recurrence." The code notes that "some specific groups are particularly vulnerable to sexual harassment," and that research indicates that lesbians and gay men are among the groups especially at risk of such harassment. The code adds: "It is undeniable that harassment on grounds of sexual orientation undermines the dignity at work of those affected and it is impossible to regard such harassment as appropriate workplace behaviour."

The extent, however, to which this Code of Practice is implemented within the British military is questionable. It would seem that policy continues to be based on the belief that the use of the normal legal process contained in the respective manuals of military law and exemplified by specific orders, regulations, and instructions is sufficient to deal with this problem.

Medical Problems

Social problems that center around issues such as cohesion, discrimination, group solidarity and so on are primarily subjective in nature. A more objective issue that has to be faced by the British military is the operational consequences of recruiting and retraining homosexuals within the military. Armed forces have a responsibility to ensure that their personnel are medically fit to undertake operational duties. For that reason, the military sets health criteria that it regularly monitors while coincidentally establishing programs of health care, the scope and nature of which far exceed the provision of civilian organizations. A rationale for this is derived from the nature of military service, which may involve postings overseas at short notice under adverse conditions, even if actual combat is not involved.

Underlying this concern with operational efficiency is the conclusion that personnel with certain medical conditions pose a major risk. The nature of this concern is summarized by the New Zealand Defence Forces (NZDF) as "having in the body organisms of causing illness."[11] This includes personnel who have such diseases or conditions as Acquired Immune Deficiency Syndrome (AIDS) and hepatitis B or C, illnesses that can inadvertently be transmitted through unscreened blood transfusions. The risk of this occurring is much greater in the British armed forces than in the general community because of the very nature of operational military service. Under certain conditions, particularly in combat situations, every British service person is a potential blood donor for another. While nonblood products are available for use in emergency situations, these are plasma expanders, which, while they are acceptable in the short term, do not replace blood.

Consequently, there are two problems: (1) the use of unscreened blood clearly presents a risk, and (2) rapid HIV testing is not appropriate for battlefield situations.

One solution is to submit all personnel to routine periodic HIV or hepatitis B/C testing. This is expensive and there is a danger of false positive/negative results. Even so, it can be argued that personnel should be tested for operational reasons. It is to be noted that the medical fitness of personnel for overseas duty under United Nations auspices is governed by U.N. rules. Under these rules, personnel must be tested before deployment and be HIV negative and hepatitis B/C negative.

The British government, however, has chosen to adopt a policy of recruitment and retention that seeks to minimize risk by excluding from military service certain individuals. First, these will include those, who irrespective of their sexual preference, are unable to meet the stipulated criteria of fitness for military service: military personnel who *inter alia* are infected with such diseases as AIDS, hepatitis B and C, and so on. This policy accords very closely with that adopted by other European states. What is more controversial is the second feature of British policy, whereby homosexuals are excluded from the military because of their homosexuality per se. This policy differs markedly, for example, from that adopted in Denmark, where it is argued:

> No specific health care initiatives are applied towards homosexuals. No military or civilian employees are requested to get an HIV test.

The Danish argument is that this particular illness, in common with other illnesses such as cancer, will affect the ability of the individual to perform a given task. When individuals are medically unfit for service, the normal processes of care and consideration take place. No special consideration will be given to a particular illness:

> Denmark recruits soldiers even if they state that they are HIV positive or have AIDS. The only question asked by the military organisation is, "Are you ill?"[12]

It can be argued that the British attitude in this context is contrary to those resolutions of the international community (e.g., Resolution 756 of the Council of Europe of October 1, 1981), which called on the World Health Organization to delete homosexuality from its international classification of diseases. Policy in the United Kingdom, however, appears to be based on the argument that the potential consequences of the noted medical conditions are not determined by the sexual orientation of the person concerned, for both heterosexuals and homosexuals may contract these particular illnesses. The issue is essentially one of fitness for military service. Risk-aversion theory would, however, suggest that the exclusion of homosexuals from military service would reduce the chance of a potential recruit or member of the military having, or developing, organisms that in causing illness would render the individual unfit.

Conclusions

It is the use of risk-aversion that characterizes the attitude of the British government to the recruitment and retention of homosexuals in the military. There is very little hard data to support the conclusions that are reached. According to Stonewall, although the Ministry of Defence has consulted the experience of other countries on the issue of homosexuality and the effectiveness of armed forces, the Ministry

> has never produced testimony from any of these countries to say that they have experienced any of the hypothetical difficulties which the MoD insist would follow if lesbians and gay men were allowed to serve.[13]

It is of particular interest to note that in the course of the Select Committee discussions, despite being repeatedly pressed on just this issue, the rationales and arguments outlined above concerning the negative impact of homosexual personnel on morals and discipline were defended by either anecdotal evidence or personal conviction.[14] It is not that these rationales are necessarily wrong or ill-founded but rather that, in regard to this issue as well as gender integration, policy needs to be guided by social scientific analysis of the links between personnel policy and operational effectiveness.

How much has British traditional policy changed? Clearly homosexuality has been decriminalized in the armed forces in the sense that homosexual activities of a type that are legal in civilian law should not constitute an offense under service law. This change echoes developments in other countries, not least the United States, where developments are watched closely by the MoD in formulating its own policy. However, for the time being, it remains the case that the MoD holds to the view that homosexual activities are incompatible with service in the armed forces. Until the amendment to the Sexual Offences Act of 1967 is implemented, decisions on the prosecution of personnel under existing legislation will be made on a case-by-case basis, presumably with the likelihood of prosecution being high only in the most serious of cases (as defined by the service offenses listed earlier).

To return to the distinction between disciplinary dismissals of homosexuals and administrative discharges, it remains the case that homosexuals will continue to be discharged on an administrative basis if they engage in homosexual activities, even if it is clear that no offense under service law has been committed. However, further policy changes are likely, not least because of current developments in the United States. In any case, in view of the Prime Minister's announcement in 1991 that, because of changes in social attitudes, homosexuality would no longer provide a bar to security clearance for members of the civil service, pressure groups such as Stonewall are now pressing for this policy to be extended to members of the armed forces.

Three policy options on homosexuality in the armed forces come to mind: (1) the reassertion of what might be called "traditional institutionalism," by maintaining the existing gay ban; (2) lifting the ban and instituting full equality regardless of openly declared sexual orientation; and (3) a compromise along the lines of the U.S. "don't ask, don't tell" scheme. This third option could either be a pragmatic solution for the indefinite future or linked with an explicit strategy of linking any shift in policy toward or away from option 2 to the outcome of a systematic research project on the relationship between homosexuality and operational effectiveness of military organizations.

We take the view that it will be difficult for the services to adopt option 1 given the current general shift away from core institutional military values, particularly as reflected in gender integration. Turning to option 2, this would institute the concept of full equality regardless of sexual orientation but may well, at least at this juncture, pose too radical a change for the services given the series of challenges they have to resolve whether in human resources, technology, or other fields. The question to be asked is: Would meeting the demands of one interest group be worth the disruption, or does this argument itself exaggerate the forces of resistance within the services?

Option 3, as sociologist James Burk has pointed out, means that homosexuals by being forced to remain silent about their orientation, although they would not be quizzed on the subject, would be denied benefits that they would be able to receive if they were allowed to openly declare their identities and have them accepted by their employers. Burk suggests that the "don't ask, don't tell" compromise could work from an administrative and disciplinary point of view if three rules were applied to sexual conduct in the service, whether or not it was of a homosexual kind:

> First, no unwanted sexual advances will be tolerated; second, the norm of privacy will be observed—this means that homosexual conduct, or more generally, oral and anal sex, will not be punished so long as it is done in private between consenting adults; and finally public conduct which demonstrably degrades unit effectiveness will be subject to administrative review and disciplinary action.[15]

Any sexually motivated act (whether of the homosexual kind or not) that demonstrably undermines the good order and effectiveness of a military unit would be subject to administrative or, in serious cases, disciplinary action on a case-by-case basis. The mere presence of personnel who are homosexually inclined would not ipso facto be the cause of such an action.

In all of this, what needs to be remembered is that the British armed forces are going through one of the most dramatic periods of change in their history, with adjustments to a radically different post–cold war strategic context at the same time as, at least to some, a bewildering series of personnel and organizational changes in order to adjust to the social values and expectations of the 1990s. The main problem is that these changes, stemming from the external strategic environment and the domestic social structure, are not occuring sequentially but simultaneously. As a result, the key is to create in quick time appropriate readjustments that do not damage operational effectiveness—or make the services feel that they are permanently under attack from outsiders who do not fully appreciate imperatives impinging upon them—but at the same time do not undermine the supportive links between the armed forces and society.

Notes

1. A major revue of information is the publication of the Stonewall group, a pressure group established to look after the interests of homosexuals who are members or former members of the British armed forces.

2. *Report of the Committee on Homosexual Offences and Prostitution* (also called the Wolfenden Report) (London: HMSO, 1957).

3. *Hansard* (June 17, 1991), 115–116.

4. Annex B to the *Report of the Select Committee on the Armed Forces Bill (1992)* (London: HMSO, 1992), 14.

5. *Hansard*, 116.

6. Ibid.

7. AR 135-175, *Separation of Officers*; AR 135-178, *Separation of Enlisted Personnel*.

8. John Hockey, *Squaddies: Portrait of a Subculture* (Exeter: Exeter University Press, 1986), 37–38.

9. Stonewall Group, press release, June 14, 1993.

10. Hockey, *Squaddies*.

11. Submission by Chief of New Zealand Defence Force, NZDF 1961 (12), to the Justice and Law Reform Select Committee (March 16, 1993), 3.

12. Statement of the Danish Surgeon-General, Knud Jessen, *Ekstrabladet*, 7 February 1993.

13. Stonewall, press release.

14. Select Committee Report; *Hansard*, 629–631.

15. James Burk, "Power, Morals and Military Uniqueness: Reflections on Banning Homosexuals from Military Service," *Society* (November/December 1993):29–36.

Chapter 14

Homosexuality and the Armed Forces in the Netherlands

MARION ANDERSEN-BOERS and JAN VAN DER MEULEN

"Homosexuals within the armed forces, would that be conceivable? Yes of course it would. Even more: it is a matter of course. Because the armed forces should represent society, shouldn't they? Yet a lot of people aren't sure whether this is a workable idea. A good reason to outline the argument and to get rid of hesitancies once and for all." A leaflet published by the Dutch Ministry of Defence opens with these sentences. The leaflet is an outcome and a symbol of government policy with regard to homosexuality. This policy aims not only at preventing and fighting discrimination, but also strives to bring about the cultural and social conditions under which homosexual men and women can be themselves in their daily lives, their workplaces included.

In this paper, we will describe and analyze the Dutch case with regard to homosexuality and the armed forces. Since 1974, sexual preference has no longer been a relevant category in defense personnel policies. For instance, sexual orientation is no longer used for selection purposes, whether for conscripts or career personnel. Since the mid-1980s, a far-reaching integration policy has been on the agenda. Measures have been taken on the one hand to guarantee the rights of homosexuals within the military and to lend assistance to them when necessary, and on the other hand to change the attitude and behavior of the heterosexual majority.

Dutch Society and the Emancipation Process

The way in which homosexuality is looked upon in Dutch society and the armed forces generally is the result of long-term historical processes. Throughout the ages gay men and lesbian women have been forced to live difficult lives. At worst they were persecuted, at best they were marginalized. Criminalizing was one of the strategies for stigmatizing homosexuality as deviant behavior. The other grand strategy, not yet vanished, was medicalizing homosexuality, i.e., "treating" it in the context of (mental) health and (mental) illness.

In the Netherlands the first homosexual rights movement began before World War I. It tried to create cultural and social equality for gays and lesbians by way of objective information to people in key positions, so-called emancipation from above. This approach achieved some modest successes but, in general, resistance toward homosexuality remained high. For good reasons, most homosexual men and women kept their sexual preference hidden. Of course, differences in degrees of tolerance existed between various strata of society.[1]

The cultural revolution of the 1960s, as a climax to long-term processes of secularization, democratization, and growing individualism, accelerated the acceptance of gays and lesbians. There were radical changes—at least at the level of discourse—in attitudes toward sexuality and the rise of a colorful and self-conscious gay liberation movement. The strategy now became one of emancipation from below, of demonstrating instead of consulting. Integration was still the overall goal but was no longer seen simply as a matter of adapting and accepting. At the same time, the movement became more diversified as a logical reflection of the heterogeneity in homosexual lifestyles.

In contemporary Dutch society, gays and lesbians can be more open about their sexual preferences than in the past. However, this frankness also makes them more vulnerable to discrimination, no longer as the category "gays and lesbians" but as individuals. Since about 1980 public opinion in the Netherlands has reached a virtual consensus about the position of homosexuals within society. In regularly conducted polls, more than 90 percent of the respondents agree with the statement, "Homosexuals should have as much freedom as possible to lead their own lives." Similar percentages show up with regard to equal rights for heterosexual and homosexual couples alike in matters of housing and inheritance. However, regarding adoption, a majority—53 percent—holds the opinion that homosexual couples should not have the same rights. This majority is shrinking; in 1980 it was 65 percent.

Despite this climate of tolerance toward gays and lesbians, experience suggests and research shows that many people "tolerate at a distance" without losing all their inner resistance toward individual homosexuals whom they encounter. This resistance mostly goes back to prejudices and stereotypes, general tolerance notwithstanding. Remnants of associating homosexuality with sin or sickness have not disappeared, especially among orthodox religious minorities. More common are prejudices against homosexuals that they are not "real" men or "real" women, and stereotypes of homosexual men as feminine gays and of lesbians as aggressive dykes. Especially among heterosexual men, the subconscious fear of becoming the object of homosexual desire can be stressful in face-to-face interaction. "Gay-bashing," in particular by male adolescents, still does exist.

In sum, without denying the existence as well as the importance of a tolerant public climate, living as a homosexual is not without problems, even in the Netherlands. Evidently, it makes a big difference where one lives, in terms of religious and regional surroundings, as well as in terms of socio-economic setting.

The process of societal change associated with the 1960s made urgent a different government policy with regard to homosexuality. The legal and political framework for governmental initiatives was a general antidiscrimination policy. As a concrete step in 1971, homosexual contacts between those more than sixteen years of age—as in the case of heterosexual relations— were no longer punishable. The first article of the constitution, formulated in 1983, stated: "In equal circumstances all persons . . . in the Netherlands shall be treated equally. Discrimination because of religion, political conviction, race, gender or on any other ground, is forbidden." Certainly discrimination because of sexual preference is implied. This constitutional article has been made more explicit and detailed by subsequent anti-discrimination laws.

Government policy aimed specifically at homosexuality has been formulated during the second half of the eighties, not in the least because of pressure from the gay liberation movement. This policy has a twofold aim: emphasizing the values and the self-identity of this particular group, as well as creating social and cultural room, by way of influencing its environment. In a concrete and practical way, projects have been developed to spread information, stimulate research, and professionalize counseling networks. This policy is conducted at a central governmental level, and is a municipal, provincial and departmental responsibility as well.

In the Netherlands, gay and lesbian emancipation policies are separated from AIDS policies. The latter aims at preventing the spread of AIDS as well as preventing the stigmatization of relatively high-risk groups such as homosexual men.

The Policy of the Armed Forces

Generally speaking, Defence Department policy with regard to homosexuality reflects overall government policy. This holds true for its content as well as its timing. As mentioned above, the military removed homosexuality during the 1970s as a basis for declaring inductees and personnel unfit to serve. The policy explicitly stated that there were no functional grounds for banning gays and lesbians from the armed forces. A working-group—Homosexuality and Armed Forces—was founded with conscripts as well as career personnel among its members. Its goal was to improve the climate for homosexuals within the armed forces.

A journalist, asked by the working group to do research on the subject, published a book revealing a number of sad and sometimes shocking experiences.[2] It had the merit of drawing public attention to the problem, and it underscored that much work remained to be done beyond policies of official admission and tolerance of homosexuals. In the 1980s, the working group changed into a union, the Homosexuality and Armed Forces Foundation, representing homosexual personnel in official and institutionalized contacts with the minister of defense. A departmental commission in which the union has its own official representative has been specifically assigned to watch closely the ongoing processes and to give advice on them.

In 1988 the minister of defense requested the Social Council for the Armed Forces, the official advisory board on issues of personnel and civil-military relations, to advise him further on policies concerning this issue. The council represents a broad spectrum of ideological, religious, and political views, as well as some vital institutions and organizations. Social scientists are present among its members. Traditionally the council advises on a unanimous basis. The council was specifically requested to advise on emancipation and integration of gays and lesbians in the armed forces, on the prevention of violence against them, and on the organization of counseling services. The minister accepted most of the recommendations.

In the meantime the independent Netherlands Institute for Social Sexological Research (NISSO) had been commissioned by the minister to conduct a major survey on homosexuals in the armed forces. We will summarize the most important results of this survey, though this somewhat violates the chronology because policy changes preceded the research. However, the latter gave the former its empirical justification.

Research Results

The research conducted by NISSO had two main objectives: first, to discover to what extent discriminatory attitudes are held by military personnel and whether discrimination against homosexuals actually occurs, second, to estimate if and how much discrimination hinders homosexuals in the performance of their military duties.

A representative sample of 1,238 male and 149 female personnel completed, on site, a precoded written questionnaire. In addition, in-depth interviews were held with some gays and lesbians. The response to the questionnaire was highly satisfactory. However, it proved quite difficult to trace gays and lesbians, and to persuade them to participate in the interviews. Using a wide variety of approaches, 49 gays and 16 lesbians were finally interviewed. Quantitatively, they cannot be considered representative of the gays and lesbians in the Dutch armed forces. Since all of them were officers or noncommissioned officers (NCOs), they also are not representative by rank.

According to the survey, 0.9 percent of the male and 3.5 percent of the female soldiers see themselves as (mainly) homosexual. Evidently, an unknown number of soldiers hide their sexual preference, so these percentages must be seen as bottom lines. Of those surveyed, 6.3 percent did not answer this question.

For the most part, the surveyed military personnel affirmed the civil rights of gays and lesbians in proportions similar to the high levels in the general public. Like the general population, service women were more tolerant of gays and lesbians than servicemen. However, this general tolerance was largely restricted to rights exercised at an "impersonal" level, such as open access to housing and the right to inherit.

In day-to-day contacts within the armed forces, heterosexual personnel, while generally accepting homosexuals as colleagues, preferred to keep gay men—and to a lesser extent lesbians—at a psychological and social distance. Servicemen were considerably more prone to stay aloof from homosexuals of their own sex than servicewomen. The more personal, rather than functional, the contact with gay or lesbian colleagues, the stronger this distancing tendency became. It was manifest in all branches of the forces, with no significant variations.

Respondents did not just keep their distance, they also enforced more narrow behavioral limits for homosexuals than for other colleagues. Putting an arm around a buddy, for instance, was said to be not uncommon in the military; however, such friendly behavior was hardly appreciated when coming from a gay colleague. Both male and female personnel tended to interact rather formally with gay and lesbian colleagues. This mode of association was more prominent among servicemen than -women.

Explicit aggressive acts against homosexuals happened only occasionally. However, almost half of the interviewed military personnel said that they "sometimes" or "frequently" heard negative statements about homosexuals in their unit. Of the male respondents, 30 percent said that they would react in a hostile or an aggressive manner if a colleague turned out to be homosexual. Only 22 percent of the male and 38 percent of the female military personnel reported that they would actively support a homosexual colleague who got into trouble because of her or his sexual preference. "I wouldn't want to get involved" typified the prevailing attitude. Women were more prepared to give support, but in view of the solitary positions that servicewomen generally occupy, their chances of actually being confronted with the victimization of a lesbian colleague were small.

No clear connection was found between the masculine image of the armed forces on the one hand and the attitude toward homosexuals on the other.

This suggests that an explanation for the lack of acceptance of homosexuals can neither exclusively nor primarily be found in the idea that homosexual men are not seen as "real men." Rather, heterosexuals tend to feel insecure and uncomfortable in the presence of homosexuals. These feelings must be seen in the context of stereotyping and prejudicing as described earlier.

Many homosexual personnel were afraid that their sexual preference could give rise to trouble. They did not have high hopes of being accepted by their colleagues—often they were the only "known one" in their units—and mostly they were satisfied if they did not encounter negative reactions. Nonetheless, most of them developed effective strategies to hold their own. Three strategies were found: masking, selective openness, and full openness. Individuals can, of course, change strategies during their careers. However, it would be virtually impossible to apply a masking strategy in a new environment, after having chosen one of openness at a previous post. The news would travel ahead of the individual.

No evidence was found that gays and lesbians were dissatisfied with their working environment. The opposite is the case. Not one of those interviewed expressed any disloyalty to the armed forces or to their unit. Apparently loyalty is a precondition for sustaining an enduring interest in a military function. Showing this loyalty is one way of keeping one's foothold. The researchers distinguished three aspects of loyalty: endorsement of the formal demands of military service, personal dedication to those formal demands, and acquiescence in the male heterosexual culture. The respondents do not contest that certain strict mental and physical demands must be met in order to fulfill a military function. One such demand is doing everything possible to be a "normal" soldier and a "good" soldier.

Against the background of these research findings, it is reasonable to expect that only the most highly motivated, loyal homosexuals will choose a career in the armed forces and persist in it. They have to try harder and pay a bigger price. Probably this is true for gays as well as lesbians, though not exactly along the same path. In the case of lesbians, additional factors appear to be at work. The main problem of lesbians is that of being accepted as a woman in a male-dominated environment. In this context their sexual identity is of secondary importance.

Current Policies

The minister of defense further evaluated and strengthened his policy in view of the NISSO research and its accompanying recommendations. In his most recent policy letter to the parliament, he referred to three broad insights won by the NISSO research:

(1) Within the armed forces, discrimination and blunt animosity towards homosexuals are rather unusual. However, a majority of men within the military

keep their homosexual colleagues at a distance. Serious incidents, seldom as they are, have to be seen against the background of this general climate.

(2) The general atmosphere within a unit is crucial for the attitudes towards homosexuals. This atmosphere is strongly influenced by the behavior and example of commanders and cadre. These personnel, however, show little inclination to deliberately improve the position of homosexuals.

(3) To some degree, these patterns can also be seen among female personnel. However, only a minority of the women keep lesbian colleagues at a distance. The problems of lesbians mainly overlap with the problems all women have in the armed forces: getting themselves accepted in an overwhelmingly male environment. (Women constitute roughly five percent of total personnel.)

These insights strengthened a policy aimed at promoting tolerance and integration. The point of departure was that the problem is not homosexuality as such but rather the reactions of others in the military environment. Patterns of stereotyping and labeling must be unlearned in order to give gays and lesbians the social and psychological room to function fully in a personal as well as a professional sense. It was seen as the organization's duty to create the conditions under which all individuals can function fully.

Coming out is a step only gays and lesbians themselves can take. Officially, they have been guaranteed that when they do, this will in no way impair their careers. Of course, whether in reality career impairment never takes place in informal and indirect ways is difficult to establish. Anecdotal evidence suggests that it does happen.

Against the background of these general points of departure and overall goals, we will describe existing and planned policies under four headings: training and counseling; information and advertising; policing and screening; and posting abroad, pensions, and housing.

Training and Counseling. A key policy initiative of the Department of Defense (DoD) is the inclusion of homosexuality as a topic in educational courses. DoD has developed readers on the topic and provided instructors extra training by professionals from gay rights organizations. To improve leadership qualities, the ministry is developing educational curricula for commanders at different levels and stages of their careers. The idea is to make officers and NCOs aware of their responsibilities in dealing with homosexuality. Attention is paid to the development of social and communicative skills and of language devoid of anti-homosexual and sexist overtones.

Evidently this training program, to be included at all educational levels, is not being implemented in all the armed forces at the same speed. In view of the rather huge task, priority is being given to training the teachers and the leaders, the former by way of "interactive methods." Of the three services, only the air force has implemented full-scale training taught by experts from outside the military. The army and the navy are developing their own curricula, to be taught by military (semi-)experts, for instance, chaplains of the different denominations trained by outside experts. The expectation is that all those in a counseling role will have taken these courses within the next two years.

There is one central office in the military where expertise from various sources is brought together. This office provides the information required to lend assistance to homosexual servicemen and -women. There is also an emergency telephone number for the counseling of homosexual personnel. To make the emergency phone number as widely known as possible, posters are displayed throughout the armed forces. A specific procedure is under development for complaints about sexual harassment, whether of a hetero- or of a homosexual nature.

Information and Advertising. Projects with regard to training and counseling are being supported by information activities. For instance, the Defence Information Service (DIS) has published and distributed a leaflet on homosexuality in the armed forces. DIS is also preparing a leaflet to inform personnel where to go with problems, including ones related to homosexuality.

In recruiting and advertising, especially at leadership level, it is emphasized that the armed forces are a heterogeneous lot, and that anyone who wants to join should have a tolerant outlook, as well as accompanying communicative skills. Key figures in the organization express themselves publicly in favor of a gay and lesbian rights policy. This has made clear, more emphatically than before, that gays and lesbians are welcome to the armed forces. The Netherlands navy has started to realize this intention by publishing an article in the periodical *Alle Hens* (*All Hands*), in which the commander of the Netherlands navy presented the policy plan, "Homosexuality in the Royal Netherlands Navy." The minister himself has given several interviews to newspapers, journals, and television to explain his policy. So far only the air force has placed recruiting advertisements in the *Dutch Gay Journal*.

Policing and Screening. The military police (MP) has a special position within the context of homosexuality and the armed forces: On the one hand, it is part of the organization in which gay rights policy is applicable; on the other, it has an executive task in the fight against discrimination and violence against gays and lesbians. The role of the military police in the fight against anti-homosexual violence is partly determined by the willingness of victims to report offenses. In Dutch society there is still little willingness to do so, and there is no reason why this should be different within the armed forces. To enhance reporting, the military police are informed about the grave consequences of anti-homosexual violence. The MPs will be trained in the specific treatment this kind of victim requires.

With regard to screening for security purposes, the officially stated policy is that no distinction is made between heterosexual and homosexual personnel. According to the directives of the Military Intelligence Service, only information relevant to a specific function or position may be collected. This is carefully monitored. Sexual behavior is only relevant when it makes the person liable to blackmail. When gays and lesbians are not forced to lead a double life, but instead can come out without fear, they can no longer be blackmailed. This is a position the minister of defense officially and emphatically has taken.

If homosexual conscripts have reasons to believe they cannot cope within the armed forces, they can be exempted. Until recently this was done on medical grounds, but now a more general category for exemption is used without stigmatizing consequences. Psychologists have been appointed to the draft boards to give advice about the placing of homosexual conscripts who are willing to serve.

Posting Abroad, Pensions, and Housing. Increasingly Dutch soldiers participate in joint operations, especially under the United Nations flag. Of course it is recognized that in some other countries and armies, the presence of homosexuals is not taken for granted. Hence, homosexual personnel are briefed about the circumstances and reactions they might encounter. They are advised to be discrete and low-profile about their homosexuality. Nevertheless, Dutch policy is that there should be no obstacle for gays or lesbians to serve under foreign commands.

Official legal equality does not preclude the possibility of unofficial discrimination. For instance, anecdotal evidence has it that a gay soldier did run into difficulties while being posted at the Dutch West Indies. That he took his partner with him, perfectly in accordance with housing rules, obviously annoyed the local authorities. They chose not to prolong his partner's visitor's permit and took intervention at the highest level to undo this measure.

One problem brought up in relation to posting abroad, especially because of the extra risks, is that of pensions. For several years, certain pension funds in the Netherlands have introduced so-called partner pensions. These apply to nonmarried couples, whether hetero- or homosexual, who have declared a status of "living together" in a notarized statement. However, until now, the pension fund for government employees, the military included, has not offered the option of a partner pension. So far, political as well as union-based pressure has not been effective in changing this. Inheritance and adoption are other instances in which the legal status of hetero- and homosexuals is not yet equalized.

Conclusion

In the Dutch armed forces, as in Dutch society, there is a gap between the official emancipated view on homosexuality—shared by public opinion—

and day-to-day interaction between heterosexuals and homosexuals. The existence of such a gap is confirmed by research, and bridging this gap is the ultimate goal of the integration policies.

Consequently, an active antidiscrimination policy is more or less in full swing to achieve attitudinal and behavioral change. This can be said for the Netherlands in general, and for the Dutch armed forces in particular. Discrimination is not really the issue at this point. Rather, the issue now is how to reach and change latent and subtle forms of gossip, (verbal) abuse, and ostracization that can be painful and damaging to those seeking to be good soldiers. In short, changing "ground level" homo-hetero interaction is at stake. How effective this program will be should become clear in two or three years, when the military conducts its follow-up evaluation.

The international debate on homosexuals within the armed forces often focuses on the supposedly unique characteristics of the military as a work environment. In this kind of semitotal institution, the typical argument goes, the interaction between members can be intense and at times intimate. Conditions of forced intimacy (sharing a pup tent, showering and the like) could make the presence of gays and lesbians disruptive or, under fire, even dangerous. Therefore, the military cannot live with homosexuals, the argument goes, nor can it afford the luxury of a "social experiment."

The typical "official" Dutch answer would be that this kind of reasoning can be traced back to stereotyping and to a lack of knowledge. The result is a self-fulfilling prophecy: When the gay or lesbian is ostracized, indeed unit cohesion is strained. However, Dutch policy suggests, this self-fulfilling circle should not be broken by banning homosexuals in the armed forces— which is impossible anyway—but on the contrary, by stimulating a general change in climate and behavior. Admittedly, this is not an easy, let alone quick, process. Forcing the issue could even be counterproductive. Certainly, the existing embarrassment and reluctance among heterosexual personnel should not be derogated or pushed aside as just being old-fashioned.

However, the heterosexual majority should accept that gays and lesbians who are motivated to serve and who fit all the criteria do belong in the armed forces. This is the official standpoint of the Dutch minister of defense in accordance with government policy in general. "Homosexuals within the armed forces, would that be conceivable? Yes of course it would. Even more: it is a matter of course."

Clearly enough, this official position is somewhat unique and more or less sets apart Dutch policies (along with those of Denmark). Although more countries (Canada, Australia, and Israel) have recently accepted, de facto and de jure, homosexuals within the military, active integration policies have not been widespread. So a very relevant question is: Why did it come about in the Netherlands? In the remaining paragraphs we will briefly analyze what we consider to be an important explanatory variable: civilianization as a basic

doctrine regarding the military. We will also discuss the possible consequences of the abolition of the draft for civilianization in general and for
minority policies and practices in particular.

Basically two (sets of) variables are crucial for explaining and understanding why and how Department of Defence policies toward homosexuals came
about. One has to do with government policy and public climate in general.
Broadly speaking, Dutch society has been characterized, especially since the
1960s, by a tolerant stand toward homosexuals. As we emphasized, the
quality of hetero-homo interaction in everyday life suggests that we characterize it as tolerance at a distance. Nevertheless, the importance of this
public feeling should not be underestimated. Together with anti-
discrimination legislation and de jure and/or de facto equal treatment of
homosexuals in all kinds of settings, this climate functions as a normative
context. Among other things, this context precludes viewing the integration
policies of the armed forces as a kind of social experiment.

The other crucial variable precluding this view is the policy of civilianizing
the armed forces as much as possible. Since the 1960s, this policy has been
pursued rather consistently. "As civil as possible, as military as necessary"
has been a motto that guided this process. If not a catalyst of social change,
certainly the Dutch armed forces have tried to follow and implement social
change. In fact, with regard to the integration of homosexuals, the defense
department is ahead of other departments of the Dutch government as well
as ahead of most of the nonmilitary world of trade and industry.

One may speculate about why this happens to be so, and certainly an
intricate explanatory web of variables and processes could be spun. A hy-
pothesis about the advantage of catching up with social change might be
defended. To put it otherwise, the armed forces must often strive consciously
to instill in their own ranks the civil norms binding in other settings. This
does not happen automatically. Therefore, we should not overlook the inter-
mediary or contingent factors between a tolerant societal climate and civilianized armed forces. For example, without the activism of gay soldiers
themselves—such as the Foundation for Homosexuals within the Armed
Forces—policies would not be as they are. The same can be said about the
active role played by the present-day minister of defense.

Like most armed forces in the Western world—not to speak of the former
East—the Dutch military is involved in a process of fundamental organizational change. It is not just a matter of downsizing. It involves a radical
redefinition of tasks and means. The decision on January 1, 1988, to abolish
the draft and to switch to an all-volunteer force is a paramount symbol of this
break in the military history of The Netherlands.

Certainly this new military will be different also in terms of mentality,
sphere, and presentation. It is hard to predict though to what degree and in
which direction these kind of changes will lead. On the one hand, there

might be some sort of traditionalist backlash seeking to do away with the supposedly sloppy sides of civilianization. Such a reaction probably would seek to reinstall classical "soldierly virtues." This might call for more discipline and uniformity (lack of diversity) than an all-volunteer force could afford. On the other hand, some "progressives" seek a more extensive cultural shake-up in the military modeled after the latest management insights. It will be interesting and important to see which one of these two impulses is going to have the stronger impact on the overall image of the Dutch armed forces.

Of course, we wonder what effect the new military will have on minority policies and practices. We suspect that the general effect will be marginal. For one thing, minority policies, in particular gay policies, are well-grounded, institutionalized, and guarded. For another, the ideal of a civilianized armed forces will be cherished as the crux of Dutch civil-military relations. A traditionalist backlash would never be so radical as to undo the essence of this ideal.

Crucial for any all-volunteer force is the success of recruitment at all levels. Research suggests that the army will have a difficult time finding its soldiers in the labor market. Incentives of a financial and educational nature will have to be used, and minority recruiting will become important. Women and ethnic minorities are clearly underrepresented in the armed forces and certainly they are going to be targeted in future recruitment efforts. Advertising will increasingly emphasize the heterogeneous character of the military. Managers of violence have to be at the same time have to be managers of diversity. All this could have a positive spin-off for the position as well as the number of homosexuals within the military.

Notes

1. R. Tielman, *Homoseksualiteit in Nederland. Studie van een emancipatiebeweging* (Amsterdam, 1982).

2. M. Bullinga, *Het leger maakt een man van je. Homoseksualiteit, disciplinering en seksueel geweld* (Amsterdam, 1984).

PART V

Implications for Policy

Chapter 15

Evolving Perspectives on the Military's Policy on Homosexuals: A Personal Note

LAWRENCE KORB

Introduction

For the past five years, the Department of Defense (DoD) policy, which excludes homosexuals from serving in the armed forces, has been a subject of intense debate within the military, the government, and the nation. Beginning in the last half of the 1980s, an increasing number of distinguished and decorated homosexual members of the armed forces publicly came out of the closet to challenge the policy. Television news programs, like "Nightline," devoted entire shows to the subject, and editorials in major newspapers, like the *New York Times*, criticized the policy. The debate reached a crescendo in November 1992, when President-elect Bill Clinton stated, two days after his election, that he would in fact keep his campaign promise to lift the ban on gay men and lesbians serving in the military.

Clinton's statements aroused the opposition of many members of the body politic, the Joint Chiefs of Staff and many in Congress, including Senator Sam Nunn (D-Ga), the powerful chairman of the Senate Armed Services Committee, and one-time Clinton ally on the Democratic Leadership Council (DLC). During the transition, Nunn informed the President that if he issued an executive order lifting the ban, he would ask the Congress to enshrine the ban into law. Clinton then asked that congressional action be delayed for six months while Secretary of Defense Les Aspin and the Joint Chiefs of Staff worked out a plan for changing the existing policy.

Clinton hoped that during those six months, the issue of gays in the military would recede from public view. The opposite occurred. The subject of gays in the military consumed more public attention during those six months than such critical issues as the economy, health care, and the war in Bosnia. No matter where President Clinton went and no matter which subject he wished to address, he received questions about gays in the military. Indeed, even at his press conference concluding the G7 meeting in Tokyo in early July 1993, Clinton was asked whether he intended to lift the ban.

Finally, on July 19, 1993, in a speech at the National Defense University, President Clinton announced an "honorable compromise" on the issue. Enlistees would no longer be asked about their sexual orientation and would be allowed to serve as long as they kept their sexual orientation to themselves. Not surprisingly, Clinton's compromise pleased no one, and in the days following his speech, there was considerable confusion about how the policy would actually be implemented in the field. As one analyst noted the policy could be labeled "don't ask, don't tell, don't pursue—and don't read the fine print."[1]

For me, this whole debate was more than academic. From May 1981 through September 1985, I had served as assistant secretary of defense for manpower, reserve affairs, installations and logistics (MRAI&L). During that period, I had promulgated the DoD directive governing the separation from active duty of homosexuals (Directive No 1332.14 of January 28, 1982). After leaving the Pentagon, I had testified or given depositions for nearly a dozen men and women who were being forced to leave the military because of their sexual orientation rather than violating any norms of conduct. In addition, I was asked to testify for five hours on the issue before the Senate Armed Services Committee in March 1993. Moreover, I discussed and debated the issue nearly a hundred times on radio and television. Finally, in his speech announcing the "honorable compromise," President Clinton referred to me and my views on the ban.

Over the past decade, my own views on this subject have changed considerably and I now feel that the nation and the military would be best served by dropping the ban entirely. In the following pages, I will attempt to outline the reasons for these changes, as well as try to frame the debate that occurred during the first six months of the Clinton presidency. But, before I do that, I need to put that entire subject in its proper historical context.

Origins of the Current Policy

There are two myths about the policy Bill Clinton promised to overturn during his campaign. The first myth is that the U.S. military has always excluded homosexuals. The second myth is that the conservative (homophobic?) Reagan administration strengthened the policy of excluding homosexuals from the military.

The fact is that for most of our history, military law and regulations did not even address homosexuality. Article 125 of the Uniform Code of Military

Justice, which specifically bans sodomy, was not enacted until 1951. Thousands of homosexuals served without difficulty and with distinction in World Wars I and II. Indeed, until the post-World War II period, military regulations on administrative separation gave commanders discretion to separate individuals for ineptness or undesirable habits or traits. Although some homosexuals were discharged on this basis, homosexuality itself was not listed as an undesirable trait.

From the end of World War II through the mid-1970s, the policy against gays became more and more restrictive. It shifted from treatment (homosexuality was considered an illness) and retention to separation. However, until early 1981, the final decision on separation of an individual serviceman or -woman was a matter of command discretion rather than mandatory policy.

The policy that made separation of homosexuals mandatory was promulgated by the Carter administration, less than a week before it left office. On January 16, 1981, Deputy Secretary of Defense Graham Claytor changed DoD policy to say that "homosexuality is incompatible with military service." Claytor wanted to ensure that homosexuals were kept out of the armed forces and that they would be separated promptly if discovered.

The change in the policy came as a result of a nearly four year review of DoD policies. This review was necessitated by two factors. First, the existing policies were being applied inconsistently between and among the services. Some units were automatically separating gays and lesbians while others were keeping some and separating others. Second, this inconsistent application of policies was causing problems in the courts. In several court cases, DoD was asked to provide detailed reasons for not exercising the discretion to retain. Indeed, Claytor noted that his new policy should enable DoD to sustain its position in courts.[2]

The real question is why did a president with a strong commitment to civil liberties, like Jimmy Carter, allow such a discriminatory policy to be enacted? According to individuals in the Department of Justice, with whom I discussed this subject, Carter's attitude toward national security changed in 1979, as a result of the Soviet invasion of Afghanistan, and the seizure of our hostages in Iran. To demonstrate that he was a hard liner on defense issues as well as a strong supporter of the military, Carter reinstituted draft registration, raised military spending substantially, and allowed the Pentagon to get "tough on gays."

Ironically, the Joint Chiefs of Staff thought that Claytor's new policy was too liberal because it said that the mere fact that an individual had a homosexual orientation should not be grounds for a less than honorable discharge. Indeed they tried to delay Claytor's policy until the hard-liners from the incoming Reagan administration took over.

I was one of those hard-liners who came to the Pentagon in 1981. To me and my office fell the task of rewriting the directive to implement Claytor's policy. None of my bosses (the secretary of defense or his deputy) showed any interest in changing the Carter policy, and indeed it would have been pretty difficult to convince the Reagan White House that Carter had been too tough on gays. Nor did there seem to be any support on the Hill or in the country in 1981 for allowing gays and lesbians to serve. Not even groups like the ACLU, which sent a representative to speak to me about changing Carter's policy of draft registration, complained about the new policy. Most individuals with whom I consulted in the Pentagon said that the new policy was merely a "legally correct" version of longstanding DoD practice. My own attention was directed to what appeared to be more pressing manpower issues like raising the quality of our volunteers (in 1980 the educational and aptitude levels of our new recruits were at dangerously low levels) and preventing the services from rolling back the gains that women had made in the 1970s. (In March 1980, the army's deputy chief of staff for personnel announced a pause in recruiting women for the army, without consulting me or anyone else in the office of the secretary of defense.)

I never imagined that this new policy would initiate an unprecedented era of witch-hunts to flush out these "undesirables." I did, however, resist pressure from the military chiefs to eliminate the honorable discharge provision for those individuals separated for homosexual orientation alone. Finally, I hoped that the courts might save us (the military) from ourselves by forcing us to focus on an individual's behavior, rather than orientation. The directive itself was issued on January 28, 1982, about one year after Claytor changed the policy, and was never ruled on by a court until twelve years later. In the court cases between 1981 and 1993, the courts either deferred to the military or made their decisions on narrow grounds.

Changes in My Own Thinking

Between 1982 and my departure from the Pentagon in 1985, there were at least two occasions when I had some serious pause about the real implications of Claytor's policy and my directive. In early 1983, I learned from a Colman McCarthy column in the *Washington Post* that air force Lieutenant Joann Newark was serving seven years at hard labor in the military prison in Leavenworth, Kansas. Her "crimes" were consensual sex with another woman in the privacy of her own off-base bedroom, and possession of an amphetamine. Not only was the sentence out of proportion to her alleged offenses, but these offenses were not even crimes in New York where the court-martial was held. Moreover, Newark was given the opportunity to resign if she would accept a bad conduct discharge. I called the secretary of the air force about the severity of the sentence and the offer of the bad conduct discharge.

A short time later, Lt. Newark was released from prison. (In 1986, her conviction was overturned by an appeals court.)

Second, in early 1985, a number of highly publicized spy cases came to light. Navy petty officer John Walker confessed to passing sensitive information about U.S. submarines to the Soviet Union; navy civilian Jonathan Pollard was arrested for passing classified information to the Israelis; and CIA employee, Larry Wu Tai Chin was accused of giving the Chinese government classified information. These three men had two things in common. They received money for spying and they all had obtained high-level security clearances based upon extensive background investigations.

As a result of these incidents, the secretary of defense established a task force to examine, among other things, the criteria by which individuals obtained these security clearances. As a member of the task force, I urged the group to conduct serious empirical research on what constituted a security risk. It seemed to me that the existing procedures focused too much on the person's sexual life and not enough on such areas as an individual's financial health. Eventually the task force recommended establishing a research facility in Monterey, California to study personnel security breaches. In 1987, this Defense Personnel Research and Education Center (PERSEREC) was directed to examine, among other things, homosexuality as a condition related to trust violation.

PERSEREC chose Ted Sarbin, professor emeritus from the University of California at Berkeley, and Kenneth Karols, a navy captain and resident psychiatrist, to conduct the study. Sarbin and Karols quickly concluded that trust or security risk was also related to a larger question, namely, the suitability of homosexuals for military service. Thus, when Sarbin and Karols completed their study in December 1988, they commented both on security and suitability. They found unequivocally that gay men and lesbians pose no security risk and are every bit as suitable for military service as heterosexuals.[3]

The Pentagon reacted angrily to the study, telling PERSEREC director Carson Eoyang that he had exceeded his authority. Officials in the office of the secretary of defense labeled the report as a draft, so that it would not have to be released to the public, and directed PERSEREC to redo the report omitting the section on suitability. In the fall of 1989, I became aware of these sorry episodes and after appealing to my successor in DoD to release the whole report, decided to become actively involved in the public debate over the issue.

For me, the PERSEREC report was clearly the straw that broke the camel's back. The Newark sentence was clearly cruel and unusual punishment. At worst she should have been discharged. Instead she received a sentence more appropriate for high treason. The spy cases showed that DoD was so hung up on sexual orientation and activity that they were missing the forest on account of the trees. Had Walker's background investigations even suggested he was a gay, he would have been put out of the navy or into the brig. But since he was straight, none of the naval investigators checked his life-style, his bank accounts, or his credit card bills.

However, the PERSEREC report provided compelling, empirical evidence that there was no good reason to exclude gays and lesbians. As a social scientist trained to let research impact policy, I found it unthinkable that Pentagon leaders would try to shoot the messenger. It made me realize once and for all that this was a clear case of blind prejudice and bigotry rather than a readiness issue, and that I had to do something about it or I could not call myself a social scientist, or live up to my obligations as a former public official.

My involvement took the form of media debates with such people as Representative Robert Dornan (R-Calif.) and Lt. Gen. Thomas Kelly, Colin Powell's deputy for operations (and media briefer during the Gulf War); speeches before such groups as the Human Rights Campaign Fund; editorials critical of the Pentagon's civilian leadership on this subject; and lobbying such public figures as then chairman of the House Armed Services Committee, Representative Les Aspin (D-Wisc.). In addition, I worked with the lawyers defending those military people challenging the ban here and in Canada.

During the period from 1989 to 1992, several things became clear to me. First, the PERSEREC reports were not the first ones that the Pentagon had buried. In 1957, navy captain, S. H. Crittenden, Jr., completed a 639-page report on the navy's policies toward homosexuals. Crittenden concluded that there is no correlation between homosexuality and suitability or attainment. Some twenty years later the chief of naval personnel replied in the negative when he was asked by the navy's judge advocate general whether the navy had any empirical proof that homosexuality in the navy has an adverse effect on mission completion.[4] Reports like this came to light only through pretrial discovery proceedings. I was never made aware of them in my years in the Pentagon.

Second, the Claytor policy of excluding gays was doomed. The only question was when. American public opinion was changing; state and local laws were changing; and other countries, including most of our NATO allies and Israel, allowed gays to serve openly. In 1992, Canada and Australia, former English colonies like us, dropped their bans. The courts were becoming less willing to accept the ban at face value. Major corporate law firms began representing homosexual members of the armed forces challenging the ban. Indeed, on January 29, 1993, a federal district judge in California found no rational basis for the policy, declared the ban unconstitutional, and ordered the navy to reinstate an openly gay petty officer, Keith Meinhold.[5] However, I never expected the issue to come to a head so quickly.

The 1993 Debate

During the presidential campaign, Bill Clinton made over one hundred specific promises. None received less attention before the election, nor more after it, than his promise to end the ban on gays in the military.

I first heard about Clinton's promise in January 1992 when a reporter called to get my reaction to his statement on the issue, which Clinton made at a forum at Harvard's Kennedy School of Government. I subsequently learned that he had first addressed the issue in October 1991 at a luncheon with twenty gay donors.[6] Clinton publicly reiterated his promise at least two more times during the campaign, once at a dinner in Hollywood and once at a town meeting in Seattle when Col. Greta Cammameyer asked him about it. At that time, Col. Cammameyer was being separated from the Army National Guard for admitting to a defense investigator, in the course of a routine background check, that she was a lesbian.

Political candidates routinely make promises that they do not keep. Candidate Clinton, for example, promised to cut taxes for the middle class. President Clinton decided to try to keep his promise on gays for several reasons.

First, if Clinton stands for anything, it is nondiscrimination or civil rights, the pivot point of politics during his upbringing in Arkansas. As a governor, he was in the forefront of obtaining equal opportunity for African-Americans and women. He also tried unsuccessfully to push a gay rights bill through the Arkansas legislature. Moreover, he had made this promise to the gay leaders in October 1991 without any prompting or lobbying because this was not a big concern of gay leaders, many of whom were involved in the peace movement.

Second, he underestimated the political and public opposition to the proposal. Since the Republicans did not raise the issue of gays in the military in the campaign, Clinton mistakenly believed that it was not a controversial proposal. He failed to realize that the Republicans never made a big issue of this because their convention in Houston had backfired on the question of cultural values. Clinton also failed to realize that Senator Nunn and Gen. Colin Powell were not just "Washington bureaucrats." Nunn is "Mr. Defense" on the Hill. Democrats and Republicans alike take their cues on defense issues from the Georgia legislator because of his expertise, independence, and long involvement with national security. Similarly, Powell is the most charismatic and well-connected military leader since Douglas Mac-Arthur. The Harlem-born general captured the imagination of the American public during the Gulf War for the Horatio Alger quality of his life, and his military expertise. Moreover, since he had served as President Reagan's assistant for national security affairs, he was wise in the ways of the media and the Congress.

Third, Clinton ran a very specific issue-oriented campaign and he detailed hundreds of these promises in a book called *Putting People First*. Moreover, since he does not appear to have any core political identity, he is defined by his promises. But, after being elected he was forced to renege on many of these campaign promises. Therefore, Clinton needed to point to at least one specific but difficult promise he kept, if he were not to destroy his political viability. Every president gets tested in his early days in office by the bureaucracy and the Congress. For example, the air traffic controllers dared Reagan to fire them in the early days of his administration. Similarly, the Senate let Bush know that it would not confirm John Tower, his original nominee for secretary of defense, but Bush refused to withdraw the nomination.

Clinton also failed to understand that while it was primarily a civil rights issue for him, others saw different sides of the issue, and that there was little room for an honorable compromise between these competing views. For the Joint Chiefs of Staff, the ban on gays was a readiness issue. They feared that the introduction of openly gay men and lesbians would create a controversy over the issue of privacy and undermine the morale and unit cohesion necessary for combat effectiveness, because military personnel are intolerant of homosexuality (about 75 percent opposed Clinton's position on the issue.[7] The military leaders were already concerned about the turbulence being caused by downsizing the armed forces by 25 percent. Moreover, the chiefs had also resisted the integration of blacks and the expansion of opportunities for women on virtually the same grounds. They personify the principle of the dangerous precedent enunciated by F. M. Cornforth: "Nothing should ever be done for the first time."[8]

For Senator Nunn, it was a question of the prerogatives of the Congress. The Constitution (Article I, Section 8) gives the Congress the power to raise and support armies and to provide and maintain a navy and to make rules for the government and regulation of the land and naval forces. For example, Congress prohibits women from serving in many combat positions and establishes the educational and aptitude requirements for new recruits. To allow President Clinton, or any president, to make such a monumental change as allowing openly gay people to serve by means of an executive order would in Nunn's view undermine Congress's ability to control the armed forces in the future.

For the gay community, allowing openly gay men and lesbians to serve in the armed forces meant their full acceptance by society. It was not so much that large numbers of gays and lesbians wanted to serve in the military, it was that they wanted the opportunity. Service in the military was, after all, a vehicle for black Americans and immigrants to prove that they were full-fledged Americans. Any compromise on this issue was like being a little bit pregnant. Either you were a full-fledged American or you were not.

Finally, for a small but vocal and strongly committed group of people, admitting gays into the military was a moral issue. For these people, homosexuality is a moral aberration, and any governmental action that appears to sanction the gay life-style is a moral abomination. Presidential power, congressional prerogatives, and unit cohesion are mere abstractions. The issue for them is morality. As "evidence" for their position they point to studies that show gays are more promiscuous, more inclined toward alcoholism, and more likely to be suicidal than other groups in society.[9]

Lessons

There are several lessons that can be drawn from this unhappy episode. They can be placed into six categories.

First, the military has and will continue to be a reflection of society. Despite what many military people believe, the armed forces exist not to defend a piece of geography, but a way of life. As society's attitudes toward the role of women and minorities in the workplace and conscription changed, the military had to accommodate these changes. Similarly, as openly gay men and lesbians become more accepted by society, and as scientific research demonstrates that homosexuality is nonpathological, not chosen, and immutable, the military must accommodate the homosexuals.

Second, the power of a president is limited both by the Constitution and by his own history. Clinton ran into resistance from a powerful senator and a legendary chairman of the JCS. While the American public did not focus during the campaign on Clinton's promise to end the ban on gays, they did note his lack of military experience. Therefore, Clinton had to confront not only the resistance of the Congress and the bureaucracy, but his own past. If Senator Bob Kerry (D-Neb.), Medal of Honor winner in Vietnam, had been elected, Nunn and Powell would have been far less willing to challenge him openly. In many ways, Clinton was the worst person to try to end the ban. Just as only Nixon could go to China, only a military hero or a strong supporter of the military could change such an entrenched policy without provoking a strong backlash.

Third, in order to fulfill controversial campaign promises, presidents must move quickly and forcefully. Had Bill Clinton signed the executive order during the inaugural parade, and dared Congress to override a presidential veto, there's a reasonable chance he would have prevailed. With a fifty-three to forty-seven majority in the Senate, and the likely support of at least four Republicans on the issue (D'Amato, Chafee, Cohen, Kassenbaum), he would have needed only thirty Democratic votes to prevail. The Congress was never able to override George Bush's vetoes of a provision in the Defense Authorization Bill that would have allowed military women to have abortions at their own expense at overseas military hospitals. Similarly, the Congress never even attempted to overturn Jimmy Carter's order granting amnesty to Vietnam draft evaders, which was signed literally before Carter left the reviewing stand on Inauguration Day in 1977. Indeed, Clinton himself signed an executive order ending the gag order on abortion counseling at federally financed clinics immediately upon taking office.

Fourth, empirical evidence or systematic research and analysis has very little impact on such controversial and emotional issues as gays in the military. Since the military leadership was against admitting gays, it ignored the Crittenden and PERSEREC reports. Similarly, during the six months leading up to the "honorable compromise," it gave no credence to a Rand report commissioned by Secretary Aspin, because this 518-page report, the most comprehensive treatment of the subject to date, concluded that military commanders should not consider sexual orientation by itself as germane to determining who may serve in the military.[10] This is especially ironic since Rand, a Pentagon creation, has helped DoD select targets for nuclear weapons, the appropriate mix of land- and sea-based strategic platforms, and the balance between active and reserve forces. Retired admiral William Crowe, Powell's predecessor as Chairman of the JCS, noted that arguments against allowing homosexuals in the armed forces are generated more by emotion than reason.[11]

Fifth, public officials need to be much more willing to challenge the accepted wisdom of the bureaucracy. I should have asked many more questions about the Carter policy, and should have sought out gay and lesbian leaders before signing the implementing directive. The Claytor policy was not merely a codification of existing practice, but a hunting license for military leaders to ferret out anyone suspected having a homosexual orientation.

Sixth, on certain issues of principle, the compromise between right and wrong is not morally correct (honorable). Lasting moral victories cannot be won by clever political compromises. If excluding a person on the basis of race, creed, color, religion, gender, or sexual orientation is wrong, then it is not honorable to say you will not be excluded as long as you deny who you are. If Bill Clinton believes what he said in the campaign, and in his speech on July 19, 1993, that discrimination on the basis of sexual orientation is wrong, he should not have taken halfway measures. As one author has noted, the real winners in this battle were the generals and admirals and their allies who harnessed their fears and ours.[12]

Notes

1.   Thomas Friedman, "Clinton's Gay Policy: Cave in or Milestone," *New York Times*, 25 July 1993.

2.   The history of the policy of the U.S. Government toward homosexuals in the military is outlined in several places. See, for example, David F. Burrelli, *Homosex-*

uals and U.S. Military Policy, CRS Report for Congress, 93-52F (January 14, 1993); Remarks of Senator Sam Nunn (D-Ga.), *Congressional Record—Senate* (January 27, 1993), 755; and Randy Shilts, *Conduct Unbecoming: Gays and Lesbians in the U.S. Military* (New York: St. Martin's, 1993).

3.   Theodore Sarbin and Kenneth Karols, *Nonconforming Sexual Orientations and Military Suitability* (Pers-TR-89-002), Defense Personnel Security Research and Education Center, December 1988.

4.   Shilts, *Conduct Unbecoming*, 281–83.

5.   Volker, Keith Meinhold vs. United States Department of Defense et al, United States District Court, C.D. California, January 29, 1993.

6.   Burt Solomon, "In Juggling Tough Ones, Clinton Picks Pragmatism Over Principles," *National Journal*, 24 July 1993.

7.   Melissa Healy, "Military Using Pollis in Debate over Gays," *Los Angeles Times*, 9 February 1993.

8.   Quoted in Peter Gomes, "Back in the Military Closet," *New York Times*, 22 May 1993.

9.   John Lancaster, "Why the Military Supports the Ban on Gays," *Washington Post*, 28 January 1993.

10.   Thomas Lippman, "Pentagon's Studies on Gays Conflict," *Washington Post*, 27 August 1993.

11.   John Lancaster, "Crowe Discounts Military Objection to Homosexuals," *Washington Post*, 11 April 1993.

12.   Gomes, "Military Closet," 19.

Chapter 16

Sexual Orientation and the Armed Forces: Lifting the Ban with Caution

ALLAN J. FUTERNICK

It is the central thesis of this paper that several societal changes external to the military must precede any future decision to permit homosexuals to serve openly in the armed forces, if lifting the ban is to be successful.[1] These changes would be predicated upon a significant reduction in the current level of ambivalence on the issue of homosexuality in general, and the concomitant establishment of a supportive legal environment for homosexuals at all levels of government. Although the American military has previously been successful in leading the way for significant social change beyond its own institutional boundaries, in this case the military most likely would be ineffective as a societal change agent, and the effort itself would engender significant organizational and institutional strain within the armed forces.

The Military as a Vehicle for Social Change

While the military has not readily accepted the role of social change agent, the American public has viewed this role of the armed forces as appropriate. Furthermore, military service also has become a vehicle for social and economic equal opportunity. Throughout the sexual orientation debate, there have been many attempts to establish a parallel between the role the military could play in integrating homosexuals and successful past roles in integrating blacks following World War II and women in the 1970s.

The integration of blacks in the armed forces is, perhaps, the most frequently cited example of the military's ability to bring about social change beyond its institutional boundaries, and in which the civilian society could not or would not act effectively. The military had offered numerous arguments against President Truman's plans to integrate the armed forces, including the "prejudicial-to-good-order-and-discipline" refrains echoed later in response to directives to integrate women in the 1970s, (and most recently in support of the ban against homosexuals).[2] However, military commanders were duty-bound by their oaths of commissioning to carry out the orders of their commander-in-chief, and they responded accordingly. Similarly, when ordered to lead the way for sexual equality two decades ago, the chain of command responded effectively to eliminate most existing barriers to women in the armed forces.

It is often argued that, had these changes not taken place within the military first, it is highly unlikely that the economic, social, and political gains recognized by minorities and women today would have occurred as rapidly as they did. In each of these cases, the desired end was to effect change throughout civilian society, and not just within the military itself.

In order to be successful, both the executive order directing the integration of blacks and the administrative changes necessary to more fully integrate women required changes internal and external to the institutional boundaries of the military. In addition to strong support from the executive branch, both the courts and the Congress worked over the years (through interpretation of the Constitution and enactment of federal legislation) to require states and municipalities to eliminate the last remaining vestiges of discrimination permitted by statute or ordinance.[3] These actions were critical to the ultimate success of the integration efforts, in that they established the necessary supportive legal environment nationwide within which the military would carry out its social mission.

Perhaps even more significant, there were no behavioral proscriptions in the Uniform Code of Military Justice (UCMJ) that had to be eliminated in order to integrate blacks and women. In the case of racial integration, many difficult years passed before there was significant progress in changing life outside the post gates. However, military commanders were still able to devote the bulk of their leadership energies toward reducing prejudice and eliminating discrimination in military life. Underlying the military's actions was the basic premise that successful interracial contact would eliminate both prejudice and discrimination, with attitudinal change following behavioral change.[4]

At this point, the similarities between the military as a vehicle for achieving subsequent acceptance of homosexuals in American society and both earlier cases fade rapidly. A presidential executive order (or a directive from the secretary of defense) to lift the ban against homosexuals serving in the armed forces would not be sufficient to enable military commanders to accomplish the task of successful integration, even if they made the most professional effort to do so. Unlike the myriad social problems surrounding the integration of blacks and women, unique legal obstacles that currently exist would continue to prohibit any sense of full integration of homosexuals in the armed forces from occurring, unless change first came from outside the military institution. This situation is primarily a reflection of the American public's ambivalence on the overall issue of homosexuality in society.

Society's Ambivalence on the Homosexual Issue

Within American society, there seems to be a feeling of support for rights and benefits for homosexuals in specific areas. At the same time there exists a clear reluctance by the public to support homosexuality as an acceptable life-style. In addition, there is uncertainty as to what approach to follow in order to provide those rights and benefits for which public support does exist. This ambivalence is reflected in three areas: public opinion polls, internal debates within social institutions, and state and municipal legislation.

A plethora of public opinion polls conducted during 1992 and the first half of 1993 on homosexuality in the United States reflect society's ambivalence on the general issue.[5] Illustrative is a June 1992 Gallup poll, which indicates that, while there has been a significant increase in support for homosexuals in housing and employment (from 59 to 74 percent since 1982), support is clearly lacking with regard to American society's view of homosexuality as an acceptable life-style (a marginal increase from 34 to 38 percent since 1982) and acceptance of legalizing homosexual relations (up from 43 to 48 percent since a dip to 33 percent occurred between 1985 and 1986, as concern with AIDS increased). Public support for homosexuals serving in the armed forces (as measured by several polls during 1992 and 1993) has ranged between 42 and 59 percent.[6]

Looking at these findings from another perspective, it appears that this ambivalence tends to be least when the rights in question accrue to homosexuals as individuals (as in employment), rather than to homosexuals as couples (as in marriage). Rights involving couples imply acceptance (at least tacitly) of the homosexual act, which the American public currently finds itself unable to do.

This same public ambivalence continues to be reflected by prominent and visceral internal debates within virtually every social institution in America.[7] This ambivalence appears to be greatest (and acceptance of the homosexual life-style appears to be least) within the most conservative institutions and organizations. However, there are efforts within each institution to separate the homosexual qua individual from homosexuals as a class (as had even been the case in the 1993 Senate Armed Services Committee hearings on lifting the ban) in order to find some basis for acceptance. The difficulty lies in resolving the conflict that inevitably occurs at the nexus of the organizational norms and the sexual behavior that defines gays and lesbians.

Finally, the lack of state and municipal legislation dealing with homosexuals reflects this same ambivalence, as do inconsistencies among and within the fifty states and the District of Columbia when such laws do exist. These inconsistencies exist within several legal areas of significant importance to the armed forces, such as anti-sodomy statutes, same-sex marriages (or partnerships), benefits (i.e., health insurance), inheritance rights, same-sex adoption, employment, housing, and public accommodations.[8] While some progress has been made (generally since 1970) in advancing homosexuals' rights in most of these areas, gains have not been established nationwide in any single area, and most gains are not in effect statewide.[9] Parallel to these gains have been efforts to roll them back or even bar any future legislation that would provide protection for homosexuals as a social class.[10] The future direction of these parallel trends will significantly impact the sociolegal environment in which the military would subsequently have to function.

Explanations of the Ambivalence

To expect the American public to warmly (or even reluctantly) embrace homosexual conduct is to ask most individuals to strip away personal values and morals inculcated in them through a lifetime of socialization. For this portion of the population, any attitudinal shift toward acceptance of homosexuality as an alternative life-style may be perceived as requiring a concomitant move away from their core values. For many, the perceived cost of such an attitudinal shift may be too great. Rather than accept these costs, they may seek ways to reduce the dissonance that could result from maintaining a social position that denies the civil rights, freedom, and dignity of others. The result may be a significant shift toward even less acceptance, in order to reaffirm their position on the issue.

As an example, the onset and subsequent spread of AIDS and the HIV virus may reduce such dissonance for a large number of Americans who might otherwise have shifted their opinions toward greater support for homosexual rights. AIDS and the HIV virus continue to be disproportionately associated with the homosexual life-style in the public's mind.[11] As noted above, an effort is consistently made to separate the homosexual individual from the homosexual act which, of course, can never be accomplished successfully. Yet most Americans continue to confront the issue in this manner. In fact, this was clearly the basis for the "don't Ask, don't tell, don't pursue" alternative to lifting the military ban completely.

Part of the ambivalence may stem from the debate over the basis of sexual orientation. Just prior to the announcement of President Clinton's new policy for the military, the National Institute of Health made public a study finding a strong positive link between genetics and sexual orientation in males. The study set off another flurry of comments on the issue by supporters and detractors alike.[12] If an individual's sexual orientation is one of "social" choice, then such choice is less likely to be viewed as being acceptable, if at the same time the homosexual act itself continues to be perceived as being illegal, immoral, or repugnant.[13] If both nature and nurture are eventually determined to influence sexual orientation, societal attitudes and the courts' responses likely will continue to mirror a "nurture-only" perspective, since social choice probably would still be perceived as the major component of the explanation.

Finally, even with overwhelming scientific evidence that an individual's sexual orientation is biologically predetermined, society's view of homosexual conduct itself still might not change. In any case, whether the Supreme Court would then grant homosexuals the status of a protected class and prohibit discrimination based upon sexual orientation would remain to be seen.[14] The net result is that, regardless of the scientific explanations of the basis for homosexual behavior, the public's overall attitude toward homosexuality will most likely continue to be one of ambivalence.

Legal Problems Impacting the Military by Lifting the Ban[15]

Virtually all of the myriad problems the military would face if the ban were summarily lifted would stem from the fact that there is no constitutional basis for guaranteeing individuals equal rights and protection against discrimination based upon their sexual orientation.[16] Court challenges continue, however, based upon the due process clauses of the Fifth and Fourteenth Amendments (requiring that laws be at least rationally related to some government interest), the equal protection clause of the Fourteenth Amendment (requiring that all persons similarly situated be treated alike), and the implied right to privacy in the Fourth and Fifth Amendments. Challenges have also been made based upon First Amendment guarantees (freedom of association, expression, and speech).[17]

Homosexual Conduct: The Heart of the Issue

Members of the United States armed forces who commit consensual sodomy can be charged with violations of the UCMJ under Articles 125, 133, and 134.[18] The heart of the issue impacting orders to lift the ban is clearly "sodomy," and the Supreme Court made it strikingly clear through Bowers v. Hardwick in 1986 that the Constitution does not guarantee the right to consensual sodomy, which is the self-defining aspect of being homosexual.[19]

Department of Defense directives 1332.14 and 1332.30, ostensibly aimed at orientation, were clearly intended to provide commanders with a more effective administrative tool for eliminating potential consensual sodomy (by homosexuals) within the armed forces. These directives cleverly reduced the need to focus on actual behavior, which has always been the real concern vis-à-vis the status of homosexuals in the armed forces. Similarly, the current policy continues to define such conduct as being incompatible with military service.

Therefore, the lifting of the ban carries a concomitant need to eliminate the current UCMJ proscriptions against consensual sodomy within the armed forces (regardless of sexual orientation).[20] However, authority for change resides with Congress, and the probability of sufficient votes to bring about such change presently is extremely low.[21] As discussed above, public opinion has consistently failed to reflect acceptance of homosexuality as an acceptable lifestyle, and Congress is keenly aware of these poll results.

If the Supreme Court does not reverse its position on consensual sodomy, military commanders will face the conundrum of differing state statutes that would impact the lives of service members. If the current military proscriptions against sodomy were lifted, service members would still be subject to civilian prosecution in some states for consensual sodomy off the military installation.[22] As of June 1993, twenty-three states and the District of Columbia had proscriptions of some sort against consensual sodomy (prohibiting anal and oral sex), and six states limit these statutes to same-sex couples.[23] All fifty states and the District of Columbia had such statutes until 1961, when Illinois was the first to eliminate it. While the most recent state to remove its statute was Nevada in 1993, the last state prior to this was Wisconsin in 1983. The District of Columbia also voted to repeal its sodomy ban in April, 1993, but Congress could reverse this decision (as it did previously in 1981).[24]

Even if Article 125 were to be eliminated, such behaviors may be subject to military prosecution under Article 134 through the Federal Assimilative Crimes Act.[25] Furthermore, permitting on the military installation a behavior that is not clearly a part of military life (such as employment of weapons) and that is not permitted off base could cause camp versus town friction. If the current military proscriptions against sodomy were not eliminated, service members would still be subject to punishment under the UCMJ, both on and off the military installation, regardless of whether consensual sodomy was prohibited by state statute.[26] In addition, it should be noted that since military retirees continue to be subject to the UCMJ even after leaving the service, homosexuals are actually subject to these proscriptions for the rest of their lives.[27]

The existing inconsistencies in state statutes regarding consensual sodomy would change the nature of command vis-à-vis homosexual service members. Commanders would be forced to apply different standards of behavior for heterosexuals and homosexuals, based upon the location of each military installation. With military installations situated in all fifty states, the normal, frequent transfer of personnel to new locations would certainly present a challenge to commanders, and perhaps draw undesired command attention to homosexual military personnel.

Other Potential Problem Areas for the Military

As in the case of state statutes regarding sodomy, there are inconsistencies both among and within the states in a number of other critical areas (recognition of equal benefits for same-sex partners, inheritance rights, same-sex adoption, and nondiscrimination in employment, housing, and public accommodations). Additionally, there is no indication that the Supreme Court or Congress will soon act to eliminate these inconsistencies. Potential problems for commanders would be most salient in the areas of rights that affect homosexuals as couples, rather than as individuals. Furthermore, these potential problems would tend to be compounded if both partners were service members.

Military commanders would face potential problems that could arise as a result of the legalization of same-sex marriages or "partnerships."[28] While no state currently recognizes marriages by people of the same sex, such unions are expressly prohibited by several states. Previous challenges in state courts have failed, and the Supreme Court has not ruled on this issue. However, the possibility of the legalization of such unions in the future does exist. At this writing, the constitutionality of such proscription is being seriously reviewed by the courts in Hawaii.[29] If the court challenge is successful, each state would then be required to recognize same-sex marriages that are legal in Hawaii (or subsequently, in any other state), which would then entitle these couples to all benefits afforded heterosexual couples in any state (i.e., health benefits, inheritance rights, tax breaks, etc.). However, even if legally married, homosexual couples would still be subject to the proscriptions of any state anti-sodomy statutes that may be in effect. Furthermore, these service members would continue to be subject to UCMJ proscriptions against sodomy (both on and off base).

Gay and lesbian couples would also continue to be subject to potential discrimination off the military installation in housing, employment, and denial of services in establishments that are not determined to be "public accommodations," as long as such discrimination based on sexual orientation was not prohibited by state, county, or municipal legislation. Finally, there is the potential for unique problems for homosexual military personnel that could result from the dissolution of same-sex unions, depending on the legal guidelines in effect at their current geographic location and their legal domiciles at the time.

How would the military deal with the issue of benefits for same-sex partners? While there have been some gains in recent years in the civilian community, there presently is no federal support for such benefits and minimal support exists at the state, county, or municipal levels.[30] For those "partnerships" (both heterosexual and homosexual) that are currently recognized in a number of municipalities across the country, whatever benefits accrue to each partner do so only within the confines of the particular municipality in which the unions were registered, and are not "portable."[31] However, as noted above, legalization of same-sex marriages by any state would require all states to provide such benefits.

Without a uniform nationwide policy on this issue, the military would have difficulty establishing its own internal policy guidelines. The Department of Defense would have to establish a policy as to what constitutes a union that would entitle the service member and partner to pay, allowances, housing, benefits (to include retirement pay and survivor benefits) that presently only accrue to married service members and those with legal dependents. In this regard, although unsuccessful thus far, some homosexuals have looked to adoption of one partner by the other as a viable alternative to marriage in order to legitimize their family status, secure inheritance rights, and accrue other benefits.[32]

The issue of inheritance rights would become most critical to military commanders during time of war. The military could be involuntarily drawn into disputes between the surviving same-sex partner of a service member and family members of the deceased (particularly if the surviving partner is also a service member). For example, if a will is not in effect at the time of one partner's death, there is no right to inheritance by the partner. Even in cases where there has been a will designating a same-sex partner as the beneficiary, there have been successful challenges by blood relatives. Finally, if a same-sex partner's will fails to provide for his or her companion, there is no legal recourse for the companion against the estate. Once again, clear guidelines would have to be established, to include entitlement to survivor benefits.[33]

Adoptions by same-sex couples could provide additional problems for commanders in dealing with a redefined concept of a military family. Currently, there is a general absence of support for same-sex adoption across the states. Two states, Florida and New Hampshire, specifically prohibit adoption by gay and lesbian partners, but a state trial court subsequently declared the Florida statute unconstitutional. Only six states (Alaska, California, New York, Oregon, Washington, Vermont) and the District of Columbia permit same-sex adoption. However, most instances of adoptions by gays and lesbians are by a single parent rather than by the couple. In addition to the interpersonal problems in integrating these families within military communities, the currently varying legal status of same-sex adoptions from state to state could open them to custody challenges by a biological parent.[34] In a related area, the estimated ten thousand children being raised by lesbians who conceived them through artificial insemination represent an increasing trend that could impact the military.[35]

Military commanders would also have to deal with the issue of equal opportunities for off-duty employment of homosexual service members and their same-sex partners. There is no federal law that precludes any private employer from discriminating against gays and lesbians solely on the basis of their sexual orientation. However, with the exception of the armed forces, homosexuality or homosexual acts in and of themselves cannot be used to exclude an individual from employment with the federal government.[36] Only seven states (California, Connecticut, Hawaii, Massachusetts, Minnesota, New Jersey, and Wisconsin) ban such discrimination, in addition to most large cities, the District of Columbia, and a number of counties and municipalities.[37] With respect to state and local governments, although federal guidelines should apply with equal force at these levels, there are cases in which the courts have upheld the right of specific agencies to discriminate based solely on an individual's sexual orientation.

Commanders have been able to put pressure on civilian establishments that discriminate in their hiring practices by placing them off-limits to military personnel. However, if there are no prohibitions against discriminating against persons on the basis of sexual orientation, the military would find it difficult to establish such sanctions against civilian establishments. In addition, clear policy guidelines would have to be established for any on-base priority hiring practices to same-sex partners that may apply to heterosexual spouses at military installations.

As in the case of employment, while the military can ensure that there is no discrimination in assigning housing on the military installation, the same cannot be guaranteed off-base. In most parts of the country a landlord can refuse to rent or a homeowner can refuse to sell to a person solely because of their sexual orientation. California, Connecticut, Massachusetts, Minnesota, New Jersey, and Wisconsin are the only states with statutes that expressly ban such discrimination based upon sexual orientation (as do the District of Columbia and a number of large cities and municipalities). In addition, the Unruh Civil Rights Act is a California statute that the courts have interpreted to provide protection for homosexuals against discrimination by landlords. Protection against discrimination in obtaining a mortgage is also limited to those states and municipalities that specifically ban such discrimination based solely upon sexual orientation.[38]

Off the military installation, housing discrimination against homosexuals (individuals or partners) could not be precluded if there were no legal prohibitions against such practices. Voluntary (or involuntary) segregation of homosexuals into isolated neighborhoods in the civilian community could result (which would clearly be counter to the intent of the integration effort).

Of additional concern to commanders would be the treatment of homosexual service members (and their partners) in public accommodations off-base. A public accommodation is "an item, service, or benefit offered generally to the public."[39] However, the operational definition of public accommodation differs from place to place. Hence, a practice may be a violation in one jurisdiction but not so within another. Statutes in California, Connecticut, Massachusetts, Minnesota, New Jersey, and Wisconsin (as well as the District of Columbia and a number of cities and municipalities) prohibit discrimination in public accommodations. However, a store, hotel, or restaurant outside these areas may refuse a person a room, meal, or any item for sale solely on the basis of sexual orientation.[40] Once again, the opportunities for "legal" discrimination based on sexual orientation vary across the nation and within states and counties.

Equal Employment Opportunity, Quotas, and Discrimination Suits

Lifting the ban on homosexuals in the armed forces would not necessarily require the military to recognize homosexuals as a protected minority group. Not discriminating on the basis of sexual orientation is quite different from being required to provide special consideration in the form of either "windows" or quotas for each important aspect of a service member's career for which selection criteria are established. It also seems unlikely, given the Supreme Court's most recent decisions on the issue, that homosexuals will be granted substantive constitutional protection in any area in the near future. In addition, there also is very little likelihood that Congress will enact legislation entitling homosexuals to protection under the Civil Rights Acts of 1964 and 1968, as amended, since it has not seen fit to do so thus far.[41] The Equal Employment Opportunity Commission has ruled that discrimination based upon sexual orientation is not prohibited by Title VII.[42]

Even if the Supreme Court did apply such status to homosexuals, and if Congress did amend Title VII of the 1964 Civil Rights Act, for those former servicemen and -women whose sexual orientation was not known to their superiors while they were on active duty, there could not have been any career opportunities missed as a result of the military's discriminatory policy. However, those homosexuals who were clearly discharged as a result of their sexual orientation (but not as a result of any violation of the UCMJ) could possibly seek redress successfully on the basis of past discrimination.

On the other hand, it would appear that those service members discharged as a result of violations of Articles 125, 133, 134 (or any other article) of the UCMJ were aware of both the proscriptions and sanctions for such conduct. Similarly, for those service members who were discharged for falsely denying their homosexuality in signed documents, it would appear that there would be a low probability of redress, since these personnel clearly knew they were making false statements. For those former service members who could establish that at the time of such declaration they were not aware of their sexual orientation, and although not guilty of any violation of the UCMJ were discharged once their sexual orientation became known, there could be some probability of redress. Such suits brought against the government for past discrimination could result in compensation, reinstatement, or both.

Finally, individuals who sought military service, but who were denied entry as a result of their sexual orientation, represent another group that could seek redress through litigation for career opportunities missed. The outcomes could be compensation, the opportunity to serve (for those who otherwise meet the military's entry requirements at the time the litigation is decided), or both.

Conclusions

Current Department of Defense policy on homosexuals and military service reflects the continued reluctance of American society to accept homosexuals into its mainstream. Indeed, if societal ambivalence on homosexuality could be eliminated (or at least reduced significantly), and a "social imprimatur" of acceptance of homosexuality could be obtained, the probability of eventual change within America's institutions (to include the military) would certainly increase significantly. Furthermore, the necessary constitutional interpretations by the courts and passage of supportive governmental legislation to legitimize the homosexual life-style and eliminate discrimination would be more likely to occur. Given a social environment of this nature, and the absence of military or civilian proscriptions of homosexual conduct, the military could then effectively carry out a directive to allow gay and lesbian personnel to serve openly.

However, in light of the minimal changes over almost two decades in public attitudes toward the self-defining act of homosexuality, and the limited gains that have been made to date in supportive legislation for homosexual rights across any governmental level nationwide, it seems unlikely that the current level of ambivalence will ebb sufficiently in the near future for any substantive changes in the social status of homosexuals to take place. The net result is that, if the ban on homosexuals serving in the armed forces is lifted by an executive order (or other directive) in the near future, the legal framework currently in place in American society will not permit openly homosexual men and women to serve anywhere in the United States as full and equal service members. Therefore, unless the Supreme Court and Congress act swiftly and in tandem to eliminate the existing legal impediments to equality for homosexuals, the military cannot be expected to successfully perform its traditional institutional role.

Notes

1. This paper focuses solely on the environment external to the military and its impact on the armed forces' ability to integrate gay men and lesbian women effectively if the ban on homosexual conduct were lifted. Most studies of sexual orientation and the military focus on the internal environment and the potential impact of gays and lesbians on unit cohesion, morale, good order, and discipline.

2. See "Their Words: Discrimination, 1948 and 1993," *New Republic* 208, 8 (February 22, 1993):15, for comparative quotes from opponents of racial integration in 1948 and opponents of lifting the ban on homosexuals in 1993.

3. For example, see Loving v. Virginia, 388 U.S. 1 (1967), effectively eliminating state miscegenation statutes; Brown v. Board of Education, 347 U.S. 483 (1954), ruling separate but equal education unconstitutional; and the Civil Rights Acts of 1964 and 1968, amended (protection against discrimination in housing, employment, public accommodations).

4. For a discussion of the effects of contact on reducing prejudice, see Gordon W. Allport, *The Nature of Prejudice* (New York: Addison-Wesley, 1958), 250–68.

5. For example, see "Straight Talk about Gays," *U.S. News & World Report*, 5 July 1993, 42; "Poll Finds an Even Split on Homosexuality's Cause," *New York Times*, 5 March 1993; "Public Opinion Divided on Gay Rights," *The Gallup Poll Monthly*, No. 321, June 1992, 2–6; "Gays under Fire," *Newsweek*, 14 September 1992, 35–41; "Difficult First Step," *New York Times*, 15 November 1992.

6. *Gallup Poll Monthly*, 2. Similar findings are reflected in the other four polls cited in note 5.

7. For examples of actions reflecting this ambivalence within major social institutions, see "A Religious Battle Too," *U.S. News & World Report*, 5 April 1993, 33; "Gay Rights, Issue of the 90's," *New York Times*, 28 April 1991; "Groups Fight Gay Ban," *Army Times*, 15 June 1992; "Homosexuals in Academe: Fear of Backlash Clouds Reactions to Increased Tolerance," *Chronicle of Higher Education*, 23 September 1992, A17–A20; "At the Bar," *New York Times*, 9 October 1992; "Some Papers Reject Gay-Themed Comic Strip," *New York Times*, 28 March 1993.

8. See Nan D. Hunter, Sheryl E. Michaelson and Thomas E. Stoddard, *The Rights of Lesbians and Gay Men: The Basic ACLU Guide to a Gay Person's Rights*, 3rd ed. (Carbondale and Edwardsville: Southern Illinois University Press, 1992), and also see *Harvard Law Review*, eds., "Developments—Sexual Orientation and the

Law," *Harvard Law Review* 102 (1989):1508–671, for a comprehensive overview and analysis of the rights of homosexuals in each of these areas.

9.   Ibid. See "Gay-Rights Advocates Resume Campaign for Maryland Law," *Washington Post*, 28 January 1993. Three counties and the city of Baltimore have ordinances, while nineteen other Maryland counties do not. Also see "Gay Rights Hurt by Lack of Uniform Protection," *New York Times*, 9 March 1993, as an example of the inconsistencies in such legislation across the counties and municipalities of New York State.

10.   See Mark Eddy, *Prohibiting Discrimination on the Basis of Sexual Orientation: Arguments For and Against Proposed Legislation,* CRS, Report for Congress (April 10, 1989), for an excellent presentation of the arguments for and against establishing legislation protecting homosexuals from discrimination.

11.   See *Gallup Poll,* (June 2, 1992), 2. Also see Eddy, *Prohibiting Discrimination,* 6.

12.   Dean H. Hamer et al., "A Link between DNA Markers on the X Chromosome and Male Sexual Orientation," *Science* 261 (January 16, 1993):321–27.

13.   *U.S. News & World Report,* "Straight Talk." Of the 46 percent who believed that homosexuality was the result of choice, three out of five opposed extending civil rights to gays. Of the 32 percent who viewed homosexuality as innate, more than half were in favor of civil rights for gays. See *New York Times,* "Poll Finds an Even Split," for similar findings.

14.   If sexual orientation were to be accepted by the courts as being an "immutable" characteristic, such as race, then laws that discriminate against homosexuals would have to show a compelling state interest in order to remain in force. However, immutability is a necessary, but not a sufficient factor, in predicting the outcome of a Supreme Court ruling on the issue. See "Developments," 1564–71; Major Jeffrey Davis, "Military Policy toward Homosexuals: Scientific, Historical and Legal Perspectives," *Military Law Review* 131 (1991):89–94; and Eddy, *Prohibiting Discrimination,* 3–4.

15.   The author is grateful to Col. Dennis R. Hunt, Professor and Head, Department of Law, U.S. Military Academy, for his insights in this area. This discussion is limited to potential problems within the United States and territories under its jurisdiction. The status of forces agreements between the United States and other nations will further define the potential legal problems for military personnel stationed overseas.

16.   Most of the material contained in the discussion of constitutional issues is drawn from "Developments," 1556–73, and Davis, "Military Policy," 84–99.

17.   See Eddy, *Prohibiting Discrimination,* 3, for constitutional arguments by proponents of civil rights legislation for homosexuals.

18.   *Uniform Code of Military Justice* (UCMJ), Art. 125, 133, 134 sections 925, 933, 934 (1984). See also *Manual for Courts-Martial, United States* (1984).

19.   Bowers v. Hardwick, 478 U.S. 186 (1986). See also Dronenberg v. Zech, 741 F.2d 1388 (1984), Doe v. Commonwealth's Attorney for Richmond, 525 U.S. 901 (1976). Note that while the Supreme Court has failed to recognize any right to sodomy, it stated that constitutional challenges to state anti-sodomy statutes were not affected by the Hardwick decision. See Hardwick, 190. See also *ACLU Guide,* 118–22, and "Developments," 1521–36.

20.   It is interesting to note that the Court of Military Appeals recently affirmed

its position on the issue pertaining to consenting heterosexual couples in U.S. v. Fagg, 34 M.J. 179 (CMA 1992) and U.S. v. Henderson, 34 M.J. 174 (CMA 1992). In both cases, a male service member had engaged in consenting oral sex with a female partner (not his wife).

21.   "Congress tells Clinton He'd Lose Vote," *Army Times*, 30 November 1992.

22.   The Supreme Court, in Solorio v. United States, U.S. 435 (1987), reversed its earlier ruling in O'Callahan v. Parker, 395 U.S. 258 (1969), and held that: "The jurisdiction of a court-martial depends solely on the accused's status as a member of the Armed Forces, and not on the 'service connection' of the offense charged." For example, see U.S. v. Fagg and U.S. v. Henderson in note 20.

23.   Only Arkansas, Kansas, Missouri, Montana, Tennessee, and Texas limit their statutes to same-sex couples. The other states with anti-sodomy statutes are Alabama, Arizona, Florida, Georgia, Idaho, Louisiana, Maryland, Massachusetts, Michigan, Minnesota, Mississippi, North Carolina, Oklahoma, Rhode Island, South Carolina, Utah, and Virginia. As of June 1993, the state supreme courts of Louisiana, Tennessee, and Texas were considering eliminating their state statutes on the basis of violation of their respective state constitutions. The discussion of sodomy statutes was drawn from *ACLU Guide*, 119–22, and "Developments," 1519–37.

24.   "Battle Looms on Sodomy Ban; D.C. Council Votes to Outlaw Law," *Washington Times*, 8 April 1993.

25.   18 U.S.C. section 13 (1982). *Manual for Courts-Martial, United States* (1984), IV-110, 60c (4)(c)(ii), states: "The Federal Assimilative Crimes Act is an adoption by Congress of state criminal laws for areas of exclusive or concurrent federal jurisdiction, provided federal criminal law, including the UCMJ, has not defined an applicable offense for the misconduct committed."

26.   For example, see U.S. v. Henderson in note 20.

27.   *UCMJ*, Art. 2(a)(4),(5), 10 U.S.C.A. section 802(a) (4), (5) (1983).

28.   It is interesting to note that the 1990 Census reported 69,200 lesbian couples and 88,200 gay male couples (less than 1 percent of all American households). As reported in "Gay Couples, by the Numbers," *USA Today*, 12 April, 1993.

29.   See Baehr v. Lewin, 852 P.2d 44 Hawaii (1993). The Hawaii Supreme Court ruled that under the state constitution's equal protection of the law, sex-based discrimination is "suspect," and the state must show "compelling" reasons for such action. The case was remanded to a lower court for action.

30.   Benefits provided by the federal government such as social security, disability insurance, and veterans' benefits may be paid to the surviving spouse or children in the event of the beneficiary's death or disability, but not to unmarried partners of the principal beneficiary. Some benefits have been extended to registered partners in a limited (although increasing) number of municipalities for municipal employees. A number of large corporations also offer benefits to same-sex partners. The discussion of gay and lesbian marriages and partnerships was drawn from *ACLU Guide*, 75–82, and "Developments," 1605–11.

31.   About twenty-five cities, counties or states have some form of domestic partnership. See "A Legal Threshold Is Crossed By Gay Couples in New York," *New York Times*, 2 March 1993.

32.   *ACLU Guide*, 81–82, and "Developments," 1626–28.

33.   The discussion of benefits for gay and lesbian partners was drawn from *ACLU Guide*, 94–98, and "Developments," 1618–26.

34.   In June 1993, the Vermont Supreme Court, in the first appellate-level ruling in such a case, ruled that a woman in a long-term lesbian relationship could adopt her partner's two children, without the biological parent's rights being terminated. See "Lesbian Wins Appeal on Vermont Adoption," *New York Times*, 20 June 1993. The discussion of homosexuals and adoption was mostly drawn from *ACLU Guide*, 106–8, and *Developments*, 1642–48.

35.   "Gays under Fire," *Newsweek*, 14 September 1992, 35–41. Also see "Developments," 1649–51 for a discussion of legal proscriptions impacting lesbians' use of artificial insemination.

36.   In Norton v. Macy, 349 F 2d 182, 184-85 (D.C. Cir. 1965) the court ruled that a rational relationship must be established between a person's sexual orientation and the efficiency of the government's operation in hiring and firing civil service personnel.

37.   Most of the discussion of homosexuals and employment was drawn from *ACLU Guide*, 15–27, and "Developments," 1554–84. Minnesota was the most recent state to pass such legislation (April 1993).

38.   Most of the discussion of homosexuals and housing was drawn from *ACLU Guide*, 64–69, and "Developments," 1612–18. Minnesota was the most recent state to pass such legislation (April 1993).

39.   *ACLU Guide*, 69.

40.   Most of the discussion of homosexuals and public accommodations was drawn from *ACLU Guide*, 69–71, and "Developments," 1670–71. Minnesota was the most recent state to pass such legislation (April 1993).

41.   Eddy, *Prohibiting Discrimination*, 1. Bills attempting to prohibit discrimination based upon affectional or sexual orientation in housing, employment, public accommodations, and federally assisted programs were introduced in each Congress since 1975. In the 103rd Congress, H.R. 423 was introduced on January 5, 1993, as the Civil Rights Amendment Act of 1993, and a somewhat similar bill is anticipated to be introduced in the Senate. These bills have consistently specified that use of statistical evidence to support any finding on the basis of sexual orientation would be prohibited, as would be the use of any form of affirmative action quotas to remedy alleged discrimination. Therefore, it is likely that any future bill would contain similar language, thus denying redress to homosexuals from the government related to military service.

42.   "Developments," 1579.

Chapter 17

Integration of Homosexuals into the Armed Forces: Racial and Gender Integration as a Point of Departure[1]

DONALD H. HORNER, JR., and MICHAEL T. ANDERSON

The integration of blacks and women into the U.S. military generally is a success story.[2] Most observers conclude that the military, responding to political mandates, implemented the required personnel changes without compromising military effectiveness. In Samuel Huntington's terms, the military in these cases balanced the "functional" and "societal" imperatives, with both the military and society better off for the experience.[3]

An executive order might soon allow homosexuals to serve openly in the armed forces, once again raising issues of organizational and institutional reform. This paper considers strategies for integrating homosexuals into the military, should that be the mandate of the political process. Drawing from the experiences of racial and gender integration, military planners may find general direction for accommodating homosexuals with the least cost to military effectiveness.

With this focus in mind, it is equally important to specify what this paper omits and hopes to avoid. This paper does not answer the question: Should the military integrate gays? Indeed, we approach this issue without judgment of whether gay integration into the armed forces is the right thing to do. Specifying the point of departure as the moment at which the integration of open homosexuals has been ordered essentially assumes away the debate over whether homosexuals should be integrated in the first place. This permits an open discussion of the policy implications garnered from earlier integration efforts.

The Integration of Blacks, Women, and Gays: Similarities

One could easily produce a laundry list of similarities in the integration of blacks, women, and gays into the military. Such an exercise, however, may have little practical utility unless focused on those which have policy implications. Below we review five useful similarities.

Arguments Used to Oppose Integration

The inclinations of the military favor organizational inertia when it comes to personnel policies. As a conservative American institution, the military resists making changes of a controversial nature.[4] Most senior military leaders argue that the military is not a laboratory for social experimentation and should not be used as a vehicle for solving societal problems. Military folklore has it that "big ships should not make sharp turns." The prevailing sentiment therefore is that any move to integrate homosexuals into the military "threatens the strong, conservative, moralistic traditions of the troops."[5]

Opposition to the integration of open homosexuals into the military shares rationales with those used to limit the integration of blacks and women.[6] For example, Col. Eugene R. Householder, then a spokesman for the adjutant general to then Army Chief of Staff Gen. George C. Marshall, echoed these sentiments when speaking before the Conference of Negro Editors and Publishers on December 8, 1941:

> The Army then cannot be made the means of engendering conflict among the mass of people because of a stand with respect to Negroes which is not compatible with the position attained by the Negro in civil life. . . . The Army is not a sociological laboratory; to be effective it must be organized and trained according to the principles which insure success. Experiments to meet the wishes and demands of the champions of every race and creed for the solution of their problems are a danger to efficiency, discipline and morale and would result in ultimate defeat.[7]

The notion that open homosexuals would undermine good order and discipline in military units assumes that their presence would impair group bonding—the social glue necessary for unit cohesion and morale necessary for effectiveness in combat. As in the cases of blacks and women, opponents of lifting the ban have predicted that integrating homosexuals into the ranks would create internal divisions and make the military too heterogeneous— conditions, they say, that make bonding more difficult.[8]

Routine and Practical Considerations

Routine and practical considerations for integrating openly gay service members are similar to those faced earlier by black and female service members. By practical considerations we mean those encountered on a day-to-day basis in military life. Concerns about billeting and individual privacy raised by the integration of open homosexuals are especially similar to those encountered with the integration of blacks and women. Such concerns are guided by prevailing cultural norms (and prejudices). In the 1950s, some white servicemen refused to eat, train, or share quarters with black servicemen; likewise, in the 1970s and 1980s, some servicemen objected to having women as co-workers in their military specialties.

The statement, "All we want to know is who we'll be sleeping next to next week,"[9] captures the essence of the billeting and privacy issues and the leadership challenges surrounding the integration of open homosexuals. Young, white, virile, southern males and their perceptions and feelings about blacks and women made earlier integration efforts similarly challenging for the military. If earlier integration experiences are a guide, the military might encounter varying degrees of difficulty in other areas:

(1) short-term inefficiencies and lapses in unit effectiveness;
(2) leadership challenges;
(3) difficulties in maintaining unit cohesion;
(4) minimal behavioral compliance with little or no attitudinal change; and
(5) threats or actual acts of violence against the newly integrated service members.[10]

It is reasonable to expect that heterosexual service members would anticipate the same privacy afforded men and women would likewise be available to heterosexuals and homosexuals after integration. Hence, the practical issues of room assignments, shower facilities, and housing areas are ones that must be dealt with by organizational policies and may mirror strategies used to successfully integrate blacks and women.

Negative Stereotypes and Associated Behavioral Characteristics

Perceived behavioral characteristics, in the form of negative stereotypes held by white and male service members, have affected the integration of blacks and women into the military. Those opposed to the integration of these groups into the service regularly cited predominantly negative descriptions of them. Stereotypically, blacks were categorized as dumb, lazy, sexually irresponsible, and lacking the stick-to-it-iveness necessary to succeed.[11] Women were characterized as physically weak, flirtatious, and emotionally unstable, and possessing neither the aggressiveness nor the psychological disposition necessary for successful military service.

The stereotypes of gays, like those of blacks and women, are uniformly unflattering. Gays are categorized as weak, effeminate, predatory, and— though homosexuality was removed as a mental disorder in 1972 from psychiatry's manual of diagnoses and diseases[12]—as persons having mental or physical defects that render them unfit for military service.[13]

The Right to Serve

Blacks and women have participated in every war since America's inception. (So have homosexuals.)[14] Their participation notwithstanding, blacks and women had to fight for the right to serve in America's armed conflicts in much the same way homosexuals are seeking the right to do so today.

Minority groups in this country have historically fought for the right to fight because military service brings, or is expected to carry with it, equal rights of citizenship. As sociologist Morris Janowitz has written:

> . . . I argue that, starting with the French and American Revolutions, participation in the national army has been an integral aspect of the normative definition of citizenship. . . . From World War I onward, citizen military service has been seen as a device by which minorities could achieve political legitimacy and rights. Until Vietnam, for example, blacks pressed to be armed and integrated into the fighting military as a sign that they had effectively attained citizenship and the concomitant privileges. Americans of Japanese descent, who were subject to indignities and arbitrary internment after the attack on Pearl Harbor, volunteered for all-Japanese combat units in order to demonstrate their loyalty and reaffirm their citizenship.[15]

The social exchange is obvious: Blacks, women, and gays fight for the right to serve in the armed forces because, by so doing, they earn the fairness and equality of treatment they believe they deserve—both in the military and in the larger society. Hence, military service is at once both a right of citizenship and a means of justifying requests for equality in other societal sectors. In the words of analyst Richard Kohn, "combat and service . . . undermine prejudice and discrimination."[16]

Civilian Control of the Military

Blacks, women, and gays have similarly targeted the military for integration with the expectation that the military can make this happen. A political mandate to integrate the armed forces would be promptly—though perhaps not eagerly—met with military compliance. This expectation is based on the culture of the military and its ethic of obedience, loyalty, and respect for civilian control. Earlier, for example, though the military initially opposed integrating blacks into its ranks, it ultimately developed and enforced an equal opportunity program that was second to none. The military was able to do this because of its organizational emphasis on hierarchy, surveillance, and social control.[17] When combined with its culture and ethic, the organizational structure of the armed forces makes it the logical place for groups to press for integration.

The integration of blacks in the military also provides a possible model of long-term consequences. In the case of blacks, short-term behavioral compliance with coercive military integration policies became an interim step on the path toward mid-term identification with integration policies. In the long term, identification has given way to attitudinal internalization and strong approval of integration policies.[18] A similar change in the cases of women and gays would alter the underlying assumptions about who can serve effectively in the military.[19]

The Integration of Blacks, Women, and Gays: Differences

In the fall of 1993 Congresswoman Patricia Schroeder (D-Colo.) approached Gen. Colin Powell, then chairman of the Joint Chiefs of Staff and maybe the most highly respected African-American in the United States, with a request to lift the ban prohibiting military service by homosexuals. Likewise, organizations such as the National Gay and Lesbian Task Force and the Campaign for Military Service sought political support from other previously disenfranchised groups. It would seem, the reasoning went, that blacks and women—who had been down this road before and had achieved some victories—would be sympathetic to the anti-ban cause.

However, in his reply, General Powell denied anti-ban supporters the foothold they sought. He wrote to Congresswoman Schroeder that he was aware of attempts to draw parallels between the experiences in the military of blacks and homosexuals but rejected the comparison as "convenient" and "invalid."[20] We identify and describe four circumstances that make the case of gays different from those that confronted blacks and women in earlier integration efforts.

Moral and Legal Implications

Homosexuality raises many moral and legal concerns that previous integration issues do not. Although there were assumed and often inaccurate behavioral characteristics associated with being black or female, these statuses were considered inferior rather than immoral or illegal. Being gay— unless one remains celibate—implies that one has performed or intends to perform homosexual acts that are illegal in many jurisdictions. The Uniform Code of Military Justice (UCMJ) currently proscribes sodomy and indecent assault with legal sanctions decided in military courts-martial. Recent Supreme Court decisions (e.g., Bowers v. Hartwick) have upheld the constitutionality of sodomy statues.

The legal issue of whether admission of homosexual orientation constitutes probable cause, or can be the basis for further inquiry, is only one among many that needs to be answered. Inconsistencies between military and civil law provide a complex legal challenge involving jurisdictional questions along with differences of interpretation.[21] Somewhat analogous to this is the military's experience with racial desegregation within its own boundaries while Jim Crow barriers to integration existed in surrounding communities in some regions of the country. However, the challenges faced by the military as it relates to gays would be of a different magnitude.

Legality aside, moral and religious objections to homosexual behavior remain strong in American culture. Moral objection is especially strong among those who assume that homosexuality is a choice one makes rather than a genetic predisposition to that behavior. The belief that homosexuality is a life-style choice reinforces the notion of gayness as a "perversion" and therefore morally wrong.

Desegregation vs. Integration

For blacks and women, the organizational challenge was desegregation. Blacks and women had "openly" served in the military in segregated units, and their contributions were noted for many years preceding orders to integrate. The immediate issue was not the determination of whether blacks and women had utility as soldiers—this they had already demonstrated. The issue instead was whether they could serve shoulder-to-shoulder with white male comrades without jeopardizing effectiveness or putting lives unnecessarily at risk.

It is also worthwhile to note that the segregation policies for blacks and women were a compromise that accommodated both those demanding to serve as a matter of civil rights and those who opposed integration. Nevertheless, segregation provided opportunities for blacks and women to demonstrate their worth in the performance of military tasks. Over time, as the inefficiencies of segregation practices became apparent, it was in the military's interest to desegregate. The task faced by the military, then, was how to dissolve organizational boundaries between segregated units. With time, full integration was realized in the case of blacks and is being approached in the case of women; in the case of blacks, this occurred far ahead of societal expectations.

Opponents of the gay ban recognize the need to establish a similar legitimacy for their cause. They have sought examples of gays who have served honorably and heroically to counter impressions that gays are unable to perform within a military context as soldiers. Two extensive documentaries have now been compiled by historian Alan Berube and journalist Randy Shilts.[22] For the most part, these authors have had to rely on the testimonies of those who served in the military as closeted gays,[23] for to be openly homosexual was grounds for administrative dismissal. Because gays out of necessity have had to be invisible, there were no boundaries that would define them as a group. The performance record therefore is piecemeal and post hoc.

Gays are thus caught in the Catch-22 dilemma of having inadequate evaluation because their status is not recognized as legitimate, and of not being recognized because they have not been evaluated. Because gays have never been officially recognized as a group in the military, the evolutionary model of change—from segregation to desegregation to integration—does not apply to their case.

Timing

It is not by coincidence that the integration of blacks and women proceeded more rapidly during periods when demand for military manpower was highest. Exigencies stimulated by World War II and the Korean War set the context and provided expanded opportunities for blacks and women.[24] Manpower requirements of the All Volunteer Force (AVF) since 1974 have set personnel levels that would not have been met without the successful recruitment of blacks and women into integrated units.

The historical and organizational circumstances confronting gays are quite different. The manpower crisis most currently facing military planners is the opposite: The challenge now is how to reduce personnel levels by a third in a very short period at minimum cost to organizational integrity and effectiveness. Hence, the military can be very selective about criteria for entrance and retention, and many talented and qualified servicemen and -women are being released. Military service in this context shifts away from an "obligation to serve" toward the "right to serve." Military service as an obligation provides more leverage for expanded civil rights than do situations in which the military can pick and choose. From a strategic standpoint, the timing for gays could not be worse.

Health Risks

Despite a recent memorandum from the Public Health Service to the service secretaries that there are no greater health risks or costs associated with lifting the exclusionary ban on homosexuals, the issue remains controversial.[25] Beliefs that gays are more promiscuous, sexually irresponsible, and more likely to be infected with the HIV virus than straight service members cause some to fear that the military will face higher rates of sexually transmitted diseases (most notably AIDS), a contaminated blood supply, and other medical risks.

Because AIDS in the United States was first encountered primarily within the gay community, the residual and persistent impression remains that it is essentially a "gay problem." Greg Seigle, in his survey of soldiers for the *Army Times*, found that fear of AIDS is one of the primary reasons cited by soldiers who oppose integration of gays.[26] Though some "health" questions were posed prior to the integration of blacks and women in the military— especially about the sexuality of black men and about unwanted pregnancies in servicewomen—none were of the sort raised in the case of homosexuals.

Policy Implications Based on Similarities and Differences

In this section, we outline six policy implications derived from the previous discussions of similarities and differences between the integration of blacks and women and the integration of gays. There is no attempt to make a direct linkage between a given similarity and a given policy implication, or, alternatively, between a stated difference and a stated policy implication. Instead, the six implications represent a synthesis of ideas generated from the discussions of similarities and differences between the integration of blacks, women, and gays.

Policy Implication 1: Implement the Policy Vigorously and Quickly

Should they be mandated to lift the ban, the armed forces should move vigorously and quickly to integrate open homosexuals. Lethargic implementation is unlikely to alter political realities and would serve to breed contempt for the new policy by recalcitrant service members. By acting promptly and with conviction, the military would send a clear message that the policy will be implemented and enforced. Even with timely enactment, past experiences with the integration of blacks and women suggest that the integration process might take as long as three decades.[27]

A systemic means of verifying compliance should be incorporated into the evaluation reports of officers (OERs) and noncommissioned officers (NCOERs). This systemic compliance check provides an institutionalized means for tracking the leadership and responsibility of those who are to enforce. A similar mechanism has proven an efficient and effective method for monitoring service members' commitment to and enforcement of earlier integration policies.

On an individual level, the military must be willing to coerce service members in order to gain immediate behavioral compliance with the policy's intent. The armed forces should manifest absolute commitment to the policy in a manner consistent with "zero defects" enforcement. Behavioral transgressions should not be tolerated. This implies that the policy should be enforced with neither disclaimers nor qualifications. To do otherwise would be to dilute the policy's legitimacy and potency.

Policy Implication 2: Craft Consistent, Comprehensive, and Unequivocal Guidelines for Commanders

The guidelines for the policy must be crafted with commanders at all levels in mind. The guidelines must be internally consistent, easily understood, and unequivocal. They must cover the wide variety of possible contingencies to simplify the enforcement process for commanders.

To the extent that no set of guidelines can cover all contingencies, military attorneys must keep abreast of incremental changes in the policy and serve as the local repository of knowledge for policy enforcement, application, and interpretation. In this vein, close working relationships between military attorneys and commanders are essential and must be fostered. Such relationships will ensure more uniform application of the policy between units and save commanders from having to waste hours analyzing seemingly unique situations in order to apply the policy properly. The intent is to eliminate situations in which commanders fail to enforce the policy because they are unsure of what to do.

Policy Implication 3: Inform Policy from a Social and Behavioral Science Perspective

The military must be willing to permit, fund, and conduct research pertaining to the policy and its enforcement from the outset. Implications from research in the form of data, observations, and findings should be used to clarify and modify the policy so that it can be more easily and uniformly enforced and to overcome problems with its operationalization. Such results could also prove useful when educating service members about the overall effects of the policy within the military.

Although the intent is not to put a researcher in every battalion or on board every vessel, the military must be open to information based on valid scientific inquiry. The prohibition of research would deny senior officials the information important for evaluating and effecting necessary changes in the policy. In the past, sound research and valid data have proven valuable when fine tuning or reformulating integration policies relevant to blacks and women, and should be no less so in the case of integrating gays.[28]

Policy Implication 4: Develop and Formulate Practical Solutions at Higher Organizational Levels than Normal

The "nuts and bolts" policies that will govern how soldiers will live and act toward each other must be crafted carefully and thoughtfully. Special attention should be directed to rules that govern off-duty conduct—the behavior least influenced by military leaders. The previous integration experiences of blacks and women, as well as a wealth of social science research (especially in the area of group dynamics), should inform military planners and leaders as they develop the instructions to accompany the mandate of gay integration.

First, policy should be constructed that addresses interests and concerns of both heterosexuals and homosexuals. The end product or policy, however, should be presented and implemented as strictly a "soldier policy." By this we mean it must avoid the impression there are separate rules that apply to either gay or straight personnel. Any differentiation would only serve to exacerbate the tensions that will no doubt initially exist. "Rules of the barracks" need to be simple, easily understood, enforceable, and nonspecific with regard to sexual orientation.

Second, policy ought to focus as much as possible on modifying the physical context within which off-duty behavior will occur. This indirect approach to modifying group dynamics is not new and is more easily accomplished when compared to direct efforts at attitude and behavioral change. All soldiers should have the right to the same minimum level of privacy and modesty, and should be able to live without fear or threat of personal invasion. If living facilities (e.g., barracks, latrines, showers) do not currently guarantee this then they will have to be modified. Lessons learned from female integration will undoubtedly be of some value, and those who have experienced this firsthand should be consulted.

Third, it will be important that policies guarantee uniformity and consistency from post to post and across the services. This will be a departure from customary implementation practices in the military where broad decisions are reached at higher levels, relying on field commanders to implement them with the provisions at their discretion. Successful integration will require consistency, and the only way to do this is to spell out the details at the top. In sum, practical solutions to practical problems will have to be developed at higher levels than normal.

Policy Implication 5: Avoid Morality Debates by Focusing on Behavioral rather than Attitudinal Changes

The interactive relationship between attitudes and behaviors has been extensively researched in the behavioral and social sciences. The integration of blacks and women was facilitated by a dual approach of trying to alter attitudes and, in some cases, to direct behavioral change. The thinking was that service members would more easily work out differences that interfered with open association and cohesion if their attitudes could be changed. The military sought to change service members' attitudes by providing them specific information and sensitizing them to others. The early "Equal Opportunity and Race Relations" training seminars and sensitivity sessions are examples of this approach to behavioral change through changing attitudes and perceptions.

Although similar seminars have been conducted during the integration of women, more reliance was placed in this case on developing criteria for defining sexual harassment and detailing the role commanders would play in the enforcement of policy. The assumption here was that rules should be established and enforced and that over time, with more frequent contact and interaction, prejudicial attitudes would change.

The model of dealing directly with behavior would seem the more appropriate for the integration of gays into the military. Because religious and moral considerations are linked to value judgments of homosexuality, overt attempts by the military to effect attitudinal change would be inappropriate, unnecessary, and ineffective—and would likely generate intense resistance.[29] It would also place military leaders in a position that may conflict with their own moral values. If attitudes about gays are to change, this must occur as a natural and unforced aspect of normal group development.

Policy Implication 6: Address Health Risks and Concerns through Education and Testing

Finally, close attention must be paid to any potential health risks that may accompany the integration of gays into the military. First, military leaders must learn and remain fully informed about the transmission of sexually transmitted diseases. Leader knowledge of factually based data will help dispel irrational fears and anxiety in the ranks. Leaders should be required to regularly disseminate this information to their subordinates in the form of classes and other educational forums.

Second, military medical officials should intensify efforts to identify soldiers who become HIV-positive. This will involve more frequent tests than are currently conducted. The purpose of this, in addition to curbing the spread of AIDS, is to make soldiers aware that the military is doing everything possible to ensure the personal safety of uninfected soldiers.

Closing Statement

The military has historically disdained its role as a laboratory for social experimentation because it may interfere with its purpose and focus to fight and win wars. It resents having to serve as a context for solving what it regards as societal ills, even though it has shown its effectiveness to make it happen. The military is also a conservative institution with a conservative mind set, made that way by the function it performs and prohibitions against risky ventures. This is reflected in the popular adage used frequently in the military: If it ain't broke, don't to fix it. However, the military serves at the behest of civilian authority, who may legitimately require institutional change and repair.

This paper has drawn parallels and contrasts between the previous integration of blacks and women with those facing the military should civilian authority mandate a lifting of ban against homosexuals. The purpose is not to arrive at a value judgment about whether the integration of gays into the military is the "right" thing to do. Its more limited purpose is to alert policy planners and military leaders that the military, in fact, has been down this road before—even if the road does not look exactly the same. Previous integration experiences, as well as a wealth of social and behavioral science research in this area, may be drawn upon to inform policy and implementation. There are also many issues, unique to the prospect of gay integration, that will demand innovative perspectives and solutions. If these can be identified in advance, it will significantly reduce the happenstance of a trial-and-error approach to institutional change.

As a case study, the issue of gay integration also provides insights into the political process. The integration of open homosexuals into the military lends itself easily to cross-cultural comparisons with other societies having militaries at different stages in the process. Of particular interest is the expanded role the military has assumed in the political process, as well as the expanded role of civilian decision-makers into affairs that historically have been the territory of the military. The interplay between military and societal forces is clearly illustrated by this major institutional change. If full gay integration in the military is achieved, it will be interesting to observe the effect on other institutions and public acceptance in general. As the black experience illustrates, the military can be a powerful agent for societal change.

Notes

1.   The views contained herein are solely the authors'. These views are neither endorsed nor rejected by the Department of Behavioral Sciences and Leadership, the United States Military Academy, or the Department of the Army.

2.   This view is held widely and specifically addressed in David R. Segal, *Recruiting for Uncle Sam* (Lawrence, KS: University Press of Kansas, 1989); Charles C. Moskos, "Army Women," *Atlantic Monthly* (August 1990): 71–78; Charles C. Moskos, "The Army's Racial Success Story: How Do They Do It?," *New Republic* (August 5, 1991), 16–20; Greg Seigle, "Ending Gay Ban May Be Toughest Legal Challenge Yet," *Army Times*, 11 January 1993; David F. Burrelli, *Homosexuals and U.S. Military Personnel Policy* (Washington, D.C.: Congressional Research Service, 1993).

3.   This classical distinction was first made in Samuel P. Huntington, *The Soldier and the State* (Cambridge, MA: Harvard University Press, 1957).

4. This opinion was highlighted in Defense Personnel Security Research and Education Center (DPERSEREC), *Nonconforming Sexual Orientations and Military Suitability* (Monterey, CA: DPERSEREC, 1988).

5. Catherine S. Manegold, "The Odd Place of Homosexuality in the Military," *New York Times*, 18 April 1993, Science Section.

6. The most recent expression of this is in Robert L. Maginnis, "A Case Against Lifting the Ban on Homosexuals," *Army* (January 1993): 37-39. Alternatively, see United States General Accounting Office (USGAO), Defense Force Management, *DOD's Policy on Homosexuality* (Washington, DC: USGAO, 1992) and Burrelli, *Homosexuals and U.S. Military*.

7. Morris J. MacGregor, Jr., *Integration of the Armed Forces: 1940–1965* (Washington, DC: Center of Military History, United States Army, 1981), 23.

8. Manegold, "The Odd Place of Homosexuality," 1.

9. Jane Gross, "Gay Sailor's Colleagues Unsettled and Unheard," *New York Times*, 5 April 1993.

10. Gary W. Berry, "Only Time Can Bring Acceptance of Gays," *Army Times*, 26 April 1993; Richard H. Kohn, "Women in Combat, Homosexuals in Uniform: The Challenge of Military Leadership," *Parameters* (Spring 1993):2–4; Grant Willis, "The Pressure Intensifies: Gay Ban's Backers, Opponents Both Vie for Attention," *Army Times*, 26 April 1993.

11. For depictions of this view see Stanley M. Elkins, "Slavery and Personality," in *Social Processes and Social Structures: An Introduction to Sociology*, ed. W. Richard Scott (New York: Holt, Rinehart, and Winston, 1959), 242–51; Daniel W. Rossides, *Social Stratification: The American Class System in Comparative Perspective* (Englewood Cliffs, NJ: Prentice Hall, 1990).

12. Burrelli, *Homosexuals and U.S. Military*.

13. James F. Kelly, "A Right to Serve?" *Proceedings* (May 1993):81–84.

14. A variety of secondary sources have illustrated successful homosexual participation in military service. Most notable are Allan Berube, *Coming Out Under Fire* (New York: Free Press, 1990); Kohn, "Women, Homosexuals in Uniform"; Randy Shilts, *Conduct Unbecoming: Gays and Lesbians in the U.S. Military* (New York: St. Martin's, 1993).

15. Morris Janowitz, *The Last Half-Century: Societal Change and Politics in America* (Chicago: The University of Chicago Press, 1978), 178, 180.

16. Kohn, "Women, Homosexuals in Uniform," 3.

17. Moskos, "Army Women" and "The Army's Racial Success Story."

18. This was noted by Herbert C. Kelman, "Three Processes of Social Influence," *Public Opinion Quarterly* 25 (1961).

19. The conception of culture that we find especially useful and relevant is outlined in Edgar H. Schein, *Organizational Culture and Leadership*, 2nd ed. (San Francisco: Jossey-Bass, 1992).

20. Gen. Colin Powell, letter to Congresswoman Patricia Schroeder.

21. See Allan Futernick's contribution, this volume, for a more detailed analysis of these and other issues.

22. Berube, *Coming Out Under Fire*, and Shilts, *Conduct Unbecoming*.

23. See, in addition to Berube and Shilts, Joseph Harry, "Homosexual Men and Women Who Served Their Country," *Journal of Homosexuality* 10 (1984):117–25.

24. This is prominently documented in the work of Janowitz, *The Last Half-Century*.

25. This was reported recently by Soraya S. Nelson, "Finding on Gay Health-Risk Questioned: Gay-Ban Supporters Disagree with Military Health Chief's Report," *Army Times*, 26 April 1993.

26. Greg Seigle, "In the U.S.: Fear and Loathing," *Army Times*, 11 January 1993.

27. Segal notes that in the military "the major constraints of race as an ascriptive characteristic were overcome more than three decades ago" (*Recruiting for Uncle Sam*, 124). He goes on to say "that the extension of similar treatment to women would lag by that three-decade period" (ibid.). For our purposes, the salient point is that a policy stipulating full integration of homosexuals will not transform the military's social or organizational landscape overnight. In reality, even with prompt and vigorous enforcement of a new policy, the process of integrating homosexuals is likely to be a rather long one.

28. In the case of blacks, see Moskos, "The Army's Racial Success Story." In regard to women, see Segal, *Recruiting for Uncle Sam*.

29. This is especially true given the emotional nature of the homosexual integration issue. For a thorough discussion of psychological reactance, see J. W. Brehm, *A Theory of Psychological Reactance* (New York: Academic Press, 1966).

Conclusion: Directions for the Future

SANDRA CARSON STANLEY and WILBUR J. SCOTT

The contributors for this volume identify and examine issues and concerns associated with the military service of gays and lesbians. Significantly, we have solicited their commentaries in the wake of President Clinton's attempt to lift the exclusionary ban. Among other things, this attempt has forced the country to confront military policies and practices publicly. The rules for the "Don't ask, don't tell, don't pursue" policy announced by the Pentagon in early March 1994 are not likely to be the final resolution, just as a return to the early policy based on "homosexuality is incompatible with military service" is unlikely.

Americans are not the first to consider the debate regarding the military service of homosexuals, as the same controversy has occurred in one form or another in most Western industrial democracies. These nations share in common an industrializing process that is destructive of traditional arrangements and a democratic ethos that extends the rights of citizenship and equal protection under the law to previously excluded groups. Thus it was only a matter of time before Americans, like others, faced the issue. The question now is: Where does the United States go from here?

In this light, President Clinton's contribution was to make public an issue that had been developing for some time. This volume, therefore, is timely because American society and the military face ongoing challenges as solutions to the consequences of continued modernization are sought. The contributions in this volume reflect diverse backgrounds, experiences, and perspectives on how this plays out in the military. As such, the contributors communicate the complexity of the controversy. The concerns are both specific to the military and broad with implications extending beyond the military's institutional boundaries. The issues affect and reflect fundamental social values, and related social processes and practices in the larger society. The multiple dimensions—historical, moral, religious, social, political, legal, and medical—illustrate the complexity and are sources of divisiveness.

Following is a broad summary of observations. Three themes that provide

directions for the future of military service by gays and lesbians are
identified.

Direction: The Case of the United States

Directions for future policies and practices regarding gays and lesbians in
the U.S. military must be considered in the social-historical context of the
nation, the military institution, and the relationship between the two.

Issues surrounding the extension of rights and equal opportunity to homosexuals are complex and divisive. Homosexuality, as an orientation with
behavioral implications, challenges society's fundamental values and traditional assumptions about morality, religion, and gender roles, especially
masculinity. In each area, heterosexuality is the norm.

We suggest that homosexuality proffers challenges, not as the initiating or
causal agent, but as one of a series of changes wrought by twentieth-century
modernization. For example, it has been argued that functions of the family
as an institution (e.g., reproduction and economic) had to be redefined
before homosexuality could find some degree of tolerance. Modernization
has also resulted in the weakening of other institutions such as religion and in
collective ties as well. Relative to the latter, there is greater emphasis on
individuality, personal freedom, and satisfaction than on group interests.

At the same time, the democratic ethos encourages open expression of
individual and collective views. The contentiousness of issues associated
with homosexuality is reflected in positions of those representing the conservative right, who emphasize moral imperatives, versus gay activists and the
gay liberation movement, who emphasize civil rights and equal opportunity.

Changing views of homosexuality—from seeing it as a disease to seeing it
as a life-style, deviant or alternative, chosen or predetermined—have been
accompanied by increased tolerance. Many Americans support equal opportunity for homosexuals in public arenas (e.g., in employment and housing),
but are more reluctant to extend acceptance of specific rights to more private
and personal areas, such as the right to marry or adopt children. This cultural ambivalence and the lack of a supportive legal environment in the more
personal areas have implications for the status of homosexuals in American
society.

Changing the exclusionary ban in the U.S. military, however, pits powerful sentiments and constituencies against each other, both within the military and in the larger society. Power struggles appear on multiple levels and
across institutional boundaries: between various interest groups in the larger
society, between civilian and military leaders, and between the president
and members of Congress.

The impact of modernization on the military has implications for the service of homosexuals. Institutional boundaries have been weakened and become more permeable and the relationship between the military and society has changed. The meaning of military service has been redefined. No longer is service seen as a civic responsibility, a rite of passage for males. Service has begun to be viewed as a citizenship right, a vehicle through which other rights in society can be earned. It may also be viewed as a "job" offering employment opportunities and benefits, rather than a "calling" (for men).

Similarly, the role of the military in society has been redefined. In the past, the central mission of the military was clear—to protect and defend the nation (especially women and children). The success of this mission required a ready force with emphasis on traditional warrior skills essential for effective combat participation. This unique mission contributed to the view of the military as a special institution, separate from society, and not subject to practices operating in other social institutions.

While the underlying reason for the existence of the military is still operational readiness to protect and defend, the character of military operations in the post–cold war period has changed. They are more likely to be multinational in focus and often involve humanitarian functions such as relief, rescue, and peacekeeping. The need for traditional skills associated with masculinity is replaced by demands for technical, administrative, clerical, social work, and health care functions. The changing mission and subsequent redefinition of the military's role in society facilitates the inclusion of previously excluded groups, especially women.

Changes in the more practical aspects have affected social-psychological conceptions, the social construction of the military and service. No longer is the military viewed as a masculine terrain, a proving ground for masculinity. While it supports the inclusion of women and homosexuals, this reconstruction has met with resistance from military men. Evidence indicates that opposition to gays and lesbians in the military is much greater among male than female service members. Servicemen report concerns about potential threats to morale, cohesion, and effectiveness associated with gay integration. It is suggested here that the perceived threats are likely to be based more on the social construction of homosexuality—conjecture, assumptions, and stereotypes—than the actual behavior of homosexuals.

Direction: Evidence from Other Nations

Since many Western nations have dealt with the integration of homosexuals in the military, there is a growing body of information that can provide direction to the current debate in the United States. The status of homosexuals in the military reflects the social-historical context of military service and the general position of homosexuals within the host society. Variations in policies exist with policies being more liberal than practices in most countries.

In the Dutch and Canadian cases, the status of homosexuals was established constitutionally in the larger society first, then extended to the military. The Dutch have the most open formal policy. They actively recruit gays and lesbians and offer seminars designed to change attitudes toward homosexuals, rather than simply ensuring behavioral compliance. In Canada, gays and lesbians are permitted to enlist and serve openly. The focus of policy implementation is on behavioral compliance rather than attitudinal change. Despite the open policies, most homosexual military personnel do not make their sexual orientation public.

There is a long history of exclusion of homosexuals in the British military. Societal attitudes have become more tolerant and homosexual acts have been decriminalized in the larger society and the military. Official military policy, however, bans the service of homosexuals for reasons of "military necessity." Military practice represents "limited tolerance." If homosexual orientation becomes known, the personal may be counseled and warned or discharged, depending on the explicit nature of behavior. The highly traditional organizational culture of the British military provides a framework in which military regulations are interpreted and enforced. The situation in the United States is probably most similar to the British case.

The Israeli case provides an interesting example of the relationship between the social-historical context of military service and military policies and practices regarding homosexuality. The rights of homosexuals and their presence in the military has not been a major issue in Israel since the formation of the state and its military some forty-six years ago. Security concerns and other pressures in daily life are much more central to Israelis. The former require an effective military in a constant state of readiness. The Israeli Defense Force is a full draft system that brings together diverse segments of society. Official policy has never excluded homosexuals from the military, but previously there were restrictions on their assignment to sensitive areas. Policy implementation was left to unit commanders, who were more concerned with satisfactory performance than sexual orientation. Further, military service is highly valued in Israel's normative system. As a result, most Israelis are highly motivated to serve and are willing to put the military ahead of personal interests.

Evidence from research in the militaries of other Western nations suggests that the performance of homosexuals is comparable to that of heterosexuals and their presence does not interfere with military effectiveness. In fact, there has been little reaction to the removal of restrictions where such has occurred. While the specific social-historical contexts of the nation, its military, and the relationship between the two differ among Western nations, there are general similarities that suggest their experience may provide direction for the United States.

Direction: Implications from Recently Enfranchised Groups

Implications from the integration of previously excluded groups can provide direction for homosexual integration. It is not suggested that the issues are parallel: Similarities as well as fundamental differences have been observed. For example, similar reasons for the exclusion of African-American men, women, and homosexuals have been given. Most notable perhaps, are assumptions about the negative effect of their presence on male bonding, morale, cohesion, and, ultimately, military effectiveness. Proponents of the inclusion of members of these groups have based their position on the extension of civil rights and equal opportunity.

A number of differences also have been observed. One of the most central is society's response to racial and gender differences versus those related to sexual orientation. Skin color is non-behavioral, and race and gender are biological traits viewed as relatively benign according to some who have discussed the analogy. While society's view of homosexuality and its origin has changed, it is still likely to be viewed as deviant. Further, there are clear behavioral components that challenge values as expressed in traditional assumptions about morality, sexuality, and masculinity. While the presence of women, especially in combat, challenged the definition of the military as a masculine domain and the definition of the warrior archetype, the presence of homosexuals does so to a greater extent, as it stands counter to the prevailing norm of heterosexuality. Further, there are legal impediments that would impact the integration of homosexuals that did not affect the integration of racial minorities and women.

Despite these differences, there are lessons to be learned from past experiences with integration. First, the integration of homosexuals, if it occurs, is likely be accomplished slowly—as has been so in the cases of African-American men and of women. In fact, it may occur even more slowly because of the greater resistance to the inclusion of homosexuals. Acceptance of a group does not necessarily accompany policy change. Second, minority integration is facilitated by military necessity. As a result of manpower demands after World War II and after the shift to the all-volunteer force in 1974, the military was motivated to integrate African-American men and then women into its ranks, and has successfully done so. The consequences have extended beyond the military and promoted social, economic, and political gains in the larger society for both groups.

The military and social environments are not as congenial for homosexuals. The timing for homosexual integration could not be worse: The reduced manpower needs of a downsizing military do not ease the inclusion of homosexuals. (The reduction in manpower needs may also slow the gains made by minorities and women.) Further, military personnel are more resistant to gay integration than they were to the presence of African-American men and women. Cultural ambivalence and the lack of a supportive legal environment will likely impede the improvement of the position of gays and lesbians in the larger society.

It is difficult to predict specifically the future direction for gays and lesbians in the military. Recent rules announced by the Pentagon are not likely to signal the end of the controversy. Current trends in society and the military preclude the return to the "homosexuality is incompatible with military service" policy but also are likely to continue to distinguish homosexual integration from that of race and gender. The issue probably will provide many challenges in the military, the courts, and the larger society. Ideally, the guiding principle will be to provide the nation with the most effective military force.

Biographical Sketches of the Contributors

Barry D. Adam is Professor of Sociology at the University of Windsor (Ontario, Canada) and author of *The Survival of Domination* (Elsevier/Greenwood) and *The Rise of a Gay and Lesbian Movement* (Twayne/Macmillan). He is currently doing research in new social movement theory and working (with Alan Sears) on a book on impacts of HIV on personal, family and work relationships to be published by Columbia University Press.

Marion Andersen-Boers is a psychologist and a staffmember at the Social Council for the Armed Forces. She has specialized in minority integration in the armed forces. She edited the Councils advice on *Homosexuality and armed forces* (1991).

Lieutenant Colonel Mike Anderson is an active-duty military officer currently serving as an Associate Professor at the United States Military Academy. He is a West Point graduate of 1973 and received his Ph.D. in Sociology from University of Chicago in 1981. He currently teaches a variety of sociology courses at West Point.

David Burrelli is a Specialist in National Defense for the Congressional Research Service at the Library of Congress. He received his Ph.D. from the University of Chicago in sociology. He has recently completed work on another M.A. in National Strategic Studies from the National War College, Ft. McNair, Washington, D.C.

Margaret Cruikshank has been writing on gay and lesbian issues since 1975. She teaches gay studies at The City College of San Francisco and recently taught courses in lesbian studies at the University of California at Berkeley and the University of Maine. Her most recent book is *The Gay and Lesbian Liberation Movement* (Routledge).

Christopher Dandeker is a Senior Lecturer in the Department of War Studies, King's College London. He is author of *Surveillance, Power and Modernity* (Polity Press, 1990), co-author (with C. Ashworth and T. Johnson) of *The Structure of Social Theory* (Macmillan, 1984) together with numerous publications on human resource issues of contemporary armed forces.

M. C. Devilbiss received her Ph.D. in sociology from Purdue University, and holds an M.A. in Religion from Lutheran Theological Seminary. Dr. Devilbiss spent twelve years in the U.S. armed forces, serving first as a basic training instructor in the U.S. Army during the Vietnam War, and later as an aircraft armament systems specialist for the Air Guard on the F–4 and F–16 fighter aircraft. Her many writings on the subject of women in the military include *Women and Military Service: A History, Analysis, and Overview of Key Issues* published by Air University Press.

Allan J. Futernick received his Ph.D. in sociology from the University of Alabama. As a career Army officer he served on the faculties of the U.S. Military Academy and the U.S. Army Command and General Staff College. He is currently the Associate Dean, School of Criminal Justice, Rutgers University.

Paul A. Gade is Chief of the Organization and Personnel Resources Research Unit at the U.S. Army Research Institute for the Behavioral and Social Sciences. He is a Fellow of the American Psychological Association and the Inter-University Seminar on Armed Forces and Society and is president of the Military Psychology Division of the American Psychological Association.

Reuven Gal, the former Chief Psychologist of the Israeli Defence Force, is currently the director of the Israeli Institute for Military Studies and the Carmel Institute for Social Studies. Dr. Gal has published numerous papers and articles on issues related to military and society, and especially concerning psychological and sociological aspects of the Israeli military.

Gwyn Harries-Jenkins is a former regular officer in the British Royal Air Force who retired in 1969 to join the faculty at the University of Hull in the United Kingdom. He specialized in Human Resources Development with particular reference to the Sociology of the Military.

Major Donald H. Horner is a graduate of the United States Military Academy at West Point. He received a Ph.D. from the University of Southern California and has taught a variety of courses at West Point in the areas of social psychology, military sociology, and military leadership and organizational theory.

Edgar M. Johnson, a U.S. Army veteran, is the Director of the U.S. Army Research Institute for the Behavioral and Social Sciences, and the Chief

Psychologist of the U.S. Army. Dr. Johnson is a Fellow of the American Psychological Association of the American Psychological Society, and of the Human Factors and Ergonomics Society. He has published over 50 book, journal, and magazine articles, and technical reports.

Lawrence J. Korb is Director of the Center for Public Policy Education and a Senior Fellow in the Foreign Policy Studies Program at the Brookings Institute. He served as Assistant Secretary of Defense (Manpower, Reserve Affairs, Installations and Logistics) from 1981 through 1985. He received his Ph.D. from State University of New York at Albany, and has authored numerous books and articles on national security issues. Dr. Korb served in active duty for four years as a Naval Flight Officer and retired from the Navy reserve with the rank of captain.

Laura L. Miller is a doctoral candidate in sociology at Northwestern University. She received her B.A. in European and Soviet Studies at the University of Redlands. Her dissertation is entitled "Gender Detente: Soldiers Managing Conflict in the U.S. Army." Field research has taken her to Army units in Somalia and the former Yugoslavia.

Charles Moskos is Professor of Sociology at Northwestern University and Chairman of the Inter-University Seminar on Armed Forces and Society. His most recent book (with John W. Chambers) is *The New Conscientious Objection: From Sacred to Secular Resistance* (Oxford University Press, 1993).

Thomas K. Nakayama teaches rhetorical and cultural studies in the Department of Communication at Arizona State University. His research interests focus on the constructions of 'race,' gender and sexuality in popular culture.

Rosemary Park CD MSc. served in the Canadian Armed Forces from 1972 until 1993. She was the principal researcher for a six-year program evaluation assessing the integration potential of CF servicewomen in combat support and isolation units; was classed an expert witness for legal cases involving integration issues, abuse of authority, harassment, and supervisor-subordinate relations; and continues to act as a contractor for the CF in the development of employment equity policy and information systems. During 1991–1992, LCdr (ret'd) Park was one of two policy analysts assisting lawyers in their preparation of a legal defence of the formerly restrictive CF sexual orientation policy.

Ronald D. Ray, a Kentucky attorney, is the author of *Military Necessity and Homosexuality.* A highly decorated combat veteran of the Vietnam War, he recently retired as a Colonel in the U.S. Marine Corps Reserve. He has served as a Deputy Assistant Secretary of Defense, a Marine historian and as a Commissioner on several Presidential Commissions.

Garry L. Rolison is Assistant Professor of Sociology at Arizona State University. He is continuing work on the nexus of race and class as well as researching academic achievement among African-American students.

David R. Segal is Professor of Sociology and of Government and Politics at the University of Maryland, where he directs the graduate program in military sociology. He specializes in military manpower and personnel issues.

Judith Hicks Stiehm is Professor of Political Science and former Provost at Florida International University. She is the author of *Nonviolent Power*, *Bring Me Men and Women: Mandated Change at the U.S. Air Force Academy*, and *Arms and the Enlisted Woman*.

Jan S. van der Meulen is a sociologist and a researcher at the Society and Armed Forces Foundation. He has published on public-opinion, the draft and civil-military relations. He wrote the chapter on the Netherlands, in Charles C. Moskos and Frank R. Wood, *The Military: More Than Just a Job?* (1988).

Index